ALLEGIANCE IN AMERICA:

The Case
of the Loyalists

Edited by
G. N. D. EVANS
Richmond College of the City University of New York

ADDISON-WESLEY PUBLISHING COMPANY
Reading, Massachusetts
Menlo Park, California · London · Don Mills, Ontario

THEMES AND SOCIAL FORCES IN AMERICAN HISTORY SERIES
Under the Editorship of Robin W. Winks

Purpose: To explore major influences on the development of American society and character.

/16 0209

Preface

Why does a nation have the right to draft a man? Under what circumstances is he permitted not to serve? Such questions as these clearly penetrate to the very foundations of a society, and in those nations, like the United States, which have established their government in the tradition of natural law and social contract, they call for an examination of the origins and character of the relationship between a citizen and his government.

If a citizen finds a conflict between the demands of his conscience and those of his country, how can it be resolved equitably? In this context the root of the problem is not loyalty in itself but a clash of loyalties, an example of the old observation that the hardest situations to handle are not those where good and evil are in opposition but where two "goods" seem to contest for our commitment. The social psychologist speaks of a person involved in and acting out a number of "roles." A man is husband, father, worker, veteran, team player, and a citizen of many constituencies. In his daily life he adjusts to each role and normally does not find them clashing with one another. But since they overlap, there is always a possibility that they will. It may be a minor conflict, such as whether a busy executive will spend a few hours with his wife and his children, who have seen too little of him (as their remarks make clear), or in the office with some problem whose solution may give him a promotion. He has to ask himself whether his advancement will ultimately benefit his family more than a few hours of recreation now. The problem of loyalties, stemming from his many roles, presents itself as opposing demands for scarce or limited commodities, his time and energy. The problem also arises, but in a much more vital way, when young men have to resolve the dilemma of when it is right to take life. Even if they have already agreed to serve in the Military, it is possible that they will face the conflict between disobeying an order and carrying it out by committing a "crime against humanity." The essential questions, then, are how men acquire, decide, and select their loyalties and what they may, can, or must do when some of these appear incompatible.

This book is divided into four principal sections. In the first are presented contemporary accounts of the Loyalists by themselves, by their allies, by Patriots, and by European observers. The second offers a selection of writings from the nineteenth century. The third does the same for the twentieth. In the last section the question of loyalty is handled by a number of social scientists from various disciplines. The book will not, because it cannot, provide explicit answers to all the questions raised in this preface. Some were not even clearly posed by the Loyalists. Others they asked, but did not answer with an incisiveness worthy of our attention. Yet the coming of the Revolution thrust them, just as much as the Patriots, into crises of conscience and bewilderment about conflicting duties. Their story is not only interesting in itself but instructive in its larger implications, for it should not be forgotten that it was the Loyalists who remained true to established government and hallowed traditions while their opponents created a justification for rebellion in order to found a new nation.

Like any historical work, this one deals with men of bygone days in the belief that, although the human story is a continuum wherein there can be no exact duplication, there seems to be a basic sequence. Many of the essentials in a man's life, once we are talking about the life of men in settled groups, stay the same, whether he lives in Athens, Greece, in the third century or Athens, Ohio, in the twentieth. Almost everything around him will be different, and that difference will be partially reflected in the internal significance of his life. However he will have to begin learning as a child and then become a citizen by adjustment to and indoctrination in the mores of his civilization, while simultaneously seeking his purpose and identity as an individual. Some men will be earnest, some will be apathetic, some will lead, some will follow, some will prize material rewards above everything else, and some will stubbornly cling to ideals. In the long run and in the deepest affairs, Man does not appear to have changed very much. That is why the philosophers and the preachers are still in business and the sages and the soothsayers still left with things to say.

In the history of the United States the occasions on which the question of loyalty, or opposing loyalties, have arisen have been comparatively few. Naturally most have been during times of war, because it is then that the full nature of political obligation is sharply brought home to men commanded to risk their lives for a country and a cause. After the Revolution the young Republic had a difficult job convincing the states to give up enough sovereignty to create a viable nation and convincing their citizens to give up local and petty jealousies sufficiently to regard themselves as Americans. The next test came with the Alien and Sedition Acts in which John Adams' government panicked a little and imposed new standards of "loyalty" by imprisoning such people as Republican newspaper editors. The War of 1812, one of the strangest in the history of the United States, raised the question of allegiance in a more international context than usual when the contrasting British and American concepts of naturalization and citizenship came into conflict over the issue of impressment. The Mexican War of 1845–1848 elicited from Henry David Thoreau one of the great classics on the nature of a citizen's duties, his essay on civil disobedience. Another man in disagreement with the American involvement in that war was Abraham Lincoln. Yet he found himself, less than twenty years later, in the catbird seat when some six million free Southerners decided to fight. The president's response was to insist that such an insurrection was intolerable and that the erring sheep must be brought back into the fold at any cost.

During World War I the federal government had to face the problem of nationals who put an emotional attachment to their "fatherland" before allegiance to the neutrality of their adopted country. In World War II the government moved rapidly, some would say precipitously, to prevent any possible repetition of this situation with the Americans of Japanese descent. Police and military forces swooped down on hapless Nisei and rounded them up for detention in concentration camps. In the Korean War a nation which was a century and a half old but still ingrained with the ideology on which it had been founded discovered that the loyalty of a disturbingly large number of men could be changed under intense psychological pressure. As for the war in Vietnam, evidence of the troubled dissent of many Americans, including a large proportion of the nation's intellectual and political leaders, stares at us from the front page of every newspaper on almost every day of every month. The problem of a man's loyalty has been raised again more vigorously, more verbosely, and more despairingly than ever before.

Perhaps no period of America's history other than the Revolution (with the possible exception of the Civil War) involved proportionately as large a number of people who were genuinely perplexed as to where their primary political loyalty lay. And no occasion, without exception, has involved such a large exodus of men and women who made a choice and then found themselves on the losing side. The Loyalists were not just the "guys in the black hats." On their side were about as many high-minded men, about as many self-servers, about as many caught up in the accidents of war as one will find among the Patriots.

History, especially as it is written in textbooks, tends to be a success story and therefore it is not surprising that such unsuccessful groups as the Loyalists receive little attention. They deserve better, not so much because their contribution to American history has been underrated—after all, the most active of them quit the new nation and the rest kept quiet and accepted the new order—but because through them we have an opportunity to study a question so basic that it can never be resolved. It centers around the mutual obligations of a man and his state, especially the allegiance of the citizen to his government. Many of the Loyalists did not simply drift to the British side. They chose their course, in part for concrete economic and political reasons and in part because they handled the question of loyalty with an emphasis and manner different from that of the men who became the Founding Fathers. Because the Loyalists had to ask themselves a number of probing questions, their answers and their behavior are relevant to us who live in the nation established by their enemies.

I wish to thank the various authors and publishers who have kindly given permission to print the extracts in this book. In the research and writing I was indirectly helped by grants for a second study of the Loyalists. These were made by McGill University (Social Science Research Fund and French Canada Studies Program), the Canada Council, and Southern Illinois University (Faculty Research Fund). At Richmond College Charles Hirschfeld generously agreed to the preparing of a preliminary typescript during the institution's first days. Mrs. Ana Kira cheerfully and competently undertook this task.

I have left my largest and most pleasant debt until last. On hectic car, train, and ferry rides my wife, Ursula, has kept up the pace both in sickness and in health, and somehow has also found the resources to handle a crotchety companion. Whatever the shortcomings of my expositions, I can never claim that I have not known loyalty, and so much more.

New York   G. N. D. E.
December, 1968

Contents

PART FOUR: THE NATURE OF LOYALTY

APPENDIX

Part One

Contemporary Observations

Loyalists Speak for Themselves

Carl Becker once reminded us that the American Revolution was both a war for home rule, that is, independence, and a war about who should rule at home. It was his way of saying that the Revolution was also a civil war. Although the fact that it began as a rebellion against an imperial government and before its close included a number of foreign powers makes it perhaps a special type of internecine struggle, the bipartite analysis remains useful. Just how confused matters were is revealed by recalling that France, the principal ally of the rebels, was much more foreign to them than the British against whom they were fighting. Furthermore, in the decade before Independence was declared the colonial leaders had been crying for, among other things, their rights as Englishmen.

The view of the Revolution as a civil war helps to explain its tenuous divisions, the difficulty in defining the principles at stake, the almost defiant indecision of many individuals. Out of a total population of about two and a half million only a handful were active warriors on either the Patriot or Loyalist side, and, a fact hardly ever put into the textbooks, at one point there were almost as many Loyalists serving with the British as there were men in Washington's army.* The issues were complex, the conflict of convictions genuine, and most people simply could not regard matters with the white heat bias of a Paine or the luminous prejudice of a Jefferson.

It is instructive to look for a moment at the war in Vietnam, quite different in many important respects, but also in part a civil war. With all our contemporary advantages in gathering information, in discovering and weighing public opinion, there are sincere and serious divergencies in the assessments of the exact nature of the military and political conflict. How much more difficult it is, then, to determine the causes, character, and consequences of the American Revolution, now nearly two centuries old, in

---

* The reader is here urged to consult the Appendix to appreciate the difficulties in arriving at any precise total for the Loyalists, and to read the latest, most accurate estimates.

which there was also a mixture of idealistic attitudes and the specific interests of individuals, groups, classes, sections, and religious denominations.

Historians continue to debate its character (including the extent to which it was a civil war), and because the Revolutionary spirit is a meaningful phrase, evoking rich traditions and inspiring ideals, their discussions are not just academic exercises. What we think were the fundamental purposes of the War of Independence has a potent effect both on our understanding and interpretation of the course and spirit of American history and on our analysis of what America is, and is doing, today. What was at stake in 1776? Each of us must still ask if the war was fought for freedom and if so freedom for whom, from what, and for what ends. Is our rebellion comparable with the wars popping up in each newscast with the apparent frequency of bread in our breakfast toasters? The distressing situation, that this nation "conceived in Liberty and dedicated to the proposition that all men are created equal" today ends up so often supporting the forces of reaction and repression, requires the best analysis our history can offer.

The outstanding rebel leaders have become enshrined as demigods and their ideas almost entombed in a mausoleum of reverential acceptance. They would not have wanted it so. Jefferson, for example, suggested the usefulness of fundamental reassessments every twenty years. But the American schoolboy is brought up on a largely uncritical diet of the glory of the Revolution. Glorious it was, but the story is usually told from one side only. In the following pages the other Americans, the Loyalists or Tories, are given a chance to say a little of their piece.

SAMUEL SEABURY

Many Loyalists, not born and educated in England or committed by the holding of royal office, were as distressed with the growing rupture between the mother country and the colonies as many of those on the Patriot side. They had not been much happier with British policies since 1763 but whatever their discontent they stopped short at rebellion. Consequently, they emphasized the need to stay within the bounds of the law, and more and more in the last two years before war broke out they stressed the possibilities of legal redress and the illegality of several actions embarked upon by various groups of colonials.

Samuel Seabury, Jr., (1729–1796) was born in Groton, Connecticut, but when he was nearly thirteen the family moved to Long Island, New York. Two years later Samuel went to Yale, where he graduated in 1748. He was interested in missionary work and the better to prepare himself studied "physic" (medicine) for a year at Edinburgh University before his ordination in 1753 by the Bishop of London, who was responsible for the activities of the Anglican or Episcopalian church in the American colonies. Although his father had been a Congregational minister before becoming an Anglican in 1730, young Seabury from the first took the side of New York's established church in the literary battles which had been waged on and off since the last years of the seventeenth century. Protagonists in these disputes tended to inject secular notes into their religious debate. Certainly a number of the Anglican clergy saw themselves as fighting for the unity of church and state and keeping the colonies within the British Empire, as well as the successful defense of their denomination.

Since religion was the major path to Seabury's stand on the Revolution, the form and style of his contribution to the Loyalist position may come as a surprise. He adopted the title of "A Westchester Farmer" and stayed true to his pseudonym by taking pains to write in the words and sentiments of an educated yeoman. His statements are bluntly phrased, direct, to the point, and pitched to appeal to property loving classes who did not want to see their prosperity and prospects overturned by a bunch of reckless political plotters.

The following extracts* are taken from three pamphlets published in 1774 and 1775 by the New York printer James Rivington who tried, with little success, to keep his newspaper, the **Gazetteer,** an impartial forum for the views of both sides. Under (A) are grouped excerpts from Seabury's **Free Thoughts on the Proceedings of the Continental Congress,** which was released on November 24, 1774. Much of the work dealt with the specific problems created for farmers by the congressional ban on the exportation of flax seed and the slaughtering and sale of sheep. Passages of more general interest have been chosen for inclusion here.

Several replies were made to the pamphlet, the most important being one written by the youthful Alexander Hamilton under the title, **A Full**

---

* Samuel Seabury, *Letters of a Westchester Farmer,* ed. by C. H. Vance in Westchester County Historical Society *Publications,* VIII (1930), 65–66; 90–91; 106; 109–111. Used by permission.

Vindication of the Measures of the Continental Congress*. Rivington also printed this pamphlet, which was a remarkably brilliant statement of the Patriot case. While Hamilton's work was still in the press Seabury issued, through the same printer, **The Congress Canvassed**, with the hope of persuading New York merchants to nullify the measures of Congress by not observing them. Extracts from this publication are grouped as (B).

Early in the new year, 1775, Seabury presented a direct reply to Hamilton's work. He called it **A View of the Controversy between Great-Britain and her Colonies,** and selections from this pamphlet have been headed (C).

Hamilton responded with **The Farmer Refuted,** which came out about March 1, 1775. Seabury drafted a counter argument, to be called **The Republican Dissected or the Anatomy of an American Whig,** but before it could appear the battle had proceeded from quills to more dangerous weapons. Seabury fled New York and helped in rousing Westchester County citizens to pledge allegiance to the King. In November, 1775, he was captured by Isaac Sears (head of the New York Sons of Liberty), detained for a month in jail at New Haven, Connecticut, released, harrassed, and then driven to seek refuge with the British troops on Long Island in September, 1776.

A) Anarchy and Confusion, Violence and Oppression, distress my country; and I must, and *will* speak. Though the open violator of the laws may escape punishment, through the pusillanimity of the magistrates, he shall feel the lash of my pen; . . .

But perhaps you will say, that these men are contending for our rights; that they are defending our liberties; and though they act against law, yet that the necessity of the times will justify them. Let me see. I sell a number of sheep. I drive them to New-York, and deliver them to the purchaser. A mob interposes, and obliges me to take my sheep again, and drive them home for my pains, or sell them there for just what they please to give me. Are these the rights, is this the liberty, these men are contending for? It is vile, abject slavery, and I will have none of it. These men defend our rights, and liberties, who act in open defiance of the laws? No. They are making us the most abject slaves that ever existed. The necessity of the times justify them in violating the first principles of civil society! Who induced this necessity? Who involved the province in discord, anarchy and confusion? These very men. They created that necessity, which they now plead in their own justification.

Let me intreat you, my Friends, to have nothing to do with these men, or with any of the same stamp. Peace and quietness suit *you* best.

---

* It will be found in *The Papers of Alexander Hamilton,* ed. by Harold C. Syrett and Jacob E. Cooke (New York, 1961–), I, 45–78.

Confusion, and Discord, and Violence, and War, are sure destruction to the *farmer*. Without peace he cannot till his lands; unless protected by the laws, he cannot carry his produce to market. Peace indeed is departed from us for the present, and the protection of the laws has ceased. But I trust in God, there is yet one method left, which, by prudent management, will free us from all our difficulties; restore peace again to our dwellings, and give us the firm security of the laws for our protection. Renounce all dependence on Congresses, and Committees. They have neglected, or betrayed your interests. Turn then your eyes to your *constitutional* representatives. They are the true, and legal, and have been hitherto, the faithful defenders of your rights, and liberties; and you have no reason to think but that they will ever be so. . . . You can trust their wisdom and prudence, that they will use the most reasonable, constitutional, and effectual methods of restoring that peace and harmony, between Great Britain and this province, which is so earnestly wished for by all good men, and which is so absolutely necessary for the happiness of us all. . . .

B) Government was intended for the security of those who live under it;—to protect the weak against the strong;—the good against the bad;—to preserve order and decency among men, preventing every one from injuring his neighbour. Every person, then, owes obedience to the laws of the government under which he lives, and is obliged in honour and duty to support them. Because, if *one* has a right to disregard the laws of the society to which he belongs, *all* have the *same* right; and *then* government is at an end. Your honour was therefore previously engaged to the government under which you live, before you promised to abide by the determinations of the congress. You had no right to make a promise implicitly to obey all their regulations, before you knew what they were, and whether they would interfere with the public laws of the government, or not. And you are so far from being bound in honour to *obey* any determinations of the congress, which interfere with the laws of the government, that you are really bound in honour to *oppose* them. Now, a little consideration will render it evident, that there is no such thing as carrying the regulations of the congress into execution, without transgressing the known laws, and contravening the legal authority of the government:—without injuring and oppressing your neighbours, who have as good a right to the protection of the laws, as *you* have.

Let it also be considered, that as no man has a legal right to do what the laws forbid, so every man has a legal right to do what they permit.

Now, by enforcing an observance of the determinations of the congress, in this province, you abrogate, or suspend, several of its laws, some of them essential to the peace and order of the government: You contravene its authority: You take the government of the province out of the hands of the governor, council and assembly, and the government of the city, out of the hands of the legal magistrates, and place them in a CONGRESS, a body utterly unknown in any legal sense! You introduce a *foreign* power, and make *it* an instrument of *injustice* and *oppression*. . . .

C) It has ever been esteemed the privilege of Englishmen to canvass freely, the proceedings of every branch of the legislature; to examine into all public measures; to point out the errors that are committed in the administration of the government, and to censure without fear the conduct of all persons in public stations, whose conduct shall appear to deserve it. The exercise of this right has always been considered as one of the grand pillars which support our present happy constitution. . . . I will also agree with you, "that Americans are intitled to freedom." I will go further: I will own and acknowledge that not only *Americans,* but *Africans, Europeans, Asiaticks,* all men, of all countries and degrees, of all sizes and complexions, have a right to as much freedom as is consistent with the security of civil society: And I hope you will not think me an "enemy to the *natural* rights of mankind" because I cannot wish them more. We must however remember, that more liberty may, without inconvenience, be allowed to individuals in a small government, than can be admitted of in a large empire.

But when you assert that "since Americans have not by any act of theirs impowered the British parliament to make laws for them, it follows they can have no just authority to do it," you advance a position subversive of that dependence which all colonies must, from their very nature, have on the mother country.—By the British parliament, I suppose you mean the supreme legislative authority, the King, Lords and Commons, because no other authority in England has a right to make laws to bind the kingdom, and consequently no authority to make laws to bind the colonies. In this sense I shall understand, and use the phrase *British parliament.*

Now the dependence of the colonies on the mother-country has even been acknowledged. It is an impropriety of speech to talk of an independent colony. The words *independency* and *colony,* convey contradictory ideas: much like *killing* and *sparing.* . . . To suppose a part of the British dominions which is not subject to the power of the British legislature, is no better sense than to suppose a country, at one and the same time, to be, and not to be a part of the British dominions. If therefore the colony of New-York be a part of the British dominions, the colony of New-York is subject, and dependent on the supreme legislative authority of Great Britain. . . .

The right of colonists to exercise a legislative power, is no natural right. They derive it not from nature, but from the indulgence or grant of the parent state, whose subjects they were when the colony was settled, and by whose permission and assistance they made the settlement.

JOSEPH GALLOWAY

In Joseph Galloway (c. 1731–1803) we see personified the sort of blind neglect which has been accorded the Loyalist leaders. Few appreciate that his statesmanlike political thinking is worthy of a place far higher than that customarily given such patriotic heroes as Patrick Henry or Sam Adams. In Galloway we also see reflected the interesting split among the colonial lawyers, a group which for all its impact on the Revolutionary era still awaits its historian.

At a very early age he rose to prominence at the Bar of Pennsylvania and this, together with his marriage to the daughter of one of the colony's wealthiest and most influential merchants, propelled him toward a successful political career. After his first election to the provincial Assembly in 1756 he served continuously for two decades. The only exception was the year 1764–1765 when he joined with Benjamin Franklin in a move against the Penn family by petitioning the Crown to change the colony's form of government from proprietary to royal.

During the period when the British government tried to reorganize the administration of its American colonies, Galloway came to occupy an increasingly important role in Pennsylvania's affairs. Each year between 1766 and 1775 he was elected Speaker of the Assembly, a position which gave him probably the most powerful single voice in the colony's politics. He also served as chairman of the Assembly's committee for correspondence with the colony's agent in London. Galloway tried to maintain harmony between Great Britain and his colony, but while acknowledging the need for the British to raise more revenue from within North America, he was no advocate of parliamentary taxation and disapproved of many of the regulations imposed upon colonial commerce.

On the other hand, he found it impossible to reject the basic premise of parliamentary supremacy. Equally, however, as a product of the English common law, he placed emphasis on citizens' rights and the necessity of exercising all power constitutionally. Looking at what was actually taking place he concluded that in some matters the British government was acting unconstitutionally and, looking to the remedy, he sought a written constitution for the empire. Indeed, his most significant contribution as a delegate to the First Continental Congress (1774) was a scheme for an imperial legislature which would thrash out the details of such a document. For a time it seemed that Galloway's plan had a chance, but consideration of it was postponed, as he claimed "by a majority of one colony." Eventually it was rejected and not even allowed to be entered in the minutes. Congress then proceeded on the radical course Galloway had feared, coming up with such measures as a nonexportation plan to add to the resolution on nonimportation which it had passed on September 27, the day immediately preceding its hearing of Galloway's plan and motion. Many have since wondered whether the passing of his instrument for a balanced distribution of legislative power, a means for legal and orderly redress of grievances, might not have prevented or at least postponed the rebellion.

When war did break out Galloway, even though he fled to the country because he thought Philadelphia was too hot to hold him, desired to stay neutral. He loved his native Pennsylvania, yet he could not believe that the American rebellion was any more constitutional, any more just, than some of the actions of British ministries had been. He joined General Howe not so much because he liked the British or was enamored of their cause but with the hope of retrieving America from the disorder into which it had fallen. After Philadelphia was taken he headed its civil administration.

Too late, Joseph Galloway was made to realize that he was too vocal a spokesman, too honest a person, and too deeply involved in a war for independence, not a war for a new disposition of imperial power. When the Continental army reoccupied the city in 1778, he sailed to England and there became the chief apologist for the Loyalists. He had already produced a severe criticism of the First Continental Congress in **A Candid Examination of the Mutual Claims of Great-Britain, and the Colonies** (1775), and now he gave a critical analysis before the House of Commons of the way in which the war was being waged (**The Examination of Joseph Galloway . . . ,** 1779 and the attacks on British military commanders, for example **Letters to a Nobleman,** 1779). More positive efforts were his continued attempts to bring about a reconciliation between Britain and the colonies on the same bases as he had proposed earlier (See his **Historical and Political Reflections,** 1780 and **Cool Thoughts on the Consequences to Great Britain of American Independence,** 1780).

The peace of 1783 finally killed his hopes, and speaking for the Loyalists in general he put into words their shock and dejection. He also expressed their bitter conviction that the British, who during the war had not fought hard enough, were now lightly selling their allies down the river. Shame and deceit were the two characteristics of the treaty most evident to Loyalist eyes. His

American estates confiscated, Galloway became dependent upon his pension from the British government, an unhappy existence which encouraged him to petition the government of Pennsylvania to permit him to return. He was not allowed to do so, and therefore spent his last years in England.

The following extract is taken from **A Candid Examination** (London edition, 1780).* It deals directly with the question of allegiance and produces a philosophical framework for Galloway's comments on the relations between Britain and the American colonies.†

All the officers of Government, every member of Assembly, every foreigner before his naturalization, had always taken the oaths of allegiance, under the directions of the statutes that have been made for that purpose. The words of the oath are the same with that administered to the subject in Britain, on the like occasions; and consequently must be of the same import, and carry with them the same obligations in every respect. Both in Britain and America the oaths are taken to the King, not in his private, but politic capacity; they are taken to him as representative of the whole State, whose duty it is to superintend the administration of justice, and to see that a faithful obedience is paid to the laws. These oaths are no more than renewals of the original covenant, upon which all Governments are formed: for in the constitution of all societies two covenants are essential; one on the part of the State, that it will ever consult and promote the public good and safety; and the other on the part of the subject, that he will bear fidelity and true allegiance to the *sovereign,* or *supreme authority.* . . .

In every Government, protection and allegiance, or obedience, are reciprocal duties. They are so inseparably united, that one cannot exist without the other. Protection from the State demands, and entitles it to receive, obedience and submission to its laws from the subject: and obedience to the will of the State, communicated in its laws, entitles the subject to its protection. A just sense of this truth has governed the conduct of the State towards the Colonies, and that of the Colonies towards the State, ever since their settlement. The Colonists have not

---

* [Joseph Galloway], A *Candid Examination of the Mutual Claims of Great-Britain, and the Colonies* (New-York, 1775 "and now reprinted" London, 1780), pp. 26–28; 52–54.

† This leads logically into Galloway's schemes for imperial union. Students interested in looking into his various plans will find them most conveniently in the study of Julian P. Boyd, *Anglo-American Union* (Philadelphia, 1941).

only settled upon the lands of the State, under its licence and authority, granted by its representative; but they have been fostered, nourished, and sheltered under its wings, and protected by its wealth and power. And as they have ever yielded obedience to its laws, they have, whenever in danger, called for its protection; and in the last war were saved from all the misery and slavery which Popish superstition and tyranny could inflict, when their inability to save themselves was universally known and acknowledged. . . .

The subjects of a free State, in every part of its dominions, ought, in good policy, to enjoy the same fundamental rights and privileges. Every distinction between them must be offensive and odious, and cannot fail to create uneasiness and jealousies, which will ever weaken the Government, and frequently terminate in insurrections; and these, in every society, ought to be particularly guarded against. If the British State therefore means to retain the Colonies in a due obedience on her Government, it will be wisdom in her to restore to her American subjects the enjoyment of the right of assenting to, and dissenting from, such bills as shall be proposed to regulate their conduct. Laws thus made will ever be obeyed; because by their assent they become their own acts.—It will place them in the same condition with their brethren in Britain, and remove all cause of complaint; or, if they should conceive any regulations inconvenient, or unjust, they will petition, not rebel. Without this, it is easy to perceive that the union and harmony, which is peculiarly essential to a free society, whose members are resident in regions so very remote from each other, cannot long subsist.

The genius, temper, and circumstances of the Americans should be also duly attended to. No people in the world have higher notions of liberty. It would be impossible ever to eradicate them, should an attempt so unjust be ever made: their late spirit and conduct fully prove this assertion, and will serve as a clue to that policy by which they ought to be governed. The distance of America from Britain, her vast extent of territory, her numerous ports and conveniencies of commerce, her various productions, her increasing numbers, and consequently her growing strength and power, when duly considered—all point out the policy of uniting the two countries together, upon principles of English liberty. Should this be omitted, the Colonies will infallibly throw off their connexion with the Mother Country.—Their distance will encourage the attempt, their discontent will give them spirit, and their numbers, wealth, and power, at some future day, will enable them to effect it.

ROBERT PROUD

Robert Proud (1728–1813), like many of the Loyalists, was born in England but, unlike others in this group such as Jonathan Boucher and Thomas Hutchinson, he was able to remain in America after the hostilities of independence ended. Well regarded among Friends (Quaker) circles in England, he came to Pennsylvania in 1759. Two years later he became master of the Friends Public School in Philadelphia. Although the war disrupted his career by compelling him to the Loyalist side, he was able to resume his position at the school in 1780. He held it for another decade at the not inconsiderable salary of two hundred and fifty pounds per annum.

Slowly gathering together an outstanding collection of source material, he began long-range labors to prepare a history of Pennsylvania. It was published in two volumes in 1797–1798, but unfortunately it is almost entirely devoted to the colony before 1742. Proud tacked on a sort of epilogue, titled "A View of the Province of Pennsylvania . . . between . . . 1760 and 1770," but he never really examined the Patriot-Loyalist quarrel.

In the following letter* we deal with another aspect of wars (especially civil ones) which is frequently forgotten in the epics of valor and glory, the harsh tales of ravage and death. This is the role of Fortune. On the battlefield he who lives may be no more skillful, no more courageous than the friend or the enemy who dies. This may also be true of those who try to stay out of the thick of things. The letter from Robert Proud to his brother William, then in England, shows this point very well. Its date is December 1, 1777.

. . . On the Commencement of open Rebellion here, I had so great Reason to fear, having not only been obnoxious to the Incendiaries and Usurpers, but also particularly pointed out and threatened by them, more than many others, who are now suffering more than I do, thro the Anarchy and Tyranny that has reigned here or for their not joining in the Rebellion and acknowledging the Usurpation. But as I have always since that time lived in a very private and retired Way, even like a Person dead amidst the Confusions, and conversing more with my Books than with Persons, who are so universally tainted more or less with the general Evil, and scarcely ever departing above two Miles from my Place of Abode for several years. Contrary to my Expectation I have suffered no Abuse, nor ever been molested, which I consider as a Providential, and very remarkable Favour; and tho this Manner of Life may have subjected me to much Disadvantage as to my temporal Interest, by accustoming myself so much to an inactive Habit, to which

---

* "Letters of Robert Proud," *Pennsylvania Magazine of History and Biography*, XXXIV (Philadelphia, 1910), 63–65. Used by permission.

I have been thought to be naturally too much addicted, yet I believe it has been a great Means of singularly preserving me from imminent Danger, to which I considered even my Life to be nearly engrossed.

But it has not fared so well with a Number of my Friends and Acquaintances; twenty of whom, mostly Friends, and all Citizens of this Place, a few days before the King's Troops approached nigh the City, were suddenly seized by the usurpation and banished into the back Parts of Virginia; . . . It will perhaps be needless here to say, that these Persons, who were thus banished from their nearest Connections were regarded as not favoring the Rebellion, and by their Persecutors called Enemies to their Country, otherwise to their Proceedings; but that they with many others, notwithstanding the general Revolt, had remained entirely inactive either for or against it, excepting some of them, I mean such as were Quakers, occasionally using their Persuasions to Peace; which was the most that could prudently be expected from Persons in their Situation, is, I believe, a truth, that may, with great Certainty be mentioned and relied on; and that nothing criminal was, or could be proved against any of them even by their Enemies nor the supporters of the Usurpation itself; of which they were so conscious as to send them into Exile without so much as a Hearing tho' loudly called for by the sufferers. But the Arrival of the Royal Army prevented further Proceedings of this kind; . . .

I have done little or nothing in my private Affairs during these Troubles, on Account of which principally, since Bro. John's Departure, I have with so much Reluctance staid in this Country: my debts being mostly yet uncollected by Reason of the distressing Circumstances of the Times, and no present Prospect of getting them in; all Paper Currency having long ago been depreciated several times its value occasioned by the large Quantity of the new Continental Cash, which every Body's obliged to take in Payment, where the King's Troops are not in Possession; no other Money being scarcely to be seen; and, as, for the same Reasons, I expect never to receive a great Part of the Principal due to me in this Country, so I have still less expectation of recovering any Interest; which it is here expected the Merchants in England will duly consider and favour their Creditors here accordingly, in that particular; hence and in Consideration of the present Dubiousness of being able to buy Bills even with our lawful Paper Currency, the only Capital that many of us have, and which seems now to be at a stand. . . .

JAMES ALLEN

The Allens were one of the "great families" of Pennsylvania in the years before the Revolution. James (c. 1742–1778) was the third son of Chief Justice William Allen. The Allen family had an abundance of wealth, status, and esteem. It tended to the Loyalist side in defense of established government, law, and property. Yet the family's members had also breathed the fresh air of American protest—even the father had remonstrated against the Stamp Act—and their support for the colonies continued up to the eve of independence. One of the boys, Andrew, was a member of the Committee of Safety in Philadelphia. In 1775, he was appointed a delegate to the Continental Congress, but he never attended once he realized that it was set on a break with Britain. Indeed, all the four sons of the chief justice seem to have drawn the line at independence. In his diary for July 26, 1775 James Allen wrote: "It is a great & glorious cause. The eyes of Europe are upon us; if we fall, Liberty no longer continues an inhabitant of this Globe: for England is running fast to slavery. The King is as despotic as any prince in Europe, the only difference is the mode; & a venal parliament are [sic] as bad as a standing army." It would seem that such thoughts would make him a Patriot, but a separation from England and the act of rebellion were too much for him to stomach, as the following diary entries show.*

March 6, 1776.—The plot thickens; peace is scarcely thought of —Independancy predominant. Thinking people uneasy, irresolute & inactive. The Mobility triumphant. Every article of life doubled. . . . I love the Cause of liberty; but cannot heartily join in the prosecution of measures totally foreign to the original plan of Resistance. The madness of the multitude is but one degree better than submission to the Tea-Act.

May 15, 1776.—I am now a political character; having been chosen a Representative in Assembly the first of this month for Northampton County, without any opposition; having 853 votes & only 14 against me. The 20th of this Month the Assembly meets but I believe we shall soon be dissolved. The Congress have resolved to recommend it to the different Colonies to establish new forms of Government, to get rid of oaths of allegiance &c. I think the Assembly of this province, will not consent to change their constitution; and then heigh for a convention!

---

* "Diary of James Allen, Esq., of Philadelphia," *Pennsylvania Magazine of History and Biography*, IX (1885), 186–187, 280–281, 288–289. Used by permission.

A Convention chosen by the people, will consist of the most fiery Inde-pendants; they will have the whole Executive & legislative authority in their hands. . . . Every article of life is extravagantly dear. I am very obnoxious to the independants; having openly declared my aversion to their principles & had one or two disputes at the coffee-house with them. I am determined to oppose them vehemently in Assembly, for if they prevail there; all may bid adieu to our old happy constitution & peace.

June 16, 1776.—This day I set off with my family for Northamp-ton, with the Chariot, Phaeton, and Sulky. I have met the Assembly & sat from 20th May to this time & have been very active in opposing Independance & change of Government; but the Tide is too strong, we could not prevent a change of instructions to our Delegates. . . .

[Feb. 17, 1777] My particular situation has been of late very un-easy, owing to the Battalion of Militia of this district, assembling in the Town of Northampton, to the number of 600 men, where they con-tinued a fortnight & marched off the day before yesterday viz. 15 Feby inst—They are generally disorderly, being under no discipline; & I was particularly obnoxous [sic], on account of my political opinions, & the conduct of my brothers, but particularly for the late assault I made on the Lieut: Coll. when my chariot was attacked & which the whole Bat-talion highly resented. Eight or nine parties of 15 or 20 men each came to demand Blankets, one party of which, was very uncivil. But by prudence I escaped without any insult, having parted with 10 Blankets. The principal officers behaved with great civility & the Coll. Boehm whom I had the encounter with, came to my house, to assure me he was innocent of the attack on my chariot & we buried the affair in Oblivion. He assured me, that the soldiers were ripe for doing some violence to my house, which he with difficulty prevented, & upon the whole I had great good fortune to escape without some injury from a riotous incensed soldiery, & am at present pretty easy on that head. Notwithstanding this I am uneasy & wish to be in Philad[a]. My wife is often alarmed; I am afraid to converse with persons here, or write to my friends in Philad[a]; & a small matter, such as a letter intercepted or unguarded word, would plunge me into troubles. I never knew, how painful it is to be secluded from the free conversation of one's friends, the loss of which cannot be made up by any other expedients. I am considering whether I shall not leave this place in May & adjourn to Philad[a] & am in that state of uncertainty, that has hitherto distressed me so much. I should prefer continuing here, were I not in so conspicuous a point of light. It is odd to reflect that I am taking as much pains to be in obscurity, as others are to blaze in the publick Eye & become of importance. . . .

Oppressions multiply & it seems determined to make this country intolerable to all who are not actively its friends. The most discreet, passive, & respectable characters are dragged forth & tho' no charge can be made, yet a new Idea is started, (which like all other beginnings of oppressive schemes soon become general,) of securing such men as hostages. This circumstance makes me think my brothers happily out of the way. I daily expect, notwithstanding my present parole, to be further harrassed, as I am extremely obnoxious. Men's former characters for integrity, & virtue, instead of availing them only expose them, as it is supposed their influence must be greater. . . . These oppressions on men who have never given offence are justified by the Whigs as necessary for the security of all Government; while the Tories think, that few cases can happen, where men of virtue ought innocently to [be] persecuted. If necessity is a plea, who created it, or where will it stop? Massacres, proscriptions & every species of iniquity may be justified by necessity.

I returned 2 days ago from a visit to Shrewsbury where I went with Mr T. Lawrence & his brother Stacy—& spent 10 days. We had a pleasant tour; & tho' considering my known sentiments, I run some risk in continuing in Jersey, where, the wantonness of oppression has exceeded all description; that Government being in the hands of the most low lived, hot-brained presbyterians. I passed thro' Brunswick, & notwithstanding the charges brought against the Enemy for wilful devastation, there did not appear to me to be more than what might have been expected from so large an army; especially considering it was an Enemy's country. The prospect of next Winter is terrible; the quantity of paper currency has together with the total stoppage of trade, risen all articles to a monstrous pitch. Green tea £20, Bohea £5 Sugar £50 pr Cwt. Loaf Sugar 25/ per lb, shoes 35/ & every thing in proportion. But this is not felt by those in employment, who are paid accordingly, & money is plenty in every department. Men who could scarcely maintain their families, now live in splendor. In short this Country is agitated to its foundations, & will probably soon be overturned.

WILLIAM EDDIS

His loyalty thrust William Eddis (fl. 1769–1777) into a bit part on the stage of history. Not even the dates of his birth and death can be given, and almost everything we know about him comes from his own correspondence with friends in England which was published in London in 1792 as **Letters from America . . . Comprising Occurrences from 1769 to 1777.***

He came to Annapolis, Maryland in the autumn of 1769 and at once took up the duties of secretary to the governor, Robert Eden. From this vantage point he developed an informed view of the colony's affairs, close relationships with its political leaders and, from his frequent travels, love for the beauty of the countryside and seashores. All these were reflected in his letters which minutely describe the life of the times. He had an artist's eye for detail whether he was speaking of marriage or menus, Maryland's economic resources or the elegance of its ladies. The events leading up to the Revolution were inevitably a subject of great concern to Eddis. We see in him a moderate man who, despite his official positions, recognized the virtue of meeting many of the colonial demands. For example, he believed all the Townshend Acts should be repealed without qualification, so that Great Britain and the American colonies might again enjoy harmonious relations. He accepted the validity of many of the colonies' grievances but felt that their way of obtaining redress was neither good sense nor good law. In 1777 Eddis was forced to leave Maryland, and back he went to his native England and obscurity.

[Letter XIX, March 13, 1775] I have even attempted to moderate the enthusiasm of intemperate zeal, by the following appeal to Common Sense and Common Equity; which, through the medium of the Maryland Gazette, has been submitted to public inspection; . . .

"TO THE PRINTERS.

"The present unhappy contention between the *mother country* and her *colonies,* is a matter of the deepest concern to every honest, every feeling mind: it is, therefore, the indispensable duty of every friend to society, to study and to pursue those methods, which may lead to a perfect reconciliation, and the establishment of a permanent union between *Great Britain* and *America.* . . .

"It is certain that there are many in *this,* and other *provinces,* who object to the spirit of violence, which seems at this time too predominant. Convinced of the propriety of their sentiments, and the integ-

---

* William Eddis, *Letters from America, Historical and Descriptive* (London, 1792), pp. 190–191; 193; 197–198.

rity of their hearts, they conceive the cause of America may be *totally injured* by a precipitate, and unnecessary defiance of the power of Great Britain: they firmly believe, that a respectful behaviour to their *sovereign* and their *mother country*—a dutiful and constitutional application to the *throne*—and a firm perseverance in *virtuous,* though *pacific principles,* will, in the issue, be productive of the most felicitous consequences. . . .

"If I differ in opinion from the multitude, must I therefore be deprived of my character, and the confidence of my fellow-citizens, when in every station of life I discharge my duty with fidelity and honour? DEATH—the certain tax on all the sons of men, were preferable to so abject a state.—No—'twere better to suffer all that "age, ach[e], penury, imprisonment, can lay on nature," than resign that glorious inheritance of a free subject—the liberty of *thinking—speaking—* and *acting,* agreeable to the dictates of conscience! I frankly acknowledge no man has a right to disturb the peace of the community, by broaching tenets destructive to the *true interests* and *welfare* of his country; but at the same time, it cannot be justifiable to compel others to adopt *every system* which we esteem conducive to the public good. Let us therefore be unanimous in *virtue*—in *frugality*—and in *industry;* let us conduct ourselves on the christian principle of "doing to others as we would have done to us;" let us not, in the frantic moments of intemperate zeal, mistake *libertinism* for *liberty,* and commit outrages, which we shall recollect with *shame,* and condemn with *heart-felt anxiety.* While we contend for the inestimable blessings of British subjects, let us not assume a *tyrannical authority* over each other. In a word, let *reason* and *moderation* hold the scale in every important determination—so shall every *real grievance* be effectually redressed— every man shall sing the song of gladness under his own *vine,* and we shall at once be free—be loyal—and be happy! . . .

Annapolis,
Feb. 14, 1775.   *A Friend to Amity."*

JONATHAN ODELL

The Revolution produced an astonishing amount of poetry, but hardly one piece can be classed as a great work and most of it does not rise above the level of doggerel. The bulk of this poetry was written in the interests of propaganda. Below is reprinted a poem by Jonathan Odell, one of the two best versifiers on the Loyalist side.

Odell (1737–1818) was a graduate of the College of New Jersey (now Princeton) who served as a surgeon in the British army during the Seven Years War. He then trained for the ministry in England and came back to Burlington, New Jersey. To help his family's finances he also practised as a doctor. When his verses made him well-known, the Patriots limited his movements. However, after some months of such circumscribed living, he broke parole and escaped to the British lines in New York City (1778). From there he continued to pour out sharp poetical slaps at the Patriots. Many of his verses appeared in Rivington's **Royal Gazette.** In addition, he became involved in a number of military-political matters. He played an important role in the discussions between Benedict Arnold and the British, served as chaplain to a regiment of Pennsylvania Loyalists, and was assistant secretary first to the Board of Associated Loyalists and then to Guy Carleton, the British commander-in-chief. When New York was evacuated Odell left with Carleton for England but shortly afterward came back to New Brunswick, Canada (1784). In its newly created government he was appointed registrar and clerk of the province and occupied a seat on the governor's council. He held public office for nearly three decades in the staunchly Loyalist province.

The following poem was written by Jonathan Odell in honor of the King's birthday, June 4, 1777.

A BIRTHDAY SONG*

Time was when America hallow'd the morn
On which the lov'd monarch of Britain was born.
Hallow'd the day, and joyfully chanted
    God save the King!
Then flourish'd the blessings of freedom and peace,
And plenty flow'd in with a yearly increase.
Proud of our lot we chanted merrily
    Glory and joy crown the King!

With envy beheld by the nations around
We rapidly grew, nor was anything found
Able to check our growth while we chanted
    God save the King!
O blest beyond measure, had honour and truth
Still nurs'd in our hearts what they planted in youth!
Loyalty had chanted merrily
    Glory and joy crown the King!

---

* Poem by Jonathan Odell, printed in Winthrop Sargent (ed.), *The Loyal Verses of Joseph Stansbury and Dr. Jonathan Odell* (Albany, 1860), p. 11.

But see! how rebellion has lifted her head!
How honour and truth are with loyalty fled
Few are there now who join us in chanting
    God save the King!
And see! how deluded the multitude fly
To arm in a cause that is built on a lye!
Yet are we proud to chant thus merrily
    Glory and joy crown the King!

Though faction by falsehood awhile may prevail,
And loyalty suffers a captive in jail,
Britain is rouz'd, rebellion is falling:
    God save the King!
The captive shall soon be releas'd from his chain;
And conquest restore us to Britain again,
Ever to join in chanting merrily
    Glory and joy crown the King!

Patriots Look at Loyalists

"A TORY IS A THING WHOSE HEAD IS IN ENGLAND, AND ITS BODY IN AMERICA, AND ITS NECK OUGHT TO BE STRETCHED"*

In this section our concern is with what the Patriots, especially some of their leaders, wrote about the Loyalists. At first thought one might expect a massive amount of commentary on fellow Americans who had, in their eyes, betrayed the cause of liberty and independence. In reality, one has to dig rather deep to find lengthy analyses of the Tory and his position. Perhaps the reason is that most of the Patriot standard-bearers were too busy either conducting the war or summoning up the sinews of the halfhearted, disputatious states. Another, more complicated reason could be that they did not feel any rabid animosity toward those who had been fellow colonials and in many cases personal friends, old companions from the days when they had stood together in opposition to the various British measures.

Some Loyalists, of whom Galloway is an example, tried to remain neutral but found that they were not left alone. They were in a war, not a tea party. Many were driven from their homes, saw their estates confiscated, their homes pillaged, their barns burned, their livestock stolen, their families separated from them. A few even suffered the cruel, painful indignity of being tarred and feathered.† Patriots in Loyalist strongholds were held in the same suspicion and suffered many of the same harrassments. In this war, as perhaps in most, there was plenty of cruelty on each side.

But this was still an eighteenth-century conflict, one in which there was no total mobilization of the nation's population and resources. Many men and women lived their daily lives in 1778 much as they had in 1773. This fact needs to be balanced against the observation that the majority of those whose comments are printed here were directly involved as leaders in the fight for American independence.

---

* *New York Journal,* February 9, 1775, quoted in Frank Moore, *Diary of the American Revolution* (2 vols., New York, 1859–60), I, 19.

† A good description of this horrible treatment will be found in the novel by Kenneth Roberts, *Oliver Wiswell* (New York, 1940; also available in paperback).

BENJAMIN FRANKLIN

Benjamin Franklin (1706–1790) in the following passages* accurately repre-
sents the general feelings of moderate Americans toward the Loyalists. We
should note that there is no doubt in his mind as to who started the war and
that, even in a friendly letter, he comes close to equating the Loyalist with a
hired murderer.

The last paragraph of the first selection is fairly well-known for the distinction Franklin makes between royalist and loyalist. Although there is more
to it than mere semantics, he really begs the question of loyalty. According
to Franklin the Americans knew better than the British what the British constitution was and what was meant by English liberties. Furthermore, as a
central figure in the Revolution, Franklin also supported a doctrine of rebellion arising from the natural rights philosophy, so loudly proclaimed by Jefferson in the Declaration of Independence. He, together with all the other
founding fathers, believed it was legitimate to resist the British government.
But he did not really address himself to the difficult, yet key problem: at what
time and under what precise circumstances is rebellion justified and resistance to his government incumbent upon the good citizen. One may speculate
whether his vehemence was not partly due to the fact that his son William,
governor of New Jersey from 1763 to 1776, was a Loyalist. The father saw
his son declared "an enemy to the liberties of this country" by the provincial
congress of New Jersey, arrested, detained in Connecticut, ill-treated, and
ultimately exiled. After the war the two partially reconciled their differences,
but William never came back to America and lived out his life as a pensioner
of the Crown.

[Letter to Francis Maseres, June 26, 1785] But we differ a little in our
sentiments respecting the loyalists (as they call themselves), and the
conduct of America towards them, which, you think, "seems actuated
by a spirit of revenge; and that it would have been more agreeable to
policy, as well as justice, to have restored their estates upon their taking the oaths of allegiance to the new governments." That there should
still be some resentment against them in the breasts of those, who have
had their houses, farms, and towns so lately destroyed, and relations
scalped under the conduct of these royalists, is not wonderful,† though
I believe the opposition given by many to their re-establishing among
us is owing to a firm persuasion that there could be no reliance on
their oaths; and that the effect of receiving those people again would

---

* *The Works of Benjamin Franklin,* ed. by John Bigelow (12 vols., New
York, 1904) XI, 64–66; XII, 58–59.
† A matter for wonder.

be an introduction of that very anarchy and confusion they falsely reproach us with. . . .

The war against us was begun by a general act of Parliament declaring all our estates confiscated; and probably one great motive to the loyalty of the royalists was the hope of sharing in these confiscations. They have played a deep game, staking their estates against ours; and they have been unsuccessful. But it is a surer game, since they had promises to rely on from your government, of indemnification in case of loss; and I see your Parliament is about to fulfil those promises. To this I have no objection, because, though still our enemies, they are men; they are in necessity; and I think even a hired assassin has a right to his pay from his employer. It seems, too, more reasonable that the expense of paying these should fall upon the government who encouraged the mischief done, rather than upon us who suffered it; the confiscated estates making amends but for a very small part of that mischief. It is not, therefore, clear that our retaining them is chargeable with injustice.

I have hinted above, that the name *loyalist* was improperly assumed by these people. *Royalists* they may perhaps be called. But the true *loyalists* were the people of America, against whom they acted. No people were ever known more truly loyal, and universally so, to their sovereigns. The Protestant succession in the House of Hanover was their idol. Not a Jacobite was to be found from one end of the colonies to the other. They were affectionate to the people of England, zealous and forward to assist in her wars, by voluntary contributions of men and money, even beyond their proportion. The king and Parliament had frequently acknowledged this by public messages, resolutions, and reimbursements. But they were equally fond of what they esteemed their rights; and if they resisted when those were attacked, it was a resistance in favor of a British constitution, which every Englishman might share in enjoying, who should come to live among them; it was resisting arbitrary impositions, that were contrary to common right and to their fundamental constitutions, and to constant ancient usage. . . .

[1788] THE CLAIMS OF THE AMERICAN LOYALISTS; AN APOLOGUE

Lion, king of a certain forest, had among his subjects a body of faithful dogs, in principle and affection strongly attached to his person and government, and through whose assistance he had extended his dominions, and had become the terror of his enemies.

Lion, however, influenced by evil councellors, took an aversion to the dogs, condemned them unheard, and ordered his tigers, leopards, and panthers to attack and destroy them.

The dogs petitioned humbly, but their petitions were rejected haughtily; and they were forced to defend themselves, which they did with bravery.

A few among them, of a mongrel race, derived from a mixture with wolves and foxes, corrupted by royal promises of great rewards, deserted the honest dogs and joined their enemies.

The dogs were finally victorious; a treaty of peace was made, in which Lion acknowledged them to be free, and disclaimed all future authority over them.

The mongrels, not being permitted to return among them, claimed of the royalists the reward that had been promised.

A council of the beasts was held to consider their demand.

The wolves and foxes agreed unanimously that the demand was just, that royal promises ought to be kept, and that every loyal subject should contribute freely to enable his Majesty to fulfil them.

The horse alone, with a boldness and freedom that became the nobleness of his nature, delivered a contrary opinion.

"The king," said he, "has been misled by bad ministers, to war unjustly upon his faithful subjects. Royal promises, when made to encourage us to act for the public good, should indeed be honorably acquitted; but if to encourage us to betray and destroy each other they are wicked and void from the beginning. The advisers of such promises, and those who murdered in consequence of them instead of being recompensed, should be severely punished. Consider how greatly our common strength is already diminished by the loss of the dogs. If you enable the king to reward these fratricides, you will establish a precedent that may justify a future tyrant in making like promises; and every example of such an unnatural brute rewarded will give them additional weight. Horses and bulls, as well as dogs, may thus be divided against their own kind, and civil wars produced at pleasure, till we are so weakened that neither liberty nor safety is any longer to be found in the forest, and nothing remains but abject submission to the will of a despot, who may devour us as he pleases."

The council had sense enough to resolve,—That the demand be rejected.

JOHN JAY

Jay (1745–1829) was a member of a wealthy and powerful family in New York; by upbringing, personality, and outlook he was a patrician. After being tutored at home he went to King's College (the present Columbia) and graduated from there in 1764. His mind and temperament seemed ideal for the law, a profession which he entered on leaving college. Grave, hard-working, resolute, with a marvelous lucidity of reasoning, he was a man who made his mark strongly but not showily. He prospered in his law practice and delighted in the social life of New York City.

The Revolution changed everything. Jay entered a career of public life and effectively ended his career as a lawyer. He represented New York at both the first and second Continental Congresses. Both in those bodies and in the New York committee of correspondence he presented moderate or conservative views, reflecting the concern of the colony's merchants that a break with Britain would be both a setback in trade and a signal for mob rule. Yet once independence was proclaimed, no one could have been more assiduous for the cause. He helped to win acceptance for the Declaration in his home colony, led the way in drafting New York's constitution, and then served until 1779 as its chief justice. Later in that year Congress selected him to be minister plenipotentiary to Spain. A new and distinguished career in diplomacy was thus begun. Before his death, fifty years later, John Jay held almost all the important offices open to him, with the exception of the presidency.

By no means a genius, Jay's contribution sprang from the fineness of his character. In the following extract* there is an intriguing picture of the way in which a devoted public servant handled an embarrassing private friendship. He speaks frankly but with quiet dignity, honest conviction, and genuine concern. It is apposite to point out that Jay's older brother James, knighted by George III in 1763, was a Patriot during the first years of the Revolution. Indeed he was one of the principal sponsors of the New York Act of Attainder, 1779, which confiscated the property of the state's leading Loyalists. But in 1782 he deliberately allowed himself to be captured by the British troops, an incident which, we are told, led John to say that he would try "to forget that my father has such a son."

TO PETER VAN SCHAACK.

17th September, 1782.

. . . In the course of the present troubles I have adhered to certain fixed principles, and faithfully obeyed their dictates, without regarding

---

* *The Correspondence and Public Papers of John Jay,* ed. by Henry P. Johnston (4 vols., New York, 1890–1893), II, 343–345.

the consequences of such conduct to my friends, my family, or myself; all of whom, however dreadful the thought, I have ever been ready to sacrifice, if necessary, to the public objects in contest.

Believe me, my heart has nevertheless been, on more than one occasion, afflicted by the execution of what I thought and still think was my duty. I felt very sensibly for you and for others, but as society can regard only the political propriety of men's conduct, and not the moral propriety of their motives to it, I could only lament your unavoidably becoming classed with many whose morality was convenience, and whose politics changed with the aspect of public affairs. My regard for you as a good old friend continued, notwithstanding. . . . Your judgment and consequently your conscience differed from mine on a very important question; but though, as an independent American, I considered all who were not for us, and you among the rest, as against us, yet be assured that John Jay did not cease to be a friend to Peter Van Schaack. No one can serve two masters. Either Britain was right and America wrong, or America was right and Britain wrong. They who thought Britain right were bound to support her, and America had a just claim to the services of those who approved her cause. Hence it became our duty to take one side or the other, and no man is to be blamed for preferring the one which his reason recommended as the most just and virtuous.

Several of our countrymen indeed left and took arms against us, not from any such principles, but from the most dishonourable of human motives. Their conduct has been of a piece with their inducements, for they have far outstripped savages in perfidy and cruelty. Against these men every American must set his face and steel his heart. There are others of them, though not many, who, I believe, opposed us because they thought they could not conscientiously go with us. To such of them as have behaved with humanity I wish every species of prosperity that may consist with the good of my country.

You see how naturally I slide into the habit of writing as freely as I used to speak to you. Ah! my friend, if ever I see New York again, I expect to meet with "the shade of many a departed joy"; my heart bleeds to think of it. Where and how are your children? Whenever, as a private friend, it may be in my power to do good to either, tell me; while I have a loaf, you and they may freely partake of it. Don't let this idea hurt you. If your circumstances are easy, I rejoice; if not, let me take off some of their rougher edges.

BENJAMIN RUSH

Benjamin Rush (1745–1813) declared that the American Revolution was generally believed by its friends, among whom the historian would include him as one of the most ardent, to be "the most important" controversy "that had ever engaged the attention of mankind . . . the very existence of **freedom** upon our globe was involved in the issue of the contest in favor of the United States." Rush suggested the title for Paine's pamphlet **Common Sense;** was a signer of the Declaration of Independence; an advocate of slavery's abolition; a pleader for an end to the death penalty; probably the first man in American medical history to use conversations with the patient as a tool in analyzing his psychological disorders and occupational therapy as a technique for treating him. In short, he is an example of that attractive eighteenth-century American who was highly educated, ever curious, intellectually indefatigable, genuinely humane, and politically committed.

The following notes* show the penchant of the scientist for classifications. They also demonstrate a medical analyst and informed public figure's understanding of the variety of men's motivations and emotions. Yet, Rush's own political leanings emerge clearly.

. . . The people of America may be divided into the five following classes.

1. *A rank tory.* This class are advocates for unconditional submission to Great Britain. They rejoice in all the misfortunes that befall the united States. They fabricate lies to deceive and divide the people of America. They employ their utmost ingenuity to depreciate the continental money.

[2.] *Moderate men.* This class are advocates for the situation of the year 1763. They have no relish for independance. They are influenced either 1, by a connection with men who hold offices under the old Government. 2nd, by an attachment to the pomp, and hiarchy of the church of England which is reduced to a level with the other protestant churches by the Declaration of independence, or 3ly, by a fondness for those luxuries which were introduced among us by our commerce wth Great Britain. In this respect they resemble the children of Israel, who say of themselves, "We remember the fish which we did eat in Egypt freely, the cucumbers and the melons, and the leeks, and the onions, and the garlic: But now our Soul is dried away; There is nothing [torn] besides the Manna before our eyes." *Numb. xi and*

---

* "Historical Notes of Dr. Benjamin Rush," *Pennsylvania Magazine of History and Biography,* XXVII (1903), 143–145. Used by permission.

5 & 6. They think freedom too dear when purchased with the temporary loss of tea, coffee, sugar, and wine, good mutton, beef, Bread, milk, and the fruits of the earth, which are the *manna* of this country, appear as nothing at all in their eyes. Lastly it is characteristic of a moderate man to hate all true whigs, and to love all rank tories.

3. *The timid Whigs,* form a third class of the people of America. They entertain a terrible idea of the resources & power of G. Britain, and a false idea of the resources and power of America. The loss of a few riflemen in a Skirmish, or a fort, or a Village, induce[s] them to conclude that the contest is over and that America is subdued. [torn] terrified at the expense of the war as much as the sight of a musquet, they fly into the most obscure corners for safety. After a defeat, they refuse continental money, but upon the news of a victory they come forth, appear stout, and wonder that any body sh^d dread the power of Britain.

4. *furious Whigs.* This class of men injure the cause of liberty, as much by their violence as the timid Whigs do by their fears. They think the Destruction of Howe's army of less consequence than the detection & punishment of the most insignificant tory. They wish for laws & good government, not so much to collect the Strength of our country against Great Britain, as to punish our internal enemies. They think the common forms of Justice sh^d be suspended towards a tory criminal, [and] that a man who only speaks against our common defence [torn] tomahawked, scalped, and roas[ted] alive. Lastly, they are always cowards, & shrink under the cover of an office, or a sickly family, when they are called upon to oppose the enemy in the field.

5. The *Staunch Whigs,* form the 5th and last class of the people of America. They are friends to liberty from principle. They esteem the loss of property, friends, even of life itself as nothing when compared with Slavery. Perseverance & firmness belong to their character. They are never dismayed with misfortunes, or unusually elated with undecisive advantages over our enemies. They are implacable in their hatred as to the court of Britain. They had rather renounce their existence than their beloved independance. They have an unshaken [faith] in the divine justice, and they [es]teem it a mark of equal folly & impiety, to believe that Great Britain can ever subdue America. They are friends to order & good government. They despise the little acts of the tories to injure our cause, and aim at their destruction chiefly by the destruction of the army & commerce of our enemies. They are just and merciful in the exercise of power. They esteem vir-

tue & wisdom as the principal qualities in legislators, and are unwilling to trust power in the hands of "Bullies, bankrupts, and blackheads."
6. Neither Whigs nor Tories. These men change their conduct, and conversation acording to the times and their company. They have no principles of any kind.

GEORGE WASHINGTON

"First in war, first in peace, first in the hearts of his fellow citizens" was the eulogy of General Henry (Lighthorse Harry) Lee on the death of Washington (1732–1799). First in the minds of American schoolboys would be an accurate addition. The words of George Greene, a minor American historian of the nineteenth century, appear to have been believed. He declared that "A copy of Washington's letters in every school and district library of the country, to serve as a text-book in clubs and debating societies, and a manual for public men in every department of civil and military administration, would do more for the formation of our national character . . . than any other source to which we could go for guidance and counsel."*

The first president needs no introduction, but those who have been brought up on the bland diet of legend need to recall the man. Although usually restrained and content to regard the Loyalists as a military problem, Washington also spoke of them in such terms as "infamous betrayers of their country" and "abominable pests of society." Since he was the target of two Tory assassination attempts, one of which involved the mayor of New York, David Mathews, it is not surprising to find in these extracts† something less than the milk of human kindness.

TO GOVERNOR NICHOLAS COOKE

January 6, 1776.

I received a Letter from Governor Trumbull, of the 1st. Inst., by which I am informed, that the Connecticut Assembly are very unanimous in the Common cause, and, among others, have passed an Act for raising and equipping a fourth of their Militia, to be immediately Selected by

---

* Preface to *Historical View of the American Revolution* (6th ed., Boston, 1895; first edition, 1865).

† *The Writings of George Washington*, ed. by John C. Fitzpatrick (39 vols., Washington, 1931–44) IV, 214–217, 449; IX, 6–7.

voluntary Inlistments; with such other able effective men, as are not included in their Militia Rolls, who incline to inlist, to act as Minute Men for their own, or the defence of any of the United Colonies, and this under proper encouragements. Another Act for restraining and Punishing persons Inimical to us and directing proceedings therein. No person to supply the Ministerial Army or Navy; to give them Intelligence; to Inlist or procure others to inlist in their Service, to pilot their Vessels, or in any way assist them; under pain of forfeiting his Estate, and an Imprisonment not exceeding three years. None to write, speak or Act against the proceedings of Congress, or their Acts of Assembly, under penalty of being disarmed and disqualified from holding any office, and be further punished by Imprisonment &c. For Seizing and Confiscating, for the use of the Colony, the Estates of those putting, or continuing to shelter, themselves under the protection of the Ministerial Fleet or Army, or assist in carrying on their measures against us. . . . The situation of our affairs seems to call for regulations like these, and I should think the other Colonies ought to adopt similar ones, or such of them as they have not already made; vigorous and such as at another time would appear extraordinary, are now become absolutely necessary, for preserving our Country, against the strides of Tyranny making against it. . . .

[To John A. Washington, the general's brother, March 31, 1776] . . . All those who took upon themselves the Style, and title of Government Men in Boston, in short, all those who have acted an unfriendly part in this great Contest have Shipped themselves off in the same hurry, but under still greater disadvantages than the King's Troops have done; being obliged to Man their own Vessels (for Seamen could not be had for the Transports for the Kings use) and submit to every hardship that can be conceiv'd. One or two have done, what a great many ought to have done long ago, committed Suicide. By all Accts. there never existed a more miserable set of Beings, than these wretched Creatures now are; taught to believe that the Power of Great Britain was superior to all opposition, and that foreign aid (if not) was at hand, they were even higher, and more insulting in their opposition than the Regulars. When the Order Issued therefore for Imbarking the Troops in Boston, no Electric Shock, no sudden Clap of thunder. In a word the last

Trump, could not have struck them with greater Consternation. they were at their Wits' end, and conscious of their black ingratitude chose to commit themselves in the manner I have above describ'd to the Mercy of the Waves at a tempestuous Season rather than meet their offended Countrymen. but with this declaration the choice was made that if they thought the most abject submission would procure them Peace they never would have stir'd. . . .

With respect to the Tory, who was tried and executed by your order, though his crime was heinous enough to deserve the fate he met with, and though I am convinced you acted in the affair with a good intention, yet I cannot but wish it had not happened. In the first place, it was a matter that did not come within the jurisdiction of martial law, and therefore the whole proceeding was irregular and illegal, and will have a tendency to excite discontent, jealousy and murmurs among the people. In the Second, if the trial could properly have been made by a Court Martial, as the Division you command is only a detachment from the Army, and you cannot have been considered as in a Seperate Department, there is none of our article[s] of War that will justify your inflicting a *Capital* punishment, even on a Soldier, much less a Citizen. I mention these things for your future Government, as what is past cannot be recalled. The temper of the Americans and the principles on which the present contest turns, will not countenance proceedings of this nature.

THOMAS PAINE

The accolade of the Revolution's outstanding pamphleteer belongs to the English-born Thomas Paine (1737–1809). This verdict can hardly be disputed if one assesses his work by its impact, and surely there is no better way to judge a writer in this genre.

It was the American war which gave Paine his chance to match his ability and his achievements. Poverty had forced him to leave school at the age of thirteen and for six years to be an apprentice and assistant to his father, a corset maker. After a brief fling aboard a privateer at the beginning of the Seven Years War (1756), he came back to a succession of jobs ranging from customs official through schoolteacher to tobacconist and grocer. He was married twice, his first wife dying before they had been together a year and the second leaving him after three years of marriage. These were years of bitterness, struggle, and failure, and Paine kept up his confidence only by reading widely and dabbling in scientific matters.

Despairing of success in England he left for America, then very much the land of opportunity. One piece of luck had come his way. When he arrived in Philadelphia late in 1774 he brought letters of introduction from no less a celebrity than Benjamin Franklin. Paine's entry into journalism, made possible by his private studies and gift of pen, was made easy by this recommendation. Hardly more than a year after landing in the New World, Paine produced his single most important work. In **Common Sense,** published as an anonymous pamphlet in January, 1776, the self-exiled Englishman called in ringing tones for America to proclaim its independence immediately. He saw this both as a practical step toward uniting the colonies and securing French and Spanish aid, and as a necessary moral decision, breaking the ties of a great continent with a small island in order to provide the means for achieving the American destiny. So long as the colonies were linked to a corrupt, monarchical heritage, Paine declared, they would be hampered in the fulfillment of their dream of a new, uncorrupted republic.

It was the first and it has remained one of the sharpest statements of an American mission. Thomas Paine believed it realizable only through a strong federal union which transcended parochial concerns and the envies of the various states. His pamphlet sold with incredible speed. A newcomer to the land had captured the mood of the impatient, rebellious colonies and pushed the theoretical arguments and the actual events to their logical conclusion. Perhaps Paine's claim that 120,000 copies were bought within three months is a piece of author's vanity, but there is no doubt that **Common Sense** was a bestseller in a way that no previous American publication had approached. (Benjamin Franklin's **Almanack** sold about ten thousand copies a year.)

At the end of 1776 Paine, who witnessed the colonies declare their independence some six months after **Common Sense** appeared, produced the first of fifteen essays we call **The Crisis Papers** or **The American Crisis.** Written between 1776 and 1783 the first line of the first one contains the phrase we best remember: "These are the times that try men's souls." In the smallest possible number of words Paine had summed up his own and the nation's situation. He had left Philadelphia to join the small, ragged Continental army in which he occupied an extraordinary position. Not a civilian, not a soldier, not an officer, he quickly became something akin to a political commissar. Quite possibly Washington turned to the author of **Common Sense** for ideological help, and for this dispirited band of volunteers Paine produced the first of his magnificent rallying cries.* From a partisan in such a position we cannot expect much toleration for Tories; indeed Paine hardly had a kind word for them.

. . . And what is a Tory? Good God! what is he? I should not be afraid to go with a hundred Whigs against a thousand Tories, were they to attempt to get into arms. Every Tory is a coward; for servile,

---

* *The Complete Writings of Thomas Paine* collected and edited by Philip S. Foner (Citadel Press, Inc.: New York, 1945). (Extracts from Paine's *The American Crisis*), pp. 53, 69, 76–77, 90. Used by permission.

slavish, self-interested fear is the foundation of Toryism; and a man under such influence, though he may be cruel, never can be brave. . . .

What we contend for is worthy the affliction we may go through. If we get but bread to eat, and any kind of raiment to put on, we ought not only to be contented, but thankful. More than *that* we ought not to look for, and less than *that* heaven has not yet suffered us to want. He that would sell his birthright for a little *salt,* is as worthless as he who sold it for pottage without salt; and he that would part with it for a gay coat, or a plain coat, ought for ever to be a slave in buff. What are salt, sugar and finery, to the inestimable blessings of "Liberty and Safety!" Or what are the inconveniences of a few months to the tributary bondage of ages? The meanest peasant in America, blessed with these sentiments, is a happy man compared with a New York Tory; he can eat his morsel without repining, and when he has done, can sweeten it with a repast of wholesome air. . . .

A person, to use a trite phrase, must be a Whig or a Tory in a lump. His feelings, as a man, may be wounded; his charity, as a Christian, may be moved; but his political principles must go through all the cases on one side or the other. He cannot be a Whig in *this* stage, and a Tory in *that.* If he says he is against the united independence of the continent, he is to all intents and purposes against her in all the rest; because *this last* comprehends the whole. And he may just as well say, that Britain was right in declaring us rebels; right in taxing us; and right in declaring her *"right to bind the colonies in all cases whatsoever."* It signifies nothing what neutral ground, of his own creating, he may skulk upon for shelter, for the quarrel in no stage of it hath afforded any such ground; and either we or Britain are absolutely right or absolutely wrong through the whole. . . .

Here is the touchstone to try men by. *He that is not a supporter of the independent States of America in the same degree that his religious and political principles would suffer him to support the government of any other country, of which he called himself a subject, is, in the American sense of the word,* A Tory; *and the instant that he endeavors to bring his toryism into practice, he becomes* A TRAITOR. The first can only be detected by a general test, and the law hath already provided for the latter. . . .

There is not such a being in America as a Tory from conscience; some secret defect or other is interwoven in the character of all those, be they men or women, who can look with patience on the brutality, luxury and debauchery of the British court, and the violations of their army here. A woman's virtue must sit very lightly on her who can even hint a favorable sentiment in their behalf. It is remarkable that the whole race of prostitutes in New York were tories; and the schemes for supporting the Tory cause in this city, for which several are now in jail, and one hanged, were concerted and carried on in common bawdy-houses, assisted by those who kept them. . . .

"A WHIG" WRITES TO THE EDITOR

This letter, over the pseudonymous signature "A Whig," appeared in the **Pennsylvania Packet** in August, 1779. John Dunlap, its publisher, had started the paper in Philadelphia in 1771 and with hardly a break issued it every week until September, 1777. Then, when the British occupied the city, he moved to Lancaster, Pennsylvania and there published the **Packet** from November, 1777 to June, 1778. Philadelphia was returned to American control in the third week of June and, very appropriately, on the Fourth of July Dunlap republished the paper from its original location.

In general, newspapers in colonial days did not carry editorial columns but the prejudices of the owner or, if one will, the policies of the paper, were conveyed by the way in which news was selected for inclusion and, more directly, in the letters chosen for publication. On more than one occasion letters to the editor were written by himself! It is clear, therefore, that the **Packet** would provide a sympathetic forum for the arguments expressed in the letter here reprinted.*

Among the many errors America has been guilty of during her contest with Great Britain, few have been greater, or attended with more fatal consequences to these States, than her lenity to the Tories. . . . Rouse, America! your danger is great—great from a quarter where you least expect it. The Tories, the Tories will yet be the ruin of you! 'Tis high time they were separated from among you. They are now busy engaged in undermining your liberties. They have a thousand ways of doing it, and they make use of them all. Who were the occasion of this war? The Tories! Who persuaded the tyrant of Britain to prosecute it in a manner before unknown to civilized nations, and shocking even to barbarians? The Tories! Who prevailed on the savages of the wilderness to join the standard of the enemy? The Tories! Who have assisted the Indians in taking the scalp from the aged matron, the

---

* *Diary of the Revolution,* ed. by Frank Moore (2 vols., New York, 1859), II, 166–168.

blooming fair one, the helpless infant, and the dying hero? The Tories! Who advised and who assisted in burning your towns, ravaging your country, and violating the chastity of your women? The Tories! Who are the occasion that thousands of you now mourn the loss of your dearest connections? The Tories! Who have always counteracted the endeavors of Congress to secure the liberties of this country? The Tories! Who refused their money when as good as specie, though stamped with the image of his most sacred Majesty? The Tories! Who continue to refuse it? The Tories! Who do all in their power to depreciate it? The Tories! Who propagate lies among us to discourage the Whigs? The Tories! Who corrupt the minds of the good people of these States by every species of insidious counsel? The Tories! Who hold a traitorous correspondence with the enemy? The Tories! Who daily sends them intelligence? The Tories! Who take the oaths of allegiance to the States one day, and break them the next? The Tories! Who prevent your battalions from being filled? The Tories! Who dissuade men from entering the army? The Tories! Who persuade those who have enlisted to desert? The Tories! Who harbor those who do desert? The Tories! In short, who wish to see us conquered, to see us slaves, to see us hewers of wood and drawers of water? The Tories! . . .

For my own part, whenever I meet one in the street, or at the coffee house, my blood boils within me. Their guilt is equalled only by their impudence. They strut, and seem to bid defiance to every one. In every place, and in every company, they spread their damnable doctrines, and then laugh at the pusillanimity of those who let them go unpunished. I flatter myself, however, with the hopes of soon seeing a period to their reign, and a total end to their existence in America. Awake, Americans, to a sense of your danger. No time to be lost. Instantly banish every Tory from among you. Let America be sacred alone to freemen.

Some British Comments

Lady Luck smiled upon the rebels and allowed them to win the war. Perhaps this is too loose, too "unscientific," and for Americans an unpatriotic verdict, but a credible case could be made for the proposition that it was lost by the British commanders rather than won by the American armies. Certainly, in the first years of the rebellion the odds were heavily on the side of His Majesty and on more than one occasion Washington narrowly escaped final defeat. It is therefore easy to understand the anger and bitterness of Loyalists who felt that their services were not well used or fully appreciated, whether these complaints came from a nonfighter such as Seabury or active military men who often found themselves treated as inferior to their British counterparts. Quite naturally their response was a sullen ire which gnawed at loyalty and the willingness to risk life, limb, and loved ones.

CHARLES CORNWALLIS

Charles Cornwallis, first Marquis and second Earl Cornwallis (1738–1805), personifies the intimate relationship between British politics and British warfare during the eighteenth century. As an intelligent member of the aristocracy he could hardly abstain from activity in both spheres.

Cornwallis seems to have had no ambitions to become a major political figure but in 1766 he took a strong stand as one of the four members of the House of Lords who supported Lord Camden in opposing the Declaratory Bill which asserted the British government's right to tax the American colonies. As the two sides drifted toward war Cornwallis found himself constantly in disagreement with ministerial measures. He resigned his offices but did so with good grace and without shrill declaration, thereby keeping the confidence of the King who in 1775 promoted him to the rank of major general.

His Majesty called upon him once the Revolution had begun and Cornwallis, notwithstanding his opposition to the policies which had helped to bring on the war, could not refuse to serve. In 1776, under Sir William Howe, he took a leading role in operations around New York City and in New Jersey. In the following year he was victorious at the battle of Brandywine and went on to occupy Philadelphia. After a visit to England and promotion to lieutenant general, he came back to America as second in command to Sir Henry Clinton who had taken over from Howe as commander-in-chief. Cornwallis thought that Clinton was, if anything, more dilatory in pursuing victory than Howe had been. He offered his resignation, but the King refused to accept it.

Cornwallis clearly understood that the entry of the French had changed the war significantly and required a reexamination of British tactics. Control over colonial ports by occupying them and preventing French disembarkation was one of his priorities. Another was subjugation of the Southern colonies, which were sending considerable sums of money to aid Washington's armies. Cornwallis also wished to rally the as yet untested Loyalist forces in that area. All these aims together demanded a strategy that should be executed on a larger scale than either Howe or Clinton had been willing to undertake. After another visit to England (during which Cornwallis witnessed the death of his wife), he returned to America and in 1799 was finally given a chance to carry out some of his ideas.*

Clinton sailed south and in May of 1780 Charleston was captured. Shortly afterward he returned to New York, leaving the Southern colonies to Cornwallis and a small army. In 1781 Cornwallis decided to march north

---

* The confusion, even controversy, in the general staff was the subject of a pamphlet war between several of the commanders, including Cornwallis. These are not easily available but the student will find excellent modern analyses in the books by Smith (Paul), Mackesy, Robson (Chs. V–VIII), and Peckham, noted in the bibliography.

into Virginia, with the hope of meeting Clinton's army in the Chesapeake Bay region. Things started badly. Colonel Banastre Tarleton, one of the most dashing cavalry leaders on the British side, was heavily defeated by Daniel Morgan at the Cowpens.* Cornwallis, however, joined up with the troops of General Alexander Leslie and chased the colonials until he caught them at Guilford Court-house (March, 1781). The resulting battle was a Pyrrhic victory for the British. The question now, as Cornwallis saw it, was the old one of whether the British commander-in-chief wanted an all out offensive war which at this juncture would mean leaving New York and bringing the whole army into Virginia or whether the British would rest easy, "quit the Carolinas . . . and stick to our salt pork at New York, sending now and then a detachment to steal tobacco etc." Against Cornwallis' own wishes he was clearly ordered by Clinton to hold Yorktown. Washington saw his opportunity, and with a mixed force of Americans and Frenchmen marched on the offensive. The unsupported Cornwallis had no choice but to surrender and on the very day he did (October 19, 1781) Clinton left New York. He moved too late and for all practical purposes the War of Independence was at an end. After the peace of 1783 Cornwallis was sent to the largest chunk left in the British imperial pie when he accepted, with much reluctance, the governor-generalship of India. As a recent commentator has observed, of all the British commanders he was the only one who went on to greatness.

These events have been described in considerable detail since they form the background to some of the most important military activities of the Loyalists in the Revolution. A number of British officers had seen possibilities of winning victories in the South by relying on local support. Cornwallis was not the first of them, but he was the most eminent. However, the delay in putting these ideas into effect was fatal. Furthermore, in this war the British found, as Americans have in very recent times, that victory in the field does not guarantee "pacification" of the country. In addition, the rout of the Loyalist forces at King's Mountain in October, 1780 was a psychological and material setback of the first order. Since the help of the Loyalists was a vital part of British policies after 1778–79, the failure of the Loyalist troops to 'win big and often', when added to the confusion in the regular army's strategy and the lack of any military genius on the British side, assured the colonials of success. Some of the difficulties encountered by Cornwallis are apparent in the following selections.†

---

* Tarleton's account, *History of the Campaigns of 1780 and 1781 in the Southern Provinces of North America* was published in London in 1787. Scattered through its pages is a good deal of information about the military activities of the Loyalists, although the work is spoiled by the arrogance of the author.

† *Correspondence of Charles, First Marquis Cornwallis*, edited with notes by Charles Ross (3 vols., John Murray, London, 1859), I, 62–63; 89–90; 91–92.

LORD RAWDON* TO SIR HENRY CLINTON.

SIR,   *South Carolina, Oct. 29, 1780.*

Lord Cornwallis having been so reduced by a severe fever as to be still unable to write, he has desired that I should have the honour of addressing your Excellency in regard to our present situation.

For some time after the arrival of his Majesty's troops at Camden, repeated messages were sent to head-quarters by the friends of Government in North Carolina, expressing their impatience to rise and join the King's standard. The impossibility of subsisting that additional force at Camden, and the accounts which they themselves gave of the distressing scarcity of provisions in North Carolina, obliged Lord Cornwallis to entreat them to remain quiet till the new crop might enable us to join them. In the mean time General Gates's army advanced. We were greatly surprised, and no less grieved, that no information whatsoever of its movements was conveyed to us by persons so deeply interested in the event as the North Carolina loyalists. Upon the 16th of August that army was so entirely dispersed that it was clear no number of them could for a considerable time be collected. Orders were therefore despatched to our friends, stating that the hour they had so long pressed for was arrived, and exhorting them to stand forth immediately, and prevent the reunion of the scattered enemy. Instant aid was in that case promised to them. In the fullest confidence that this event was to take place, Lord Cornwallis ventured to press your Excellency for co-operation in the Chesapeak, hoping that the assistance of the North Carolinians might eventually furnish a force for yet further efforts. Not a single man, however, attempted to improve the favourable moment, or obeyed that summons for which they had before been so impatient. It was hoped that our approach might get the better of their timidity, yet during a long period, whilst we were waiting at Charlotteburgh for our stores and convalescents, they did not even furnish us with the least information respecting the force collecting against us. In short, Sir, we may have a powerful body of friends in North Carolina, and indeed we have cause to be convinced that many of the inhabitants wish well to his Majesty's arms, but they have

---

* Francis, Lord Rawdon (1754–1826) was at this time one of Cornwallis' senior commanders. For details of his career see the *Dictionary of National Biography.*

not given evidence enough—either of their numbers or of their activity —to justify the stake of this province for the uncertain advantages that might attend immediate junction with them. There is too much reason to conceive that such must have been the risk. Whilst this army lay at Charlotteburgh, Georgetown was taken from our militia by the Rebels, and the whole country to the east of Santee gave such proofs of general defection that even the militia of the High Hills could not be prevailed upon to join a party of troops who were sent to protect our boats upon the river. The defeat of Major Ferguson had so dispirited this part of the country, and indeed the loyal subjects were so wearied by the long continuance of the campaign, that Lieut.-Colonel Cruger (commanding at Ninety-six) sent information to Lord Cornwallis that the whole district had determined to submit as soon as the Rebels should enter it. From these circumstances, from the consideration that delay does not extinguish our hopes in North Carolina, and from the long fatigue of the troops which made it seriously requisite to give some refreshment to the army, Lord Cornwallis has resolved to remain for the present in a position which may secure the frontier without separating his force. In this situation we shall be always ready for movement whensoever opportunity shall recommend it, or circumstances require it. . . .

PROCLAMATION BY EARL CORNWALLIS.

Hillsborough, Feb. 20, 1781.

Whereas it has pleased the Divine Providence to prosper the operations of His Majesty's arms in driving the Rebel army out of this province, and whereas it is His Majesty's most gracious wish to rescue his faithfull and loyal subjects from the cruel tyranny under which they have groaned for several years; I have thought proper to issue this Proclamation to invite all such faithfull and loyal subjects to repair without loss of time, with their arms and ten days' provisions, to the Royal Standard now erected at Hillsborough, where they will meet with the most friendly reception; and I do hereby assure them that I am ready to concur with them in effectual measures for suppressing the remains of rebellion in this province, and for the re-establishment of good order and constitutional government.

EARL CORNWALLIS TO LORD GEORGE GERMAIN.

My Lord,   *Wilmington, April 18, 1781.*

I think it incumbent on me to be explicit to your Lordship, as his Majesty's minister, on one or two capital points. The principal reasons for undertaking a winter's campaign were—the difficulty of a defensive war in South Carolina, and the hopes that our friends in North Carolina, who were said to be very numerous, would make good their promises of assembling and taking an active part with us in endeavouring to re-establish his Majesty's government. Our experience has shown that their numbers are not so great as had been represented, and that their friendship was only passive. For we have received little assistance from them since our arrival in the province; and although I gave the strongest and most public assurances, that after refitting and depositing our sick and wounded, I should return to the Upper Country, not above two hundred have been prevailed upon to follow us, either as provincials or militia. This being the case, the immense extent of this country, cut with numberless rivers and creeks, and the total want of internal navigation, which renders it impossible for our army to remain long in the heart of the country, will make it very difficult to reduce this province to obedience by a direct attack upon it. If therefore it should appear to be the interest of Great Britain to maintain what she already possesses, and to push the war in the Southern provinces, I take the liberty of giving it as my opinion, that a serious attempt upon Virginia would be the most solid plan, because successful operations might not only be attended with important consequences there, but would tend to the security of South Carolina, and ultimately to the submission of North Carolina. The great reinforcements sent by Virginia to General Greene, whilst General Arnold was in the Chesapeak, are convincing proofs that small expeditions do not frighten that powerful province.

AMBROSE SERLE

Ambrose Serle (1742–1812) rose to political power through the favor of Lord Dartmouth. He then came to America through the post of private secretary to Lord Howe.* His comments are especially valuable since most other accounts

---

* The entry for Serle in the *Dictionary of National Biography* is in error on many details. Biographical data can be obtained from the introduction to his *Journal,* from which the following extract is taken.

of the Revolutionary period come from military men and, for our purposes, because he was in very close touch with some of the most important Loyalists.

It has often been assumed that his views were formed for him by those Americans with whom he came into contact. This was hardly the case. By 1770 he was convinced that an Anglican episcopate in the colonies would strengthen the tie to Britain, and in 1775 he was ready to publish his views. **Americans against Liberty** is an illuminating title for a tract which vigorously defended the Britsh empire as a government under law and hit hard at the colonials as "open enemies to the public and general liberty of the British empire."

Serle in America did not change his mind. In his writings* the gap between the British and American ideas on government and society is quite clearly perceptible. He was unable to appreciate the ideological nature of the conflict or view the American reasons for revolt as more than delusions or trivial concerns. Although the Revolution convinced him that colonies were more of a drain than a boon to the mother country, he was sensible enough to realize that since they were in existence they had to be governed. The American Loyalists might be friends but they were, after all, colonials, to be treated with civility but also with scepticism. In 1776 Howe's secretary expected a quick end to the rebellion, which he sincerely believed was the work of a small minority of malcontents, but by the close of 1777 he was beginning to reconsider. In the last extract one can catch a glimpse of his growing disillusionment with the might of British arms. He also appears to be questioning the value of keeping the colonies, even if Britain were to be the victor.

This Day [October 16, 1776] the loyal Inhabitants of the City & County of New York met according to Advertisement at the City Hall, and agreed to two Addresses; the one to the King's Commrs for declaring the City to be at His Majesty's Peace, and the other to the Governor [Tryon], requesting him to present their Address to the Commrs. One cannot help observing, how, in all multitudes, one or two busy men prepare the Way & lead on every Measure, while the rest gape almost at every thing, and follow the Sheep with the Bell. There need be no stronger Argument than this against Democracies in general. One or two, or at most the Combination of a few, take the Reins, and all the rest passively acquiesce in their Determinations. Which then is better; that a certain Number, authorized by a particular Constitution, and amenable to the Society, shd. direct Affairs; or an uncertain Number, skulking behind a Mob and accountable to nobody? . . .

---

* *The American Journal of Ambrose Serle, Secretary to Lord Howe, 1776–1778*, ed. by Edward H. Tatum, Jr. (San Marino, California, 1948) pp. 124–125; 163–164; 223–224. Used by permission of the Henry E. Huntington Library and Art Gallery.

One of the Mr. Allens of Philadelphia* called upon me at Tea, and gave me large & particular Information of the State of Things and the Temper of the People in the Province of Pensylvania: He is positive that three fourths of the People are against Independency; that the Continent is under the Dominion of a desperate Faction, formed by the worst Characters upon it; that the Inhabitants in general begin to have their Eyes open relative to the Nature & Consequences of the Dispute; and that the Germans and Quakers in particular have changed their Sentiments upon this Controversy.—But, alas, they all prate & profess much; but, when You call upon them, they will *do* nothing. Our Northern Army in the Spring will be of more Service to us, under Providence, than all the provincial Troops, under the Denomination of Friends, throughout America.† To govern America, it must be conquered; and it must be no lax Governmt. to retain the Conquest. It may seem an extraordinary Proposition, but I believe it a true one— It may be conquered with more Ease than governed, if no Change be made upon the Conquest in our System of colonial Policy.

Thursday 15th. [May, 1777]

Preparations still going on for the Campaign. Nothing material.—The Govr. [Tryon] told me in the Course of Conversation, that a very sanguine Gentleman had engaged to raise a Corps of 300 men for the Defence & Security of N. York City & Island only, but that he had just sent him a Lr. in which he grievously deplores his Inability to accomplish the Purpose, scarce a man enlisting in the Town. An ungrateful Set! This has been ever their Practice. G. Britain might expend her last Farthing for their Protection; and, after all, if they did not absolutely turn against her, they would leave her to shift for herself. I only grieve, that it is necessary for her to expend a Penny on account of this unprofitable Region. If she had left them to themselves, the Colonists would soon have avenged her Quarrel, and employed their Insolence and Barbarity of Temper among themselves.‡

---

* William Allen (1704–1780) was a leading member of the famous Philadelphia mercantile-legal family and father of James Allen (see pp. 15–17). Ironically, he was one of those most responsible for establishing the Pennsylvania legislature at Philadelphia and thereby contributed to the creation of "Independence Hall."

† This army met total defeat at Saratoga ten months after Serle's prediction.

‡ Deleted: "in cutting each others Throats"; "among themselves" substituted.

SIR HENRY CLINTON

Sir Henry Clinton (1738?–1795) served as commander-in-chief in North America between May, 1778 and May, 1781. He was a gallant soldier as his conduct on the European front in the Seven Years War, at the battle of Bunker Hill (1775), and at the battle of Long Island (1776) showed. Yet Clinton as a commander was a man whose "behavior was shot through with contradictions." Understanding the personality of this general is more difficult than usual, but it seems clear that he had considerable trouble accepting responsibility. This may be attributed partly to personal characteristics and partly to the fact that Lord Cornwallis, his second in command, held a "dormant commission" to succeed Clinton either if something happened to him or if he gave cause for his recall.

Vis-à-vis the Loyalists Clinton continually had to face the fact that their help was always less than the British had anticipated. Yet the most important reason for this may well have been inadequate British military support. The commander-in-chief was caught in the middle. At home the ministers expected a strong demonstration of colonial loyalty, in the colonies the Loyalists expected strong military aid and fair treatment as participants in the war against the rebels. Each waited upon the other and Clinton, never the most decisive of men, did not fully satisfy anyone.* But, as the following extracts† show, he in turn was a long way from being happy with the manner in which the Loyalists in New York conducted themselves.

[1781] . . . But, when the terms of capitulation were publicly known, it is impossible to describe the indignation, horror, and dismay with which the American refugees who had either taken up arms in our cause or flown to us for protection read the *tenth article* of that convention, *whereby* they considered themselves as not only most cruelly abandoned to the power of an inveterate, implacable enemy, to be persecuted at the discretion of party prejudice and resentment, but even as excluded from the same conditions of surrender with their fellow soldiers whenever it should happen to be their unfortunate lot to act with the King's troops in the defense of fortified places.

---

* A biography which is exciting because it seeks to use the findings of modern psychology to aid in explaining a historical personage is William B. Willcox, *Portrait of a General: Sir Henry Clinton in the War of Independence* (New York, 1964) for which an appetizer is an article by Willcox and Frederick Wyatt, *William and Mary Quarterly*, 3rd Ser., XVI (1959).

† *The American Rebellion: Sir Henry Clinton's Narrative of his Campaigns, 1775–1782*, ed. by William B. Willcox (Yale University Press: New Haven, Conn., 1954) pp. 352–353; 359–361. Used by permission.

The Board of Associated Loyalists at New York addressed me immediately on this subject through their president, Governor Franklin.*
And it was with some difficulty I could restrain their clamors until the
arrival of Lord Cornwallis, who I hoped would be able to explain his
conduct in this matter to their satisfaction. But, His Lordship's plea
of *necessity* and his having secured the *Bonetta,* sloop, as an asylum
for the escape of the most *obnoxious* being insufficient to calm their
apprehensions (or heal the wounds inflicted on their personal feelings
by the word *punished,* which seemed to *admit guilt,* and a *consequent
right* in the revolted colonists to prosecute them in their civil courts for
acts of allegiance to their lawful sovereign), I thought it proper to
endeavor to remove their fears for the future by issuing an order to the
different posts of the army under my command, directing them to pay
the same attention in all cases in every event whatsoever to the interests and security of the loyalists within their respective districts that
they did to those of the King's troops under their orders, and not to
suffer or admit any distinction or discrimination to take place between
them on any occasion. And I had the happiness to find that this had
in great measure the desired effect, especially as it was soon after
honored by His Majesty's most gracious approbation and confirmation.

There were, however, some oversanguine gentlemen† who advised
me on this occasion to issue a proclamation threatening the enemy with
retaliation in kind for every injury they inflicted on the loyalists for
joining the King's army. But a punishment of that nature appertained
more properly to the civil jurisdiction and could not, consequently, be
inflicted without opening the courts of law; for to threaten them in my
capacity of commander in chief would have been unavailing and nugatory while so many of our troops were prisoners in the enemy's power.
And, being desirous of showing every possible attention to the interests
and feelings of those unfortunate men who had relinquished their all
and were now drawn into a most alarming situation for their attach-

---

* In early November Clinton assured Gov. Franklin, orally and by letter, of
his anxiety to alleviate the loyalists' fears. The Board answered on the 14th,
over Franklin's signature, that the only way to do so was to proclaim publicly that they would receive, in any future capitulation, the same terms as
regular troops, and to threaten retaliation for any harm done to those already
captured. See Franklin to Clinton, Nov. 14, and minutes of the Board of
Associated Loyalists for Nov. 8 and 14, 1781, filed at the end of Feb.,
1782, CP[Clinton Papers]. [Willcox' footnote]
† The members of the Board of Associated Loyalists.

ment to the constitution of Great Britain, I offered to permit the revival of civil government in the New York district if retaliation was thought indispensable, and the civil courts should be judged by the crown lawyers to be equal to the inflicting of the necessary punishments. For, although I had never yet seen the moment proper for such a measure while that province was involved in the operations of war (which must ever suffer many obstructions and even disappointments when clogged by the control of civil jurisdiction), yet the loss of all the loyalists acting with our troops was a matter of too serious moment to admit of hesitation, had that been likely to be the consequence of our not being armed with the same civil weapons of terror which the enemy had the power of using against us. But Lieutenant General Robertson, the Governor of New York (after having consulted the principal refugees and civil officers of the province), being of opinion that the revival of civil government would be inexpedient at the present juncture, and all the general officers and the Admiral concurring in the same sentiments, the idea was of course dropped. . . .

[1781–82] I have already noticed that, in obedience to the King's commands transmitted to me by his Secretary of State, I had consti-tuted certain gentlemen therein named a Board of Directors of Asso-ciated Loyalists, for the purpose of forming into armed companies and troops (for the annoyance of the revolted colonists) such loyal refu-gees as pleased to associate under them, and of issuing from time to time regulations and orders for their guidance and government, sub-ject, however, to the control of the Commander in Chief, to whom all their proceedings were to be regularly reported and from whom the commissions for the officers recommended by them were to issue, in order to sanction their operations and entitle them to the usual advan-tages when taken prisoners by the enemy. A prison was also allotted to them for the confinement of the prisoners captured by their parties, and the power of exchanging or releasing them vested in themselves, but under the express condition of not putting to death or otherwise maltreating, by way of retaliation, any of the enemy who might happen to fall into their hands.

Having by these means guarded, as I thought, against all improper enormities, I did not judge it necessary to require constant reports of the prisoners taken at different times by the Associators, or how they disposed of them. I was consequently greatly surprised and shocked when I heard in the course of common rumor that one Joshua Huddy, a captain in the rebel service who had been taken prisoner by the Associators and lodged for several days in their own prison as a prisoner of war, had been delivered with two other prisoners of war to Richard Lippincott, a captain of Associators, by virtue of a written order from the Board of Directors dated the 8th of April, ostensibly for the purpose of being exchanged for three Associators [who were] prisoners with the enemy; and that, these prisoners being carried by him into the Jersies under this pretense, Joshua Huddy was there murdered and left hanging, with a label on his breast to signify he was thus treated in retaliation for one White, an Associator said to have been murdered not long before by the rebels.

This was so audacious a breach of humanity and the usual customs of war, and such an insult to the dignity of the British arms and my own command, that I should have esteemed myself extremely deficient in my duty had I neglected to take notice of it. But, as the royal sanction from whence the Directors derived their existence as a board had rendered them respectable, I judged it right, out of delicacy, to address myself first to them, and to desire that they would immediately make the necessary inquiries into the circumstances stated and report the result to me, that proper steps might be taken for punishing the delinquents and preventing such atrocities in future. For I could not conceive it possible that those gentlemen would have authorized such an act of barbarity or wished to screen the offenders. But, receiving only evasive answers from them (which were both unbecoming the serious importance of the subject and deficient in that respect which I thought due to my station), I caused Captain Lippincott to be arrested to prevent his escape. And, having submitted all the information I was able to obtain respecting the affair to the consideration of a council of war composed of the general and other principal officers of all the Hessian, British, and provincial corps in the garrison, I directed a general court martial to be convened, in consequence of their unanimous opinion, to try Lippincott for the murder of Huddy. Therefore, as the members of that court martial were selected from the most dignified ranks in the British and provincial lines in order to secure impartial justice to all concerned, I have not the least doubt that—had I remained in the command until their proceeding had been closed—both friends and enemies would have been perfectly satisfied, and neither the humanity, justice, nor dignity of this nation would have been committed by the result of their decision.

But, in taking a retrospective view of this business, I acknowledge that allowances should be made for the actions of men whose minds may have been roused to vengeance by repeated acts of cruelty committed by the enemy on their dearest friends and connections. Such sanguinary effects of their resentment might, however, have introduced a system of war horrid beyond conception; and I am really sorry to observe there were many circumstances accompanying this transaction which would almost warrant a suspicion that it was done with a view of precluding all future reconciliation between Great Britain and the revolted colonies. Having, therefore, most probably long thirsted after indiscriminate retaliation, and finding that I was disinclined to sanction it by my having refused to issue a threatening proclamation in consequence of the tenth article of the capitulation of Yorktown, these gentlemen appear to have taken this bold step for the purpose of forcing that measure.

JAMES SIMPSON

James Simpson was a second-level British official in South Carolina before the Revolution began. In 1779 he was sent on a secret mission by Lord George Germain in order to gather information and make estimates on probable Loyalist aid in the event of a second British attempt to capture Charleston.

Simpson executed his mission and reported to Clinton at his New York headquarters in the summer of 1779. He concluded that there was an excellent chance of local support and confirmed the commander-in-chief's inclination toward a southern campaign, similar to one which had succeeded in capturing Savannah in the previous year. Simpson went south with the army and after Charleston was taken, following a siege of four months, he was given a job as "intendant," presumably commander of the local police. The first extract is from Simpson's letter to Germain and the second from a memorandum he prepared for Clinton after Charleston had been captured.

JAMES SIMPSON TO LORD GERMAIN*

New York, August 28, 1779

. . . I arrived at Savannah Fifty One days after I left London, and found the Kings Troops either returned, or returning from the incursion into South Carolina. In a few days afterwards, several Flaggs were

---

* Germain Papers, Clements Library, University of Michigan. Used by permission. Some minor changes in punctuation have been made.

sent from the Rebels, to enquire after Negroes, and other property, which had been carried away when the Army had evacuated the Country, which was alleged to belong to widows, orphans, and absentees, who had never been in the Rebellion. As most of the persons who were sent were my former acquaintances, and desirous to see me on that account, as well as to enquire after Connections and Relations, which they had in Europe; my opportunities to gain the intelligence I wanted, were much better than I could have expected. The most Violent of them, without Scruple acknowledged their distress for want of both the conveniences, and necessaries of life, and that their Money was so much depreciated that it was almost of no value. Many of them exprest eager wishes for a Settlement, and Peace, and mentioned with regret the remembrance of what they called the old times. But I am convinced that there are still too many amongst them, who will use all their influence to prevent a restoration of the publick tranquility; from a Motive I neither observed, nor suspected, till after my return to the Continent, which cannot fail to operate very powerfully, for if any reliance is to be had, in representations that come from every part of the Country, there is such general resentment, raised against most of the individuals who have composed the Congresses and Committees in the different Governments, and those who have been active in enforcing their Tyrannical Edicts, that they are become apprehensive that the restoration of Legal Government would involve their ruin, and that their safety depends upon their being able to retain power.

I have seen several People from the Back Country of Carolina and made every enquiry which appeared to me necessary, both of them and the officers of the Carolina Loyalists who maintain a constant correspondence there. I was informed that those People, who had so inconsiderately assembled in opposition to the Rebels, in 1776 and 1777, and many more who were suspected for adhering to them, have been the objects of almost unremitting Persecution ever since, that some of them, had found means to make their Peace, and were become equally Tyrannical over those with whom they had formerly associated, and that others had been drove away, or otherwise fallen Martyrs to the distresses they had Suffered, but there were still great Numbers, who continued firm in their opposition, and were become most violent in their enmity to those by whom they had been oppressed. The People with whom I conversed were naturally very inquisitive to know whether any attempt would be made this Fall to reduce Carolina, and were much affected when I returned a doubtful answer to their inquiry, for they had been taught to believe that it would certainly take place, and were so confident of its success, that it appeared to me, their spirits rather required to be a little depressed than elevated; I therefore thought it proper to represent to them, that exclusive of any other reason, their situation rendered such a measure deserving mature consideration, for that altho' the Province was to be overrun, and Charles Town reduced by the Kings Troops, yet unless Government was to be so firmly established as to give security to them, without the protection of the Army, (and which could only be effected, by the Efforts of the people themselves,) the Success would be far from complete, and if upon a future emergency, the Troops were withdrawn, and they should suffer the party who now predominated, again to prevail their situation, would probably be very deplorable. But to this they replied, "they had no apprehensions on that score, that they were Numerous, and able enough to protect themselves, if they were once restored to an equality with their oppressors, by being applied with Arms and Ammunition, of both which, they are quite destitute, and which they alledge is the sole cause of their present Submission, and if they should afterwards suffer themselves to be overpowered they should think they were deserving everything they could Suffer, and would never afterwards complain they were abandoned.

These My Lord were the representations and assurances I received from those who are likely to be best acquainted with the state of the country, and most interested in the Success of any Attempt that may be made in order to Subdue it, for I may truly say the existence of themselves, and their families, will depend upon it. I am confident they meant to be sincere, and candid, in their informations, but I nevertheless make some allowances for the sanguine disposition I observed they were in by having just seen, such a handfull of Men penetrate so many miles, through the most difficult part of the Country, to the very gates of Charles Town. And upon the whole, I do not hesitate to declare to your Lordship, that I am of opinion, whenever the Kings Troops move to Carolina, they will be assisted by very considerable Numbers of the Inhabitants, that if the respectable Force proposed moves thither early in the Fall the reduction of the country without risk or much oposition will be the consequence, and I am not without sanguine expectations that with proper conduct such a concurrence of many of the respectable Inhabitants in the lower Settlements may be procured that a due submission to His Majestys Government, will be established throughout the Country.

I have been induced to form such an opinion, not from the intelligence I have received, of their private dispositions, but their conduct, and behaviour when the Army was making its progress through the Country. They in general not only Submitted, and received protections, but many of them showed more Civility, and gave more aid, than considering their Situation, was consistent with prudence, for which several are now confind in Goal and Prison Ships at Charles Town, and I am sorry to say that others, in return for their hospitality, were shamefully plundered, when the Troops evacuated the Country; but I hope the displeasure that the Commander in Chief hath exprest at such behaviour will efface any bad impression it may have occasioned, and prevent it in future.

JAMES SIMPSON TO SIR HENRY CLINTON*

Charles Town, 15 May 1780

. . . I have conversed with some of the people of the first fortunes in the province whose dispositions are as favourable as could be wished, from a conviction of their Error, and feeling too late the miseries their fatal Politiks have produced, with the necessity there is to head back the Paths, by which they have been led to their destruction. I have seen others, who without reasoning upon the subject, or perhaps being incapable of it, but by being Tools to a faction, have been of great weight in keeping up the Flames of Rebellion, that now declare their inevitable Ruin will ensue unless that Government which they all acknowledge was preferable to any they can ever hope to establish is restored. There are others, who still assert that their Cause was founded in Virtue but that it is impossible to maintain it any longer. And some there are, who say it ought never to be relinquished but by the general Consent of America. The Sentiments of the two last Classes I have only from report, for I have thought it proper to avoid a Conversation or Intercourse with any of them, unless it hath been sought for—and of the whole of them, I beg to be understood that I do not mean the Bulk of the People, but Individuals whose Influence would formerly have preponderated in turning the Scale whatever way

---

* Clinton Papers, Clements Library, University of Michigan. Used by permission. Minor changes in punctuation have been made.

they inclined; and in drawing a comparison between the four Classes, the number and consequence of the two first by far exceed the last.

The Loyalists who have always adhered to the King's Government, are not so numerous as I expected; besides those who have been drove from the Province, there are many who left the Town and settled in the Country, where they found themselves less liable to persecution. Elated with their present Triumph, and resentful for their past Injuries, they are clamourous for retributive Justice, and affirm that the Province will never be settled in Peace, until those People, whose persecuting Spirit hath caused such calamities to their fellow Subjects shall receive the punishment their Iniquities deserve. Indeed I am convinced there are some, who are deservedly so obnoxious that whatever measures may be adopted by Government, it will be impossible for them to escape the Effects of private Resentment.

With respect to the lower Class of people (which with those I have above mentioned) will comprehend all the Inhabitants I am convinced they will without trouble submit quietly to the Government that supports itself.

I am pretty confident that I am near the Truth in the above description, and that matters are not painted in more flattering terms than they deserve. The obvious consequences which appear to me are that it will be very practicable to re-establish the King's Government in S. Carolina. Altho' it will require both Time and address, whilst conviction operates upon those I first mentioned, Interest upon the second, and despair upon the third. Those whose madness would still prompt them to oppose it will sink of course, especially if that severe Vengance, which is so justly their due should be denounced & executed upon all those who, under colour of their Tyrannical Laws, under which the blood of so many of H.M. faithfull subjects hath already been shed, in future should attempt to drag out the unwilling People to oppose the King's Government. If the terror they have excited was once removed, a few months would restore this country to its former good Government.

Through Foreign Eyes

Like the French and Indian War (1754–1763), which one American historian prefers to call the Great War for Empire, the War for Independence was an international affair. The British hired foreign mercenaries, Americans entered into a treaty of alliance which for a century was a unique event in their diplomatic history, and before the peace half a dozen nations had become directly involved. The Revolution therefore brought to American battlefields people from countries other than Britain, and it became a topic of general concern in the Western world.

Most analytically minded observers concentrated on the ideology, on the special features of this, the first significant colonial rebellion in modern history. The virgin land, the natural rights philosophy, the legitimacy of rebellion, what Crèvecoeur later called "this new man, the American," these were the kind of topics which attracted comment. Few paid attention to the Loyalists who seemed to foreigners either the dull, reactionary, restrictive types among the colonial population or mere placemen, lackeys of the British government. The light of revolution was in the sky, the fire of freedom in the heart, why then bother with the deadwood? Yet some did take notice of the loyal provincials, especially those who had to fight alongside them, and a selection of their comments completes this first section of contemporary accounts.

A FRENCH VIEW

We know only that the author of the journal from which the next selection* is taken was a Frenchman who briefly visited America in 1777, the year before his country and the rebelling colonies signed their treaty of alliance. Naturally, the analysis produced as a result of the hasty visit was sketchy and on a number of important points quite erroneous. Like any other traveler in a foreign land the author was particularly susceptible to misinformation, poor estimates, and highly subjective opinions which he could not verify in the time at his disposal, even if he had so desired. This Frenchman brought with him a positive image of America, one deeply held and abundantly expounded by his contemporary intellectual leaders, the Philosophes. They viewed America through tinted spectacles, seeing her as untrammelled by the decadence and degradation prevailing in their own state. America to them was new territory where a great political and philosophical experiment was being executed. In general the value of this journal as an accurate foreign commentary is seriously marred by the overriding preconceptions of its author and the frequency with which he commits factual mistakes. However, these weaknesses are less evident in his comments on the Loyalists.

The Tories, who support the cause of the King, fall into two classes. There are those who have always been Royalists, and others who lacked sufficient popular favor to enter the congresses at the time of their formation. The latter, adhering neither to the King nor to the Americans, serve, however, from a spirit of intrigue, the party that is hostile to the one to which they inwardly belong, and which they oppose only through envy or vengeance. Whatever individuals may compose these two classes, they are highly prejudicial to the success of the Americans, some by virtue of titles or rank to which the British government elevated them, winning over to its cause their relatives, families, and dependants; the others, with a fine show of being republicans and anti-Royalists by finding ways to inform themselves of the decisions of the congresses and passing on the information to others, are thus the vexatious cause of the prolongation of hostilities and of the aid or helpful information which the enemy receive and from which they readily profit.

---

* *On the Threshold of Liberty: Journal of a Frenchman's Tour of the American Colonies in 1777*, trans. by Edward D. Seeber (Indiana University Press: Bloomington, Ind., 1959), pp. 113–114. Used by permission.

BARONESS FREDERIKA VON RIEDESEL

Baroness Frederika von Riedesel (1746–1808) was the wife of the general who commanded the Brunswick detachment of the German troops serving with the British army during the Revolution. Her journal* is remarkable for its detail and its directness. Unfortunately she was not very much concerned with the ideological content of the Revolution and her observations are almost entirely narrative in quality. Somewhat surprisingly, in view of her husband's position and function, she does not say a great deal about the Loyalists. In the following passages from her diary there is a mixture of hearsay evidence, firsthand description, and righteous indignation which may perhaps lessen the validity of her analysis but, by way of compensation, it indicates the atmosphere and attitudes of the times.

[1777–78] There was also the case of two brothers who loved each other dearly, but the one espoused the King's party, the other the republicans. The former, desiring to see his brother again, took leave and went to him. The other welcomed him joyously and said, "I am so happy to see that you have returned to the good cause." "No, my brother," the royalist replied, "I shall continue to be faithful to my King, but that cannot prevent me from loving you." Thereupon the American jumped up in rage, took a pistol, and threatened to shoot him if he did not leave the house immediately. All his good brother's assurances that a difference of opinion in politics could not injure their love were in vain. The other only cried, "It is only my old love for you which prevents my shooting you immediately, because every royalist is my enemy." And he would really have done it, had not his brother finally departed. Almost all families were thus divided, and this made it clear to me that there is nothing more terrible than a civil war. With such people we were obliged to live or to see nobody at all. I naturally preferred the latter choice. . . .

[1779] We also stopped at a very pretty place called Elizabeth Town [Elizabeth, New Jersey] opposite Staten Island, where we met a number of royalists, who were happy to have us stay with them. Being so

---

* *Baroness von Riedesel and the American Revolution: Journal and Correspondence of a Tour of Duty 1776–1783*, trans. and ed. by Marvin L. Brown, Jr. (The University of North Carolina Press: Chapel Hill, N.C., 1965), pp. 70–71; 92–93. Used by permission of The Institute of Early American History and Culture and the publisher.

near New York and sure of my husband's exchange, we thought that we had now reached our immediate goals and ate our dinner there happily in the thought that, as we intended crossing over to New York directly afterwards, we would be set free that same evening. But suddenly the door opened and an officer, who had been sent by General Washington, entered and handed General Phillips a letter, containing orders to return, as Congress had not given its approval to the exchange. The eyes of General Phillips, who was a very violent man, sparkled with fury. He hit the table with his fist, exclaiming, "This is pleasant!—and we should have expected it from these people, who are all rascals!" I was petrified and unable to speak a word. He took my hand and said, "Now, my friend, do not lose courage. Follow my example. See, I am quite composed!" "Everyone," I replied, "has his own way of expressing sadness. I conceal mine in my heart, and you express yours by violence. In my opinion, however, you would do better not to show these people how angry you are, because they only scoff at you, and besides it may only cause you still further trouble." He admitted I was right and assured me that he would bear his sorrow like I, with resignation, and was thereafter quiet.

I was pregnant and felt badly all the while, so the journey exhausted me exceedingly. I had hoped to be able to live quietly among people who would take care of me; but in vain! After only one day of rest, which had been granted us, we had to start on the return journey, and we stopped with the Van Hornes again. This time we met a nephew of General Washington there with a number of American officers, who during the three days of their stay had succeeded in so changing the minds of these people (they were of the turncoat type), that not only did we find the daughter of these so-called royalists on the friendliest of terms with these anti-royalists, whom she allowed all sorts of liberties, but in addition, as they no longer felt that they needed to spare our feelings, we heard them singing all through the night "God save great Washington! God damn the King!" It was difficult for me to conceal my annoyance about this when we departed next morning. . . .

JOHANN HEINRICHS

Captain Johann Heinrichs was one of the numerous Hessian officers who served in the Revolution. A man of education, ability, and opinions, he appears to have enlisted just to see America. His curiosity was unbounded,

his capacity for taking pains considerable, his delight in putting down his im-
pressions and writing short analytical essays great enough to overcome the
distractions and demands of war. These qualities, plus the fact that he
probably did not share the patriotic emotions of a British officer (although
the lethargy of some of the generals suggests that these were **not** always vital
characteristics on the imperial side) have given Heinrichs' accounts their importance. The first extract* is from his letter book and the second† from the
part of his diary written during Clinton's second attack on Charleston (1780).‡

TO THE HONORABLE COUNSELLOR OF THE COURT, H.

January 18, 1778

"Call this war, dearest friend, by whatsoever name you may, only
call it not an American Rebellion, it is nothing more or less than an
Irish-Scotch Presbyterian Rebellion. Those true Americans who take
the greatest part therein, are the famous Quakers. The most celebrated, the first ones in entire Pennsylvania and Philadelphia and Boston are, properly speaking, the heads of the Rebellion. I am not allowed to write to you explicitly, just how the matter developed, but
you can guess at what I have omitted, and you will hit it pretty
fairly. . . .

"For the first you must assume two Rebellions proper. The former
was fomenting fifty years ago. It was the result of a state projected
upon false principles, whose citizens consisted of seemingly hypocriti-
cal pious impostors, and downright cheats. These hypocrites are the
Quakers. I cannot tell you all of the infamy I hold these people capable
of; for I can think of nothing more abominable, than to practise, under
the guise of Religion,—malice, envy, yea even ambition, (thirst of
power). In Pennsylvania they are the first, the most respected. They
know the origin of the Colonies, and knew how to centralize the power
in themselves by degrees. By means of such cabals these manifest

---

* "Letter-Book of Captain Johann Heinrichs," *Pennsylvania Magazine of History and Biography*, XXII (1898), 137–139. Used by permission.

† *The Siege of Charleston*, trans. and ed. by Bernhard A. Uhlendorf (University of Michigan Press: Ann Arbor, 1938), pp. 321, 323. Used by permission.

‡ The diary of Captain Heinrichs, together with other Hessian accounts and
some letters, can be found in Bernhard A. Uhlendorf (ed.) *The Siege of
Charleston* (University of Michigan Publications in History and Political
Science, XII, Ann Arbor, 1938).

cheats contrived to attract the Germans who have settled here; they deceived the Germans by means of a paper printed in Germantown, whose editor was paid by them. They were the first to institute a light company; they let the Germans go in first, afterwards they extricated themselves, and left their dupes in the muddle; they bought houses and lands with Congress money and afterwards called themselves friends of the King and said their religion forbade them to fight.

"The second rebellion is that which originated amongst the rebels during the past campaign, namely that for Independence. Since then the remaining righteous ones, who were partly infatuated by the heat of their imagination, partly educated in wrong principles, and in part possibly may have been partially right in their opinion, these have left the scene of action since then, and just as Congress consists of Scoundrels, so the Army consists of people, warmed up in part by the war party, also their only support is in the war, and who are unwilling to exchange sword for last and needle, or who may fear that their former masters, whose serfs they are, would harness them to the yoke, as soon as they surrendered their Captain and Subaltern patents. This is the army proper of the enemy, numbering about 12,000 men. The remainder substitutes and Militia, of whom ten or twenty thousand are mobile at times; these fight only for the Province in which they dwell, and have been unable to resolve joining the Army and go into another province.

The Carolinians considered the laws which forbade this commerce and the customs officials' enforcement of these laws interference with their liberty and sufficient cause to take up arms. Since no other province besides South Carolina makes such excessive profits by contraband trade, which is facilitated by the situation of her harbor and the many small rivers and islands around the capital, the staple of all her trade, no group of people was more warmly interested in this rebellion than the merchant population of South Carolina. It is quite different with the inhabitants of the country, who here go under the name of "back-country people." The greater part of the rural population of this part of America are, I believe, favorably inclined toward peace, *for they gain nothing by this war*. The safe rule, according to which one can always ascertain whether a man is a loyalist or a rebel, is to find out whether he profits more in his private interests, his mode of life, his way of doing things, etc., when he is on our side or on that of the enemy. There are only very few exceptions to this rule: on the side of the enemy are a few enthusiasts and some pseudophilosophical-political dreamers who have read, but did not understand, Hugo Grotius' *Law of Nations,* while on our side there may be a small number of which one can say with conviction that love and faithfulness to God and their lawful King has brought them under the colors of their sovereign.

Part Two

Historical Commentaries

Loyalist Historians

Considering how many men were involved and how many of them were not only literate but skilled in letters, the Revolution produced a disappointing crop of histories from those who knew it firsthand. The lengthy writings of Washington, Adams, Jefferson, Hamilton, and a host of lesser lights add up to a good body of contemporary material, but hardly a participant took on the task of writing a history of the causes, events, and consequences of the war. No Thucydides graced the days of the American Revolution.

The Loyalists offered no one who could challenge for such a title but many of the best colonial chroniclers chose their side. Among their products we may cite William Smith's *History of . . . New York*, Thomas Hutchinson's *History . . . of Massachusetts Bay*, Robert Proud's *History of Pennsylvania*, and Alexander Hewat's *Historical Account . . . of South Carolina and Georgia*. The titles convey the essentially local nature of these histories, but this should not be cause for either surprise or regret. It would be too much to ask for national histories from historians who were fighting against the creation of the new nation. In addition, what they knew best were state or local affairs. They felt the need to explain their own political position and defend their Loyalist stand and were therefore impelled to make personal and local explanations. The result is that of the Loyalist literati only one or two offered a general treatment of the Revolution. The value of the writings of Loyalist historians is a clear depiction of the struggle for power within the colonies, even though many did not deal with the actual years of the Revolution.

JOSEPH GALLOWAY

The reader is referred to Part One, where Joseph Galloway is introduced. In the following selections Galloway again affirms his belief that most of the colonials were loyal to Britain in 1763, that although a few were "reduced by false pretenses into measures of violence," the vast majority were not. He deals with the events of the decade before war broke out and develops in his analysis what would now be termed a "conspiracy theory" of history (Letter I). Then he turns head-on into the question which must have occurred to his listeners: 'If you're right, Galloway, why aren't the British armies doing better?' The answer he gives is pointed and unequivocal: because the generals have fought the war badly, when they have bothered to fight at all (Letter III). The British military leaders became the scapegoat for the Loyalist analyst, just as the failure of Loyalists to raise troops had become a standard alibi of British ministers and generals. Next we have a rapid summary of how the Loyalists and their opponents acted in the last year or so of peace. Galloway's analysis shows how the Patriots had to seize the initiative and portrays the Loyalists as defenders of law and order. The last extract is from Galloway's examination before a committee of the House of Commons, where he pungently lambasts General Howe and provides an account of American affairs in keeping with his own prejudices and what he believes his audience wants to hear.

[From Letter I]* . . . During the last war, there was no part of his Majesty's dominions contained a greater proportion of faithul subjects than the Thirteen Colonies. The millions they granted to the Crown, the thousands sent into the field, the numbers of their privateers in the European and American seas, operating against the common enemy, are convincing proofs of this truth. The idea of disloyalty, at this time, scarcely existed in America; or, if it did, it was never expressed with impunity. How then can it happen, that a people so lately loyal, should so suddenly become universally disloyal, and firmly attached to republican Government, without any grievances or oppressions but those in anticipation? The tax imposed, and assigned as the cause of their disaffection, was truly a relief, not a burthen. Had it been a burthen, it was never felt, and had it been felt, it was of a most trivial nature. No fines, no imprisonments, no oppressions, had been experienced by the Colonists, that could have produced such an effect. It is a consequence that does not accord with the nature of the passions and affections of man. Reverence for a Sovereign from whom they have long received

---

* [Joseph Galloway], *Letters to a Nobleman, on the Conduct of the War in the Middle Colonies* (3rd. ed., London, 1780), pp. 8–10.

every proof of paternal regard and protection, and attachment to a Government under which they have been the happiest people on the globe, with a predilection for its laws, religion, manners, and customs, founded in reason, and riveted by habit and enjoyment, from infancy to manhood, and even to old age, are not to be eradicated by such trivial causes. They become second nature, and hard to be expelled. If we search the whole history of human events, we shall not meet with an example of such a sudden change, from the most perfect loyalty to universal disaffection. On the contrary, in every instance where national attachment has been generally effaced, it has been effected by slow degrees, and a long continuance of oppression, not in prospect, but in actual existence. Here we can conceive, that national attachment and affection, although fixed by habit, may give way at length to the superior influence and dictates of the first and most powerful principle in human nature, self-preservation; but without such a cause, it cannot be accounted for by reason, or by any antecedent example in the history of mankind.

[From Letter III]* . . . How then, since the British Commander had a force so much superior to his enemy, has it happened that the rebellion has not been long ago suppressed? The cause, my Lord, however inveloped in misrepresentation on this side of the Atlantic, is no secret in America.—It has been long lamented there, by thousands of his Majesty's faithful subjects, while the rebels have repeatedly announced it in their publications with triumphant insolence and ridicule—Friends and foes unite in declaring that it has been owing to want of wisdom in the plans, and of vigour and exertion in the execution.

To support this truth, so universally adopted in America, before I descend to particular operations, I will first treat of the general conduct of the war.—The Commander in Chief never began his operations until the middle of June. A part of that month, and the whole of April and May, when the season is moderate, and most proper for action, and the roads are good, were wantonly wasted; while a variety of the most cogent motives pointed to an early and vigorous campaign. In these months, the rebel army was always reduced to its weakest state. Its numbers were diminished by incessant and excessive fatigue, sick-

---

* [Joseph Galloway], *Letters to a Nobleman* . . . , pp. 36–37.

ness, and desertion; and those who remained were naked, half starved, and destitute of supplies. It was in the months of April and May that recruits for the rebel army were chiefly procured, who never could join it before the month of June. And it was apparent, in every year, that the operations of the British army, as soon as begun, however indolent, never failed to sink the spirits of the rebellious to such a degree, as totally to obstruct the recruiting service. In vain did these inviting, these importunate circumstances, against which nothing ought to have prevailed but some momentous and insuperable difficulty, press the General to take the field. He preferred the pleasures of indolence and dissipation, to a discharge of his duty to his country. . . .

[First Continental Congress, 1774]* The system of seditious opposition, in both countries, to the measures of Government, being thus concerted, the Congress broke up. The loyalists seeing no hope of opposing the approaching storm, retired to their families. The republicans adjourned to a tavern, in order to concert the plan which was necessary to be pursued by their party, throughout the Colonies, for raising a military force. This settled, they also returned to their respective Colonies.

And here the two parties acted upon very different principles. The loyalty of the first forbad them to join in the sedition, and taught them to look up to Government to take the lead in suppressing it. But they soon found that the powers of the colonial governments were insulted with impunity, and were daily giving way to new usurpations, without any exertion to prevent it. However, they hoped that the time was approaching, when the powers of the State would be exerted; and they knew, that those powers, if conducted with wisdom, would be more than sufficient to crush the intended rebellion. But the republicans were well apprised that they must rise into power by their own industry. They were therefore indefatigable throughout America. The discontented and factious were convened in every Colony. Provincial congresses, conventions, and committees of safety were appointed by a part of the people in every district, which, when compared with the whole, was truly inconsiderable. These illegal bodies having elected

---

* [Joseph Galloway], *Historical and Political Reflections on the Rise and Progress of the American Rebellion* (London, 1780), pp. 94–95.

men of the most seditious principles, for members of the next Congress, proceeded to other business.

The loyalists were disarmed, the most obnoxious of them imprisoned. The loyal presses were restrained, some of them seized and destroyed. Publications in favour of Government were publicly burnt, while the republican presses teemed with speeches of their friends and allies in parliament, and letters wrote from their colleagues in faction in England, with a thousand other literary performances, all tending to lead the people into a rebellious opposition to Government. Every measure that art and fraud could suggest, as necessary to delude the people into arms, was industriously pursued.

[Examination by the House of Commons]* Q. What proportion of the inhabitants of the revolted Colonies, do you think, from principle and choice, supported the present rebellion at any period?

A. I don't think that one-fifth part have, from principle and choice, supported the present rebellion.—Many of those, who have appeared in support of it, have, by a variety of means, been compelled.—I would wish to give reasons, and not fatigue the Committee. The last delegation to Congress, made by the province of Pennsylvania, and the appointment of all the officers of that state, was made by less than two hundred voters, although there are at least thirty thousand men intitled to vote by the laws of that province. . . .

Q. From your knowledge of the people of America, what proportion of the inhabitants do you think at this time would prefer a reconciliation with Great Britain, rather than assist in supporting American independence?

A. From the experience which the people have had of the superlative and excessive tyranny of their new rulers; from the distresses they have felt by the ravages of war, and the loss of their trade; from an aversion which they have to an attachment and connection with France, which they are fearful will terminate in the loss of their liberties, civil as well as religious; and from the old attachment, and I believe an earnest desire to be united with this country, I think I may venture to say, that many more than four-fifths of the people would

---

* Gt. Britain: House of Commons, *The Examination of Joseph Galloway, Esq.* (2nd. ed., London, 1780), pp. 10–12.

prefer an union with Great Britain, upon constitutional principles, to that of Independence. Many of the people, who at first took part in the opposition to Government, and were deluded by the Congress and its adherents, have severely felt every degree of distress. From those feelings they now reason, and that reason has prevailed on them to compare their old happy situation with their present misery, and to prefer the former.

THOMAS HUTCHINSON

Political events directly affected the writings of Thomas Hutchinson (1711– 1781). The first volume of his **History . . . of Massachusetts Bay,** covering the years to 1692, was published in 1764 and had a favorable reception. He was prompted to embark on a sequel to bring the history up to 1750, but his labors were interrupted when on August 26, 1765 a mob protesting the Stamp Act burst into his house and turned everything upside down. His manuscript was thrown into the muddy street and only a marvellous piece of luck allowed the author to recover most of it. In such circumstances Hutchinson's comparative objectivity was commendable, though the incident was not entirely forgotten. Probably it began the souring process which deprived the third volume (completed in 1778 but not published until fifty years later) of the balance evident in the first two. Although the history stopped short of the actual war, the author's treatment of the events leading up to it mirrored his Loyalist prejudices in such things as the analysis of James Otis' motives. Nevertheless there is a large amount of very valuable material in the **History,** including some penetrating comments on the causes of the Revolution. For example, Hutchinson may possibly have been the first historian to appreciate the incendiary role played by the colonial newspapers.

It would be difficult to convey his bias in a brief excerpt from the **History,** where the Loyalist party as such is hardly dealt with because it did not truly develop until the war had almost commenced. Instead, the selection below comes from his direct refutation of the document we know as the Declaration of Independence. It would be useful to have a copy to read alongside Hutchinson's counterthrust, only parts of which can be presented here.*

The first in order, *He has refused his assent to laws the most wholesome and necessary for the public good;* is of so general a nature, that it is not possible to conjecture to what laws or to what Colonies it refers. I remember no laws which any Colony has been restrained

---

* [Thomas Hutchinson], *Strictures upon the Declaration of the Congress at Philadelphia* (London, 1776) pp. 10–11; 19; 22–23; 28–30, 31–32.

from passing, so as to cause any complaint of grievances, except those for issuing a fraudulent paper-currency, and making it a legal tender; but this is a restraint which for many years past has been laid on Assemblies by an act of Parliament, since which such laws cannot have been offered to the King for his allowance. . . .

The laws of England are or ought to be the laws of its Colonies. To prevent a deviation further than the local circumstances of any Colony may make necessary, all Colony laws are to be laid before the King; and if disallowed, they then become of no force. . . .

This charge is still more inexcusable, because I am well informed, the disallowance of Colony laws has been much more frequent in preceding reigns, than in the present. . . .

He has forbidden his Governors to pass laws of immediate and pressing importance, unless suspended in their operation till his assent should be obtained, and when so suspended, he has utterly neglected to attend them.

Laws, my Lord, are in force in the Colonies, as soon as a Governor has given his assent, and remain in force until the King's disallowance is signified. Some laws may have their full effect before the King's pleasure can be known. Some may injuriously affect the property of the subject; and some may be prejudicial to the prerogative of the Crown, and to the trade, manufactures and shipping of the kingdom. Governors have been instructed, long before the present or the last reign, not to consent to such laws, unless with a clause suspending their operations until the pleasure of the King shall be known. I am sure your Lordship will think that nothing is more reasonable. . . .

He has erected a Multitude of new offices and sent hither Swarms of officers, to harrass our people and eat out their subsistence.

I know of no new offices erected in America in the present reign, except those of the Commissioners of the Customs and their dependents. Five Commissioners were appointed, and four Surveyors General dismissed; perhaps fifteen or twenty clerks and under officers were necessary for this board more than the Surveyors had occasion for before: Land and tide waiters, weighers &c. were known officers before; the Surveyors used to encrease or lessen the number as the King's service required, and the Commissioners have done no more. Thirty or forty additional officers in the whole Continent, are the *Swarms* which eat out the subsistence of the boasted number of three millions of people.

Cases had often happened in America, which Surveyors General had not authority to decide. The American merchants complained of being obliged to apply to the Commissioners of the Customs in London. The distance caused long delay, as well as extraordinary charge. A Board in America, was intended to remove the cause of these complaints, as well as to keep the inferior officers of the Customs to their duty. But no powers were given to this Board more than the Commissioners in London had before; and none but illicit traders ever had any reason to complain of grievances; and they of no other than of being better watched than they had ever been before. At this time, the authority of Parliament to pass Acts for regulating commerce was acknowledged, but every measure for carrying such Acts into execution was pronounced an injury, and usurpation, and all the effects prevented. . . .

For imposing taxes on us without our consent.

How often has your Lordship heard it said, that the Americans are willing to submit to the authority of Parliament in all cases except that of taxes? Here we have a declaration made to the world of the causes which have impelled to a separation. We are to presume that it contains all which they that publish it are able to say in support of a separation, and that if any one cause was distinguished from another, special notice would be taken of it. That of taxes seems to have been in danger of being forgot. It comes in late, and in as slight a manner as is possible. And, I know, my Lord, that these men, in the early days of their opposition to Parliament, have acknowledged that they pitched upon this subject of taxes, because it was most alarming to the people, every man perceiving immediately that he is personally affected by it; and it has, therefore, in all communities, always been a subject more dangerous to government than any other, to make innovation in; but as their friends in England had fell in with the idea that Parliament could have no right to tax them because not represented, they thought it best it should be believed they were willing to submit to other acts of legislation until this point of taxes could be gained; owning at the same time, that they could find no fundamentals in the English Constitution, which made representation more necessary in acts for taxes, than acts for any other purpose; and that the world must have a mean opinion of their understanding, if they should rebel rather than pay a duty of three-pence *per* pound on tea, and yet be content to submit to an act which restrained them from making a nail to shoe their own horses. Some of them, my Lord, imagine they are as well acquainted with the nature of government, and with the constitution and history of England, as many of their partisans in the kingdom; and they will sometimes laugh at the doctrine of fundamentals from which even Parliament itself can never deviate; and they say it has been often held and denied merely to serve the cause of party, and that it must be so until these unalterable fundamentals shall be ascertained; that the great Patriots in the reign of King Charles the Second, Lord Russell, Hampden, Maynard, &c. whose memories they reverence, declared their opinions, that there were no bounds to the power of Parliament by any fundamentals whatever, and that even the hereditary succession to the Crown might be, as it since has been, altered by Act of Parliament; whereas they who call themselves Patriots in the present day have held it to be a fundamental, that there can be no taxation without representation, and that Parliament cannot alter it.

But as this doctrine was held by their friends, and was of service to their cause until they were prepared for a total Independence, they appeared to approve it: As they have now no further occasion for it, they take no more notice of an act of imposing taxes than of many other acts; for a distinction in the authority of Parliament in any particular case, cannot serve their claim to a general exemption, which they are now preparing to assert. . . .

In every stage of these oppressions, we have petitioned for redress in the most humble terms; our repeated petitions have been answered only by repeated injury.

What these oppressions were your Lordship has seen, for we may fairly conclude, that every thing appears in this Declaration, which can give colour to this horrid Rebellion, so that these men can never complain of being condemned without a full hearing.

But does your Lordship recollect any petitions in the several stages of these pretended oppressions? Has there ever been a petition to the King

—To give his Assent to these wholesome and necessary Laws to which he had refused it? . . .

All the petitions we have heard of, have been against Acts of the Supreme Legislature; and in all of them something has been inserted, or something has been done previous to them, with design to prevent their being received.

They have petitioned for the repeal of a law, because Parliament had no right to pass it. The receiving and granting the prayer of such petition, would have been considered as a renunciation of right; and from a renunciation in one instance, would have been inferred a claim to renunciation in all other instances. The repealing, or refraining from enacting any particular laws, or relieving from any kind of service, while a due submission to the laws in general shall be continued, and suitable return be made of other services, seems to be all which the Supreme Authority may grant . . . Gratitude, I am sensible, is seldom to be found in a community, but so sudden a revolt from the rest of the Empire, which had incurred so immense a debt, and with which it remains burdened, for the protection and defence of the Colonies, and at their most importunate request, is an instance of ingratitude no where to be parallelled.

Suffer me, my Lord, before I close this Letter, to observe, that though the professed reason for publishing the Declaration was a decent respect to the opinions of mankind, yet the real design was to reconcile the people of America to that Independence, which always before, they had been made to believe was not intended. This design has too well succeeded. The people have not observed the fallacy in reasoning from the *whole* to *part*; nor the absurdity of making the *governed* to be *governors*. From a disposition to receive willingly complaints against Rulers, facts misrepresented have passed without examining. Discerning men have concealed their sentiments, because under the present *free* government in America, no man may, by writing or speaking, contradict any part of this Declaration, without being deemed an enemy to his country, and exposed to the rage and fury of the populace.

JONATHAN BOUCHER

Jonathan Boucher (1738–1804) was the son of a man who doubled as innkeeper and schoolmaster in a small village in northern England. From poor circumstances the boy was pushed to an education and did well enough to start night school teaching at the age of sixteen. In April, 1759 he sailed to Virginia where he had a job as private tutor. He quickly discovered that he and the Virginians were of different tastes. Interestingly, soon after his arrival he was complaining that will all their faults he felt that he could get along with them were it not for their "forward obtrusion which subjects you to hear obscene conceits and broad expression, & from this, there are times w'n [when] no sex, no rank, no conduct can exempt you."

In 1762 Boucher returned to England to be ordained as an Anglican minister and then came back to Virginia as rector of Hanover, King George's County. Later, in St. Mary's County, a stepson of George Washington was among his pupils. The stepfather and the vicar-schoolmaster exchanged a considerable number of letters (see Volume III of **Letters to Washington** in five volumes, edited by Stanislaus M. Hamilton, Boston and New York, 1898–1902 or **Letters of Jonathan Boucher to George Washington,** edited by Worthington C. Ford, Brooklyn, New York, 1899), but of course the two men gradually came to different conclusions about America's destiny. By the time the revolution began, Boucher was in charge of Saint Anne's church in Annapolis, Maryland, which in his view was then "the genteelest town in North America." There he was a leader in literary activities, chaplain of the lower house of the assembly, and a close friend of the governor, Robert Eden.

Such a combination might appear to be a clever effort at playing both sides of the political street, but this was not the case. Boucher was absolutely firm in his loyalty to England and the Crown. In his last sermon, preached, as he recalled it, with pistols lying at the ready on the plush pulpit cushion, he openly avowed that "As long as I live, yea, while I have my being, will I proclaim 'God save the King'." He left for England in the fall of 1775 and never came back to the new United States. Yet, when a collection of his addresses and sermons, given between 1763 and 1775, was published in 1797 as **A View of the Causes and Consequences of the American Revolution,** * the dedication was to the first American president as "a tender of renewed amity."

The title is a little misleading since one will not find here a historical analysis. The volume is merely a collection of thirteen sermons preached by Boucher in the colonies between 1763 and 1775. Nevertheless, the preface gave him an opportunity to comment on those who had already written histories of the Revolution, and therefore it is an important contribution to Loyalist historiography. These remarks were followed by some observations which are indicative of what the Anglican vicar **might** have said if he had produced a history of his own.

Most writers on American topics, as well as the historians of the revolt, are confident in ascribing the extraordinary prosperity of America to the skill, the industry, and the enterprising spirit of the Americans themselves. It seems to be taken for granted that, notwithstanding our protection and patronage, and notwithstanding all our bounties and benefactions, this actually was the case: and there are few who will be at the trouble to examine on what authority these opinions are founded. No man can be more willing than I am to allow to the efforts of the Americans all that they are entitled to; and I am equally ready to allow, that it is not a little to which they are entitled: but, at the same time, I am well aware how much more easy it is to assert that

---

* Jonathan Boucher, *A View of the Causes and Consequences of the American Revolution* (London, 1797), pp. xxxix–xli; lxiv–lxv; 509; 514–515.

they owe their success solely to themselves, than it is to prove it. If, however, ten, thousand reasons could be given for the rapid growth of America, the matter of fact must and would still rest just where it now does: for, all this has happened under the auspices, the protection, and the encouragement of Great Britain. All that either country has greatly to regret on this subject is, that the prudence of the one did not keep pace with her affection; and that the humility of the other was not commensurate with her prosperity. Great Britain did not consider, that, governed as her Colonies were, whilst she strained every nerve to render them opulent and powerful, she was in effect advancing them still nearer to independency. Nor did those Americans who, by the means of many false and dangerous maxims of government, were at such pains to alienate the affections of too numerous a portion of their countrymen from the Parent State, consider that the principles then so sedulously inculcated for that purpose would render the people equally indisposed towards any future government.

Among other circumstances favourable to the revolt of America, that of the immense debt owing by the Colonists, to the Merchants of Great Britain, deserves to be reckoned as not the least. It was estimated at three millions sterling: and such is the spirit of adventure of British merchants, and of such extent are their capitals and their credit, that, not many years ago, I remember to have heard the amount of their debts to this country calculated at double that sum: it is probably now trebled. Disposed, as with great propriety the Legislature of Great Britain always has been (and it is to be hoped always will be) to be careful of her commercial interests, so considerable a pledge, under such circumstances, becomes of serious moment. Enquiries can hardly be too soon instituted, how far this is, or is not, one of the few instances, in which, with equal advantage to Commerce and to the State, this spirit of enterprize may be controlled and restrained. By so unbounded a credit, that respectable body of men, the British merchants, seem to have deprived themselves, if not of their freedom of will, yet certainly of their free agency: for if, hereafter, unfortunately for both countries, disputes should again be fomented between the Americans and ourselves, (and their being so deeply in our debt, however able they may be to discharge it, is surely such a state of things as can never be thought likely to prevent disputes,) what is the part which merchants so circumstanced will probably take? The answer to this question, I conceive, may well be, that merchants will probably act as they once before did in a similar case; that is to say, rather than run the risque of losing their debts, they will side, or appear to side, with the Americans. The condescensions and the concessions which (contrary to the usual course of things) creditors in this instance made to debtors, (and in particular to the planters of Virginia and Maryland,) were not only to the last degree humiliating and degrading, but productive of other and greater evils. Low people were thus trained to be insolent and unmannerly; and were also taught, that there was hardly any thing, however unreasonable, which they could not obtain, provided only they were clamorous and audacious in demanding it. . . .

That much blame attaches to Great Britain, from her supineness in suffering Colonial mismanagements to rise to such an height of error as at length to amount to a rebellion, from her want of counsel and conduct in carrying on the war, and from her pusillanimity in concluding an ignominious peace, the most zealous of her admirers will not deny. For all these errors she is now called to account, and made to pay severely for all her misdoings. Heavy to this nation was the loss of Thirteen of the best of her Continental Colonies: but it becomes intolerable to us now only when, as one of it's consequences, another republic is about to arise at our very doors; a republic to which that of America can be compared only as an infant Hercules may be compared with an Hercules at his full growth. . . .

Hence it follows, that we are free, or otherwise, as we are governed by law, or by the mere arbitrary will, or wills, of any individual, or any number of individuals. And liberty is not the setting at nought and despising established laws—much less the making our own wills the rule of our own actions, or the actions of others—and not bearing (whilst yet we dictate to others) the being dictated to, even by the laws of the land; but it is the being governed by law, and by law only. . . .

This popular notion, that government was originally formed by the consent or by a compact of the people, rests on, and is supported by, another similar notion, not less popular, nor better founded. This other notion is, that the whole human race is born equal; and that no man is naturally inferior, or, in any respect, subjected to another; and that he can be made subject to another only by his own consent. The position is equally ill-founded and false both in its premises and conclusions. In hardly any sense that can be imagined is the position strictly true; but, as applied to the case under consideration, it is demonstrably not true.

SAMUEL PETERS

Of the Loyalists who wrote histories dealing with the Revolutionary period few were so fired up with a spirit of castigation and revenge as Samuel Peters (1735–1826) who published the first edition of **A General History of Connecticut** in London, 1781. Roundhouse attacks come easily from those possessed of an abundance of righteousness, and Peters, an Anglican missionary and minister, had more than his share. In Hebron, Connecticut the Sons of Liberty paid him two visits. On the second he was yanked out to the village green to recant his pro-British views. In short order Peters stole away and grabbed a ship for England, leaving behind his wife, his children, and a score of slaves.

Paying back his tormentors seems to have been a prime motivation for the **History**. Today no one takes it very seriously, but its barbs had stung, and proud Connecticut men from John Trumbull in 1798 to William Prince in 1898 blasted the author for what they considered an inaccurate diatribe. Yet neither his stand nor his treatment by fellow colonials stopped Peters from blaming the British for bringing about the revolution, as the following passage* taken from a more judicious section of his work makes apparent. (It is copied from the 1877 edition and differs somewhat from the original version but not in any way which affects either the author's argument or his tone.)

Many writers have endeavored to point out the motive which prompted the Americans to the wish of being independent of Great Britain, who had for a century and a half nursed and protected them with parental tenderness; but they have only touched upon the reasons ostensibly held up by the Americans, but which are merely a veil to the true causes. These, therefore, I shall endeavour to set before the reader.

In the first place: England, as if afraid to venture her Constitution in America, had kept it at an awful distance, and established in many of her colonies republicanism, wherein the democratic absorbs the regal and aristocratic part of the English Constitution. The people naturally imbibed the idea that they were superior to kings and lords, because they controlled their representatives, governors, and councils. This is the infallible consequence of popular governments.

Secondly: The English had, like the Dutch, adopted the errors of ancient Rome, who judged that her colonies could be held in subjec-

---

* [Samuel Peters], A *General History of Connecticut . . . by a gentleman of the province* (orig. ed., London, 1781; the ed. quoted here, New York, 1877), pp. 247–249.

tion only by natives of Rome; and therefore all emoluments were carefully withheld from all natives of the colonies.

Thirdly: The learned and opulent families in America were not honoured by their King like those born in Britain.

Fourthly: The Americans saw themselves despised by the Britons, "though bone of their bone and flesh of their flesh." They felt and complained of, without redress, the sad effects of convicts, the curses of human society and the disgrace of England, taken from the dungeons, jails, and gibbets, and poured into America as the common sewer of England, to murder, plunder, and commit outrage upon the people "whom the King did not delight to honour."

Hence the rebellion. Human nature is always such that men will never cease struggling for honour, wealth, and power, at the expense of gratitude, loyalty, and virtue.

Indignation and despair seized the gentlemen in America, who thought, like Haman, that their affluence and ease was nothing worth so long as they lay under the sovereign's contempt. They declared that the insult reached the whole continent, in which were to be found only two Baronets of Great Britain, while all the other inhabitants were held beneath the yeomanry of England. They added: "Let Caesar tremble! Let wealth and private property depart, to deliver our country from the injuries of our elder brethren!" How easily might the rebellion have been averted by the granting of titles! With what reason faction and discontent spring up in South-America, may be learned from the dear-bought wisdom of Spain, who transported to her colonies her own Constitution in Church and State, rewarded merit in whatever part of her territories it appeared, sent bishops to govern and ordain in every church in South-America, and they, together with the native *noblesse,* promoted harmony, the offspring of justice and policy; while North-America abounded with discord, hatred, and rebellion, entirely from want of policy and justice in their party-coloured charters, and of the honours and privileges of natural-born subjects of Great Britain.

It appears that the British Government, in the last century, did not expect New-England to remain under their authority; nor did the New-Englanders consider themselves as subjects, but allies, of Great Britain. It seems that England's intent was to afford an asylum to the republicans, who had been a scourge to the British Constitution; and so, to encourage that restless party to emigrate, republican charters were granted, and privileges and promises given them far beyond what any Englishman in England was entitled to. The emigrants were empowered to make laws in Church and State, agreeable to their own will and pleasure, without the King's approbation; they were excused from all quit-rents, all Government taxes, and promised protection without paying homage to the British King, and their children entitled to the same rights and privileges as if born in England. However hard this bargain was upon the side of England, she had performed her part, except in the last respect—indeed, the most material in policy and in the minds of the principal gentlemen of New-England. The honour of nobility had not been conferred on any of them, and therefore they had never enjoyed the full privileges and liberties of the Britons, but, in a degree, had ever been held in bondage under their chartered republican systems, wherein gentlemen of learning and property attain not to equal power with the peasants. The people of New-England were rightly styled republicans; but a distinction should be made between the learned and the unlearned, the rich and the poor. The latter formed a great majority; therefore the minority were obliged to wear the livery of the majority, in order to secure their election into office. These very republican gentlemen were ambitious, fond of the power of governing, and grudged no money or pains to obtain an annual office. What would they not have given for a dignity depending not on the fickle will of a multitude, but on the steady reason and generosity of a king? The merchants, lawyers, and clergy, to appearance were republicans, but not one of them was really so. The truth is, they found necessity on the one hand, and British neglect on the other, to be so intolerable, that they rather chose to risk their lives and fortunes to bring about a revolution, than continue in the situation they were. As to the multitude, they had no cause of complaint: they were accuser, judge, king, and subjects, only to themselves.

The rebellion sprung not from them, but from the merchants, lawyers, and clergy, who were never inimical to the aristocratic branch of the Government, provided they were admitted to share in it according to their merits. It is true, they, like Calvin, the author of their religion, maintained that no man can merit anything of the Great Eternal; nevertheless, they thought they had merited the aristocratic honours which emanate from earthly kings; while kings and nobles of the earth imagine themselves to have merited more than they yet enjoy —even heaven itself—only because they happen to enjoy the honour of being descendants of heroic ancestors.

CHARLES STEDMAN

The father of Charles Stedman (1753–1812) was a Jacobite who had been forced to flee his native Scotland to escape the wrath of the British government. The son left America, **his** native land, for precisely the opposite reason.

The elder Stedman had a successful judicial career in Philadelphia. Charles went to the College of William and Mary with the intention of joining the same profession, but had little chance to show his talents. When the war broke out between Britain and the colonies, both father and son became Loyalists. Charles was appointed commissary to the army of Sir William Howe. He had a good knowledge of German, presumably gained from contact with German-speaking colonials in Pennsylvania, and served first as an interpreter for the Hessian troops and later as commander of a rifle corps of Palatine soldiers. Stedman saw a great deal of action; he was wounded twice, captured twice, and once sentenced to be hanged as a rebel.

In 1783 he followed his father into exile in England and eventually was appointed to assist one of the commissions in settling Loyalist claims. In 1794 his **History . . . of the American War** was published in London. There was no doubt that his military accounts, like others which had appeared both during and after the war, would be challenged by somebody. On this occasion the attack came from Sir Henry Clinton who questioned Stedman's accuracy on a number of matters. The criticisms were not very serious, and as the only Loyalist analysis which attempts to cover the war as a whole Stedman's work remains of considerable interest. Its neglect by historians is scarcely deserved. The following extract* provides an excellent short summary of the significance of the Revolution, written a decade after Stedman left America.

The American Revolution is the grandest effect of combination that has yet been exhibited to the world: A combination formed by popular representation and the art of printing. So vast a force as was exerted by Great Britain had never been sent to so great a distance, nor resisted by any power apparently so unequal to the contest. The military genius of Britain was unimpaired; she rose with elastic force under every blow; and seemed capable, by the immensity of her revenues, of wearying out, by perseverance, the adversity of fortune: But wisdom, vigour, and unanimity, were wanting in her public councils. The eloquence of some legislators in opposition to government; the narrow views of ministers at home; and the misconduct of certain commanders abroad, through a series of pusillanimity, procrastination, discord, and folly; brought this country, in spite of the gallant efforts of the British

---

* C[harles] Stedman, *History of the Origin, Progress, and Termination of the American War* (2 vols., London, 1794), II, 446–449.

officers and soldiers by land and sea, the justice of their cause, the firmness of their sovereign, and the general vows of the people, to a crisis, which has not indeed been followed (so limited are our prospects into futurity) by all that calamity which was generally apprehended, but which, nevertheless, although the national character, for spirit and enterprise, was abundantly sustained by individuals, cannot be regarded otherwise than as a disgrace to the British: Since it exhibited, in our public conduct, the triumph of party over genuine patriotism, and a spirit of [s]peculation and pleasure prevailing in too many instances over military discipline, and a sense of military honour. The British minister did not possess that towering genius which is alone fitted, in difficult and turbulent times, to overcome the seditious, and rouse the remiss to their duty. Though a man of fine talents, as well as an amiable disposition, he was constitutionally indolent: And, besides this, there was not that degree of cordiality and perfect unanimity that the minister was led to suppose amongst the friends of his majesty's government in America. It is, perhaps, a matter of doubt whether the loyalists were not, on the whole, too sanguine in their expectations. But it is the nature of men to cherish the hope of relief with an ardour proportioned to the greatness of their misfortunes.

On the whole, the British government did not proceed on any grand system that might control particular circumstances and events; but studied to prolong their own authority by temporary expedients. They courted their adversaries at home, by a share of power and profit; and the public enemies of the state, by partial concessions. But these availed much more to the establishment of new claims, than all the declarations of parliamentary rights and royal prerogatives with which they were accompanied, did to maintain the rights of established government: For facts quickly pass into precedents; while manifesto is opposed to manifesto, and argument to argument. Had the measures adopted by Britain, been adopted in time*, perhaps they would not have been adopted in vain. Their concessions, as well as their armaments, were always too late. Earlier concession, or an earlier application of that mighty force which was at the disposal of the commanders

---

* Besides a mighty navy, Great Britain had a force in America, amounting nearly to 42,000 men, besides from 25,000 to 30,000 loyalists, who were actually enlisted in the several provincial corps raised during the war. [Stedman's footnote]

in chief in 1777, might perhaps have prevented or quashed the revolution.

While the natural strength and spirit of Great Britain were embarrassed and encumbered with the disadvantages and errors now enumerated, the Americans, in spite of a thousand difficulties and wants, by the energy of liberty, the contrivance of necessity, and the great advantages arising from the possession of the country, ultimately attained their object. The Americans, indeed, were not fired with that enthusiastic ardour, which nations of a warmer temperament, in all ages, have been wont to display in the cause of freedom. But they were guided by wise councils; they were steady and persevering; and, on all great occasions, not a little animated by the courage of general Washington, who has been proverbially called a Fabius, but in whose character courage, in fact, was a feature still more predominant than prudence. The American generals, having the bulk of the people on their side, were made acquainted with every movement of the British army, and enabled, for the most part, to penetrate their designs: To obtain intelligence, on which so much depends, was to the British commanders a matter of proportionable difficulty. The Americans had neither money nor credit: But they learned to stand in need only of a few things; to be contented with the small allowance that nature requires; to suffer, as well as to act. Their councils, animated by liberty, under the most distressing circumstances, took a grand and high-spirited course, and they were finally triumphant.

The Revolution of America, though predicted by philosophy, was generally considered as a remote contingency, if not a thing wholly ideal and visionary. Its immediate causes were altogether unforeseen and improbable. It came as a surprise upon the world: And men were obliged to conclude, either that the force of Great Britain was ill-directed, or that no invading army, in the present enlightened period, can be successful, in a country where the people are tolerably united.

Sympathetic Historians of the Nineteenth Century

During the nineteenth century only a sprinkling of historians paid much attention to the Loyalists or wrote of them as anything but traitors to the cause of liberty, scoundrels who had deserted the good ship America in her hour of greatest need. Whatever period one selects, the underlying note is that of patent, and often pugnacious, chauvinism. When the "scientific" methodology of American historians trained in Germany in the last quarter of the century began to make itself felt in more thorough and "objective" historical accounts, there was no rapid or radical change in outlook. Even this new training emphasized (in nearly every case) a commitment to nationalist history, which hardly inspired greater attention for those "non-Americans," the Loyalists.

An exception to the general neglect was Lorenzo Sabine, but his work had little effect on the more notable American historians of the century, whether they wrote multivolumed histories of the United States or specialized in the Revolutionary period. The Loyalists were either ignored or slighted. So prevalent were these attitudes that someone like Moses C. Tyler, writing in 1897, was extremely conscious of being a revisionist. Another very understandable result of studying history through patriotic eyes is the paucity of treatments of the Loyalists during the nineteenth century. The three best are included in this brief section.

LORENZO SABINE

Lorenzo Sabine (1803–1877) was the first American historian to give the Loyalists anything like their due. Although we know disappointingly little about him, he seems to have had at least two of his native New England's virtues, enterprise and a mind of his own. These were reflected in the career he created for himself on what he called the "eastern frontier of the union." At Eastport, Maine, he started work in a shop for ten dollars a month; then he tried to branch out on his own, went bankrupt, got another job, and tried again. Later he wrote that he "built and owned vessels, fitted out fishermen, and was a petty dealer in codfish and molasses." There was more to come: a position as a bank official, three years as a member of the Maine House of Representatives, deputy collector of customs, and editor of the Eastport **Sentinel**. Sabine's historical interests ranging from duelling to fisheries and forests, almost matched the breadth of his careers.

By the time he moved to Framingham, Massachusetts (1848) he had already produced his most notable contribution. The **American Loyalists or Biographical Sketches of Adherents to the British Crown in the War of the Revolution** appeared in 1847 and was the basis of his later, larger **Biographical Sketches of Loyalists** (1864), a work which has not yet been bettered. Consciously and vigorously Sabine resurrected the Loyalists from oblivion and the tradition of obloquy. In doing so he perhaps overstretched some points a little, a not uncommon characteristic among historical writers in the first half of the nineteenth century. None of them had received extensive professional training and they were therefore innocent of the prevalent modern vice of walking in the middle of the critical road. Sabine also produced a most interesting analysis of the origins of the Revolution, one in which he drew attention to the British side of the argument and emphasized economic matters as principal determinants. He said, "To me the documentary history, the state-papers of the revolutionary era, teach nothing more clearly than this, namely, that almost every matter brought into discussion was **practical**, and in some form or other related to LABOR,—to some branch of COMMON INDUSTRY." Speaking of the specific issue of the "tea-ships" he saw its essence not as a question of taxation but "like all the others between the merchants and the crown, one of commerce."

Sabine was a good American who believed that the colonists had substantial reasons for rebellion in 1776. He regarded the aftermath of the Seven Years war or Great War for Empire as leading "naturally and certainly to freedom." But he asked that the Loyalists be given a fair hearing, that the complexity of the war's causes be recognized and investigated in place of unthinking adherence to symbolic slogans, and that the role of class and party be examined in each of the colonies. In this last area we are only now fully taking up his suggestions and beginning to look minutely at the economic, political, and social divisions in America during the Revolutionary period. In short, Sabine was calling for Americans to be better historians, to remember in dealing with great men that although something "is due to the dignity of history" so too something "is due to the dignity of truth. The

bandaged eyes and the even scales [traditional symbols of Justice] I apprehend, are as fit emblems for the student as for the judge."
    The first selection below is from a review essay* which Sabine wrote on
the publication of John G. Simcoe's **History of the Operations of a Partisan
Corps** (1844). It shows his belief that the Loyalists dearly deserved their
historian and indicates, some three years before his own study appeared, the
spirit in which he was conducting the research. This passage is then followed
by selections from Sabine's study.†

. . . But of a spirit wholly different are the searchers after truth, and
the close students of history. These have ascertained, from the various
sources open to them, that all who called themselves "Whigs" were not
necessarily disinterested and virtuous, and the proper objects of un-
limited praise; and that the "Tories" were not, to a man, selfish and
vicious, and deserving of unmeasured and indiscriminate reproach. . . .
Men who give up home, who separate themselves from kindred, who
surrender all the happiness and expectations of life, in order to become
exiles,—if of distinguished private worth,—are never to be stigmatized,
but always to be respected, and sometimes venerated. . . .

    Every effort which has been, or which remains to be made, to
relieve the class . . . from obloquy and shame, has had our most hearty
concurrence. And while we hope that full justice will be done to such,
we would also hope that no asperity of judgment may be shown towards those who were aged, who were grief-stricken, or who adhered
to the crown from natural timidity of character, the dread of blood-
shed, or the conviction that the most united and energetic resistance
would prove unavailing; since, if blamable, they were, as a mass, severely punished. Those who clung to the cause of the king upon a
calculation of personal advantage, or from the love and expectation of
place and power, deserve to be held up to public scorn; and assuredly
we will say nothing to avert from them the full measure of reprobation
which they deserve.

    There is still another class, on whom public indignation has fallen,
and yet rests, none too heavily. The occasions are few, if, indeed, they
are found at all, which justify men in bearing arms against their native
land. This has been the sentiment in all ages, and we would endeavour

---

* [Lorenzo Sabine], Review of J. G. Simcoe's *History of . . . the Queen's
Rangers* in *North American Review*, LIX (1844), 262–263; 301.
† Lorenzo Sabine, *A Historical Essay on the Loyalists of the American Revo-
lution* (Boston, 1847), pp. 36–37; 66–67.

to confirm and strengthen it. To this end, we would not have the conduct of the Loyalists who entered the British service and fought against their brethren held excusable, either now or at any coming time. Until every distinction between right and wrong shall be beaten down, their deep sin will stand accursed. . . .

Be all this as it may, the Loyalists should have been suffered to remain in the land of their birth. Most of them would have easily fallen into respect for the new state of things, and obedience to the new laws, and, long before this time, all would have mingled with the mass. The error of England in perpetuating two distinct races in Canada just begins to be felt. There, as in our own case, the conquerors and the vanquished should have been mingled and made one. We acquired the southern possessions of France in America forty years after she yielded up to British arms her remaining territories in the North; but how different is the population of French origin in Louisiana from that in British America! To make republican Americans of Frenchmen—if we may so express the idea—was a task far more difficult, than to unite under one form of government the entire people of the thirteen States. And yet, while we failed to accomplish the latter, how very nearly have we already perfected the former!

We must leave the subject here. The doctrines of the Whigs may yet be embraced, before the century closes, by their opponents of whom we have discoursed. Colonies become nations as surely as boys become men; and of all races, the Saxon learns to rule itself the soonest. The thirteen children of England taught the lesson, we trust, that, though fire and sword may retard, they cannot prevent, the operation of this law of nature. . . .

We enter now upon a brief inquiry to show the divisions in the different classes and avocations of Colonial society. And first, those who held office. Nearly all the officials of all grades adhered to the crown. This was to have been expected. Men who lived in ease, who enjoyed all the considerations and deference which rank and station invariably confer, and especially in monarchies, and who, therefore, had nothing to gain, but much to lose, by a change, viewed the dissensions that arose between themselves and the people, in a light which allowed their self-love and their self-interest to have full play. "They were appointed and sworn to execute the laws, and in obeying the instructions of the ministry at home to enforce the statutes of the realm, they did but perform common acts of duty." These were the arguments, and they were neither the first nor the last persons in office who have reasoned in the same manner, and who have kept their places at the expense of their patriotism. Besides, they affected to believe, that the Whig leaders were mere needy office-hunters, and that the contests between them were in some measure personal. The descendants of Loyalists, whose homes are across our northeastern border, in conversations with citizens of the republic, continue to repeat the tale. They have been answered, that, were the charge true, *our* fathers were still the more patriotic of the two; since, upon this issue, it would seem that *theirs*, who were the fat and sleek possessors, would not give up the much coveted stations to the lean and hungry expectants and claimants, even to preserve the British empire from dismemberment. They have been answered farther, that *they* derive no benefit from the averment, even though Washington, and John Adams, and Jay, were just objects of the world's scorn, and though every associate they had were an Arnold in motive, and for the obvious reason, that separation from the mother country is still to be triumphantly defended on the ground of absolute necessity. For, without a dissolution of the connexion, the Saxon race in the New World could neither have developed the resources of the continent they occupied, nor have become great and happy. . . .

It has been answered, too, that few foresaw the issue to which the quarrel must come, and that the Whigs continually denied an intention to do more than obtain a peaceable redress of grievances. It has been said, also, that those who received the name of Tories were not at first, nor indeed for some years, resisting a *revolution,* but striving to preserve order, and an observance of the rights of persons and property; that many, who took sides at the outset as mere conservators of the peace, were denounced by those whose purposes they thwarted, and were finally compelled, in pure self-defence, to accept of royal protection, and thus to become identified with the royal party ever after. Again, it has been stated, that, had the naked question of Independence been discussed from the beginning, and before minor, and in many cases, local, events had shaped their course, many, who were driven forth to live and die as aliens and outcasts, would have terminated their career far differently; that many were opposed to war from religious principle; that some thought the people enjoyed privileges enough; that others were influenced by their official connexions or aspirations; that another class, who seldom mingled in the affairs of active life, loved retirement, and would, had the Whigs allowed them, have remained neutrals; that some were timid men; some were old men; and that tenants and dependents went with the landholders without inquiry; and as a thing of course. All of these reasons, and numerous others, have been assigned at different times, and by different persons. But another cause quite as potent as either of those which have been enumerated, it would seem, upon thousands, namely, a dread of the strength and resources of England, and the belief, that successful resistance to her power was impossible; that the Colonies had neither the men nor the means to carry on war, and would be humbled and reduced to submission with hardly an effort.

That motives and considerations, hopes and fears, like these, had an influence in the formation of the *last* Colonial parties, cannot be disputed, and the unprejudiced minds of this generation should be frank enough to admit it. All, both Whigs and Tories, were born and had grown up under a monarchy; and the abstract question of renouncing it or of continuing it was one on which men of undoubted patriotism differed widely. Very many of the Whigs came into the final measure of separating from the mother country with great reluctance, and doubt and hesitation prevailed even in Congress. Besides, the Whig leaders uniformly denied, that Independence was embraced in their plans, and constantly affirmed, that their sole object was to obtain concessions, and to continue the connexion with England as hitherto; and John Adams goes further than this, for, says he, *"there was not a moment during the revolution, when I would not have given everything I possessed for a restoration to the state of things before the contest began, provided we could have had a sufficient security for its continuance."* If Mr. Adams be regarded as expressing the sentiments of the Whigs, *they* were willing to remain Colonists, provided they could have had their rights secured to them; while the Tories were contented thus to continue, *without* such security. Such, as it appears to me, was the only difference between the two parties *prior* to hostilities, and many Whigs, like Mr. Adams, would have been willing to rescind the declaration of independence, and to forget the past, upon proper guarantees for the future. This mode of stating the question, and of defining the difference between the two parties—down to a certain period at least—cannot be objected to, unless the sincerity and truthfulness of some of the most eminent men in our history are directly impeached; and if any are prepared to dispute their veracity, it may still be asked, whether *the Tories ought not to be excused for believing* them? . . .

MOSES C. TYLER

Toward the end of the nineteenth century the cause of the Loyalists acquired another significant adherent, who treated them from an angle missed by his few predecessors. Moses C. Tyler (1835–1900), after a spotty academic career, became a minister, a professor of rhetoric and literature at the University of Michigan, and a journalist. In 1881, three years after he published a **History of American Literature, 1607–1765,** he accepted the offer of Cornell University to occupy one of the first chairs in American history to be established in this country. Along with the great majority of the best contemporary American historians, Tyler, even before he visited Germany, was committed to the German school of history and its emphasis on more disciplined, more methodical, more "objective" research. With a number of like-minded people he helped to found the American Historical Association in 1884.

In 1897 he published his two volumed **Literary History of the American Revolution,** an ambitious attempt to write an American version of Kulturgeschichte. A sincere patriot, he nevertheless shared with many intellectuals of his time a deep admiration for Great Britain, and these dispositions combined with his dedication to balanced and impartial history led to a work as notable for its lack of prejudice as for its abundant detail and magisterial authority. Sabine, while laboring to give the Loyalists their due, made no secret of his Patriotic inclinations and openly stated "I am of Whig descent, and am proud of my lineage. With the principles of men who, when it was ascertained that a redress of grievances could **not** be obtained, preferred to remain British subjects, I have neither communion nor sympathy." Tyler, on the other hand, endeavored to be an apologist for no group and although conscious of the inbred prejudices of his fellow Americans he dealt equally with both sides of the Revolution's literature.

His analysis mirrors his background and its limitations. The history he wrote is clearly the work of a white, Anglo-Saxon Protestant. It is weighted in favor of New England and slights the contribution from other areas, especially the South. But today, almost seventy years later, it still stands without a real rival. The information it offers is solid and usually accurate; the style is strong and reflects good taste and good judgment; the purpose is large yet well defined. This is not a work of picayune criticism but a successful attempt to depict "the majestic operation of ideas, the creative and decisive play of spiritual forces, in the development of history, in the rise and fall of nations." Tyler aptly called his study "the inward history of our Revolution—the history of its ideas, its spiritual moods, its motives, its passions, even of its sportive caprices and whims." He wanted Whigs and Tories to tell their own tale "without either of them being liable, at our hands, to posthumous outrage in the shape of partisan imputations on their sincerity, their magnanimity, their patriotism, or their courage." Very deliberately he was shifting the focus of discussions of the Revolution and giving the work of the various political bodies a secondary role and, in keeping with another major thread in the intellectual fabric of his day, he emphasized that Americans and Britishers were part of the same race and expressed the hope that his work would promote better understanding on both sides of the Atlantic. The selection comes from an article* which Tyler wrote for the very first volume of the **American Historical Review** (1895), where his statements are more succinct and more bold than in his volumes of literary criticism.

There cannot be a more authentic introduction to the Loyalists of our Revolution, than is to be had through an acquaintance with their literature. As we turn over the pages of that literature,—political essays, pamphlets, sermons, songs, satires, epigrams, burlesques, lampoons,— a literature now having almost a pathetic insignificance as it slumbers under a hundred years of dust and contempt,—perhaps the first notable fact that calls for attention is, that, in point of time, its development lags somewhat behind that of the Revolutionist party, and does not become of much value until within the twelvemonth preceding the Lexington and Concord skirmishes,—that is, until about the time of the Congress of 1774. . . .

Even yet, in this last decade of the nineteenth century, it is by no means easy for Americans—especially if, as is the case with the present writer, they be descended from men who thought and fought on behalf of the Revolution—to take a disinterested attitude, that is, an historical one, toward those Americans who thought and fought against the Revolution. Both as to the men and as to the questions involved in that controversy, the rehearsal of the claims of the victorious side has been going on among us, now for a hundred years or more, in tradition, in history, in oration, in song, in ceremony. Hardly have we known, seldom have we been reminded, that the side of the Loyalists, as they called themselves, of the Tories, as they were scornfully nicknamed by their opponents, was even in argument not a weak one, and in motive and sentiment not a base one, and in devotion and self-sacrifice not an unheroic one. While the war was going forward, of course the animosities aroused by it were too hot and too fierce, especially between the two opposing groups of Americans, to permit either party in the controversy to do justice to the logical or to the personal merit of the other. When at last the war came to an end, and the champions of the Revolution were in absolute triumph, then the more prominent Tories had to flee for their lives; they had to flee from the wrath that had come, and to bury themselves, either in other lands or in obscure places of this land. Then, of course, they and all their de-

---

* "The Party of the Loyalists in the American Revolution" in *American Historical Review* (New York, 1896) I, 24; 26; 32–33; 37–40; 44–45.

tested notions and emotions and deeds, whether grand or petty or base, went down out of sight, submerged beneath the abhorrence of the victorious Revolutionists, and doomed, as it appears, to at least one solid century of oratorical and poetical infamy, which has found its natural and organized expression in each recurring Fourth of July, and in each reappearance of the birthday of Washington. . . .

So much, then, must be said on behalf of the Tories of the Revolution,—in point of numbers, they were far from inconsiderable, and in point of character, they were far from despicable. On the one hand, they formed no mere rump party. If they were not actually a majority of the American people,—as they themselves always claimed to be, and as some careful scholars now think they were,—they did at least constitute a huge minority of the American people: they formed a section of colonial society too important on the score of mere numbers to be set down as a paltry handful of obstructives; while in any rightful estimate of personal value, quite aside from mere numbers, they seem to deserve the consideration which conscientious and cultivated people of one party never ask in vain of conscientious and cultivated people of the opposite party,—at least after the issues of the controversy are closed. . . .

Even yet it is not quite needless to remind ourselves that the American Revolution was a war of argument long before it became a war of physical force; and that, in this war of argument, were involved a multitude of difficult questions,—constitutional, legal, political, ethical,—with respect to which honest and thoughtful people were compelled to differ. All these questions, however, may, for our purposes, be reduced to just two: first, the question of what was lawful under the existing constitution of the British empire; and secondly, the question of what was expedient under the existing circumstances of the colonies. Now, paradoxical as it may seem to many of the American descendants of the victorious party, each of those questions had two very real and quite opposite sides; much was to be said for each side; and for the Tory side so much was to be said in the way of solid fact and of valid reasoning, that an intelligent and a noble-minded American might have taken that side, and might have stuck to it, and might have gone into battle for it, and might have imperilled all the interests of his life in defence of it, without any just impeachment of his reason or of his integrity—without deserving to be called, then or since then, either a weak man or a bad one. . . .

But after the question as to what was lawful under the existing constitution of the British Empire, came the question as to what was expedient under the existing circumstances of the American colonies. Now, as it happened, this latter question had two aspects, one of which pointed toward the expediency of rejecting the taxing power of parliament, even though such power did exist under the constitution; the other pointed toward the expediency of separation from the empire.

Having in view, at present, the former aspect of this question, the American Whigs went forward and took the ground that, if the claim of Parliament to tax them was indeed justified by the constitution, then so much worse for the constitution,—since it was a claim too full of political danger to be any longer submitted to: "If Parliament, to which we send no members, may tax us three pence on a pound of tea, it may, if it pleases, tax us a shilling, or a guinea. Once concede to it this right to tax us at all, and what security have we against its taxing us excessively?—what security have we for our freedom or our property against any enormity of oppression?" And what was the answer of the American Tories to this argument? "Yes," said the Tories, "you allege a grave political danger. But does it really exist? It is likely ever to exist? Are you not guilty of the fallacy of arguing against the use of a power, simply from the possibility of its abuse? In this world every alleged danger must be estimated in the light of common sense and of reasonable probability. In that light, what ground have we for alarm? The line drawn by the supreme legislature itself for the exercise of its own power, is a perfectly distinct one,—that it should tax no part of the empire to a greater amount than its just and equitable proportion. As respects America, the supreme legislature has not yet overstepped that line; it has shown no disposition to overstep that line; we have not the slightest reason to suppose that it ever will overstep that line. Moreover, all the instincts of the English race are for fair play, and would be overwhelmingly against such an injustice, were Parliament to attempt it. It is thought in England that as we, British subjects in America, receive our share of the benefits of membership of the empire, so we ought to pay our share toward the cost of those benefits. In apportioning our share of the cost, they have not fixed upon an amount which anybody, even here, calls excessive; indeed, it falls rather below than above the amount that might justly be named. Now, in this world, affairs cannot be conducted—civilization cannot go on— without confidence in somebody. And in this matter, we deem it reasonable and prudent to have confidence in the good sense and in the justice of the English race, and especially of the House of Commons, which is the great council of the commoners of the English race. . . .

And this brings us to the second aspect of the question of expediency,—the great and ultimate issue of the whole controversy,—that of Independence. Of course, no one pretended that separation from the empire was a right provided for by the constitution. All admitted that it could be resorted to only as a revolutionary measure required by some vast and commanding need in the existing circumstances of the American colonies. And what was the attitude of the American Tories respecting the project for independence?

In order to answer this question, we shall need to translate the word used for separation from the empire into its modern American equivalent. For, just as the Whig doctrine for the rejection of the taxing-power of the general government meant what in the nineteenth century we have known under the name of Nullification, so the Whig doctrine of separation from the empire meant precisely what we now mean by the word Secession. The American Revolution had just two stages: from 1765 to 1776, its champions were Nullifiers, without being Secessionists; from 1776 to 1783, they were also Secessionists, and, as the event proved, successful Secessionists. The word Independence was merely a euphemism for national disunion, for a disruption of the British Empire. What the Whig leaders resolved to do, under the name of Independence, about the middle of the year 1776, seemed to the American Tories of that time precisely the same political crime as, to the people of the Northern States, seemed the measure undertaken by certain Southern leaders, in the latter part of 1860, under the name of Secession. In short, the Tories of the American Revolution, concerning whose standing in history we are now making inquiry, took between 1776 and 1783 constitutional ground similar to that taken by the people of these Northern States and by the so-called Loyalists of the Southern States between 1861 and 1865; that is, they were champions of national unity, as resting on the paramount authority of the general government.

Finally, the whole strength and dignity of their historic claim is not appreciated until we recall the fact that, for the first ten or twelve years of the Revolution,—from 1764 to 1776,—the entire Whig agitation was conducted on a perpetual disavowal of the purpose or the desire for independence. In every form in which a solemn affirmation could be made and reiterated, it was affirmed by the Whigs during all those years that the only object of their agitation was to obstruct and to defeat a bad ministerial policy, thereby to secure a redress of grievances; that, as for independence, it was the thing they abhorred, and it was mere calumny to accuse them of designing or of desiring it. . . .

It is an error to represent the Tories of the American Revolution as a party of mere negation and obstruction. They did deny, they did attempt to obstruct; but they also had positive political ideas, as well as precise measures in creative statesmanship, to offer in the place of those ideas and measures of their fellow-colonists to which they made objection, and which they would have kept from prevailing if they could.

Secondly, it is an error to represent the Tories of the American Revolution as a party opposed either to any reform in the relations of the colonists with the mother-country, or to the extension of human rights and liberties here or elsewhere. From the beginning of the agitation, they clearly saw, they strongly felt, they frankly declared, that the constitutional relations of the colonies with the mother-country were in a crude state, were unsatisfactory, were in need of being carefully revised and reconstructed. This admission of theirs, they never recalled. Quite aside from the question of its legality, they doubted the expediency, under modern conditions, of such an exertion of parliamentary authority as the ministry had forced into life. Upon these points, there was substantial agreement between all Americans; namely, that there was a wrong, that there was a danger, that there should be a reform. It was chiefly as to the method and the process and the scope of this needed reform, that Americans broke asunder into two great opposing parties. The exact line of cleavage between these two parties, together with the tone and the spirit characteristic of each party, may now be traced with precision in the history of the Congress of 1774. . . .

Thirdly, it is an error to represent the Tories . . . as composed of Americans lacking in love for their native country, or in zeal for its liberty, or in willingness to labor, or fight, or even to die, for what they conceived to be its interests. As was most natural, the party which succeeded in carrying through the Congress of 1774 such measures and methods of political reform as, in fact, led to civil war, and, finally, to American Independence, took for itself the name of the patriotic party, its members being commonly called "patriots." Beyond question, the Whig party was a patriotic party; but it is not now apparent that those Americans who failed in their honest and sacrificial championship of measures which would have given us political reform and political safety, but without civil war and without an angry disruption of the English-speaking race, can justly be regarded as having been, either in doctrine, or in purpose, or in act, an unpatriotic party.

GEORGE E. ELLIS

The cooperatively authored, multivolumed **Narrative and Critical History of America** (8 vols., Boston, 1884–89) edited by Justin Winsor, Harvard's librarian and a founder of the American Library Association, was generally believed by contemporaries to be one of the finest pieces of historical scholarship yet produced. Winsor was keenly interested in American history and as early as 1849 wrote a history of his home town, Duxbury, Massachusetts.

Both New England's sense of regional identity and its strong intellectual traditions encouraged publishers to produce local histories. Winsor was asked to write one for Boston and accepted the assignment. Later his publisher asked him to write a history of the United States as a whole, using the same format as that used for the Boston history, i.e. a number of essays by various authors. George Ellis (1814–1894), who had previously been a contributor to the **Memorial History of Boston** (4 vols., 1880–81), was assigned the Loyalists as one of his topics.*

Ellis was an indefatigable man who fully exploited the opportunities afforded him by his close association with both Harvard College and the Massachusetts Historical Society (of which he later became president). He was not a professional historian nor a particularly acute amateur (a contemporary said that he was more antiquarian than historian), but no one could doubt his interest. His historical labors were intense and incessant, resulting in a slew of publications outside his own profession of theology.

Ellis' mother was the daughter of a Loyalist who had escaped to Nova Scotia, but there is no evidence that this connection affected his views. What is more tangible is his review of Sabine's book which appeared in the **North American Review** in 1864 where, despite recognizing the book's merits and the need for a reappraisal of the Loyalists, he had difficulty moving beyond a nationalistic, Patriotic stance. In the next twenty years there was a subtle change, as his essay in Winsor's **History** makes clear. Ellis, in essence a conservative himself, came to appreciate the virtues of the Loyalists and to recognize that a historiographical gap needed to be filled.

THE LOYALISTS AND THEIR FORTUNES

The terms Tories, Loyalists, Refugees, are burdened with a piteous record of wrongs and sufferings. It has not been found easy or satisfactory for even the most candid historian to leave the facts and

---

* Justin Winsor (ed.), *Narrative and Critical History of America* (8 vols., Boston, 1884–1889), VII, 185; 192–193.

arguments of the conflict impartially adjusted. Insult, confiscation of property, and exile were the penalties of those who bore these titles. Reasonable and grateful, akin to what is best in human nature, is our relenting over the tale of their miseries. Remembering that the most bitter words of Washington that have come to us are those which express his scorn of Tories, we must at least look to find some plausible, if not justifying, ground for the patriot party. Among those most frank and fearless in the avowal of loyalty, and who suffered the severest penalties, were men of the noblest character and of the highest position. So, also, bearing the same odious title, were men of the most despicable nature, self-seeking and unprincipled, ready for any act of evil. And between these were men of every grade of respectability, and of every shade of moral meanness. . . .

Alike in speeches and printed essays on the other side of the ocean and in the passionate protests of many of the Tories in the colonies, we meet at this time with the severest denunciations of "the Tyranny of the Rebel Congress." It was said that this was exercised over "the vast majority of the loyal people of the colonies." Unquestionably there was reason for this reproach. Candor admits that a very large number of honorable loyalists had at this crisis to meet a bitter disappointment. They had heartily sent a representation to the Congress for the purpose of securing a redress of grievances; but that Congress had proved, as was claimed, treacherous to its proposed objects, and had led them into a trap, and had abused their confidence. A considerable number of sincere men could say this in all truthfulness. And to the most conscientious of such it would be an imbitterment of the later penalties to feel that they had in any way connived at measures through a misplaced trustfulness.

There was one suggestion of practical good sense and consistency which might have been expected to have had much weight for a considerable class of the adherents of the crown. They had avowed their allegiance to established authority as a safeguard against anarchy. The plea was a good one so long as there was such authority; but it had been wrecked; even the remaining fragments of it were useless. The significant fact was undeniable, that the overthrow of the royal government had been effected fully as much, if not more, by the acts of the official representatives of that government as by the leaders and measures of the revolt. Royal governors had abdicated their chairs and taken to flight. Constitutional assemblies had been disabled and dispersed. Judicial authorities and proceedings were repudiated. Meanwhile, Congress had initiated measures for substituting a new authority and order. It realized as fully and as sternly as did the stanchest loyalists the perils of anarchy, and set itself to avert it. As things then stood, the country had no other government. So far then as the loyalists clung to order against anarchy, they had but to extend the meaning of the term loyalty from its limited reference to the British king to the recognition of Congress, which had established a government. Certain it was that no alternative offered itself, for in the failure of that effort anarchy was inevitable. And it was as certain that the malignant or the merely obstinate attitude of one class of loyalists was the most formidable obstacle to the purposes of Congress. The sort of government, or the temporary substitute for it, which Congress initiated might be regarded as a government *de facto*. France justified her alliance with the States by averring that she found them exercising government and in possession of independency. This was in conformity with the usage of nations. If the plea was good for foreigners, why not for our own citizens? Undoubtedly it did prevail with a large portion of the loyalist body. . . .

We have not to search beyond the working of human nature to explain on the one side the elements, both noble and base, that exhibited themselves in the loyalists, or on the other side to account for the vengeful treatment of them by the patriots. Patriotism needed constant reinforcement, by working up its own stern resolution, and by humiliating everything that would bring it to discomfiture. Loyalism in all its stages could find a full justification of itself till it was realized that the final struggle was inevitable. And freely admitting that even after sides were taken on the great issue, men of the highest intelligence and nobleness might still cling to Great Britain, we have equally to grant that the patriots, having resolved to have a country of their own, free from foreign mastery, might justly regard such internal foes, with all that was insidious in their influence, as more to be dreaded than a foreign army of red-coats and mercenaries. . . .

American Nationalist and English Whig Historians

Until the last few years it has been fashionable to speak of a "special relationship" between the United States and Great Britain. In its name a great deal of claptrap has been uttered and many distortions of history have been blessed. The truth is that Anglo-American relations during the nineteenth century were considerably more complicated than this simple phrase suggests; when the two nations were not at war they were frequently not far from it.

To some extent a change in the lingering animosity began during the Civil War with the British government's refusal to assist either side in any active, official way. Between this war and World War I a number of large, long-range forces tended to bring the two countries closer together so that they were able to overcome even a serious diplomatic crisis, such as the Venezuela boundary dispute (1895–97), without resort to arms. The underlying causes of this increased amity may be found in many areas. Some of the most important were: the closing of the economic gap between the two nations, mutual concern with the problems of peace in a world of rising new nations industrially equipped to make large-scale war, and the strengthening of established financial and commercial ties. There was also a less tangible and more complicated intellectual force in the recognition of an Anglo-American culture. Some of this recognition was, unhappily, based on racism and the acceptance by many American historians and social scientists of the "germ" theory of their nation's history. Such writers were very likely to find an important part of the explanation of the undoubted American greatness in the European heritage and, more specifically, in English institutions.

In this section are grouped together earlier and later examples of American "nationalist" writing and extracts from the "Whig" school of historians. It is interesting to see that by the end of the century a number of English Whig historians (e.g., George O. Trevelyan) were writing the history of the Revolution from much the same approach as the American nationalists (e.g., George Bancroft). Both saw the War for Independence as a crucial struggle for liberty. Each viewed man as a political animal in a never-ending quest for freedom. While Bancroft, the American patriot and fervid democrat, found the Revolution and the consequent Constitution as the glorious dawn of freedom on this continent, Trevelyan, the genteel English-man, found in many of the same events justification for the actions of his ancestors and for his own view of history. When he examined the period 1763–1775 he found a small group of liberty-loving English Whigs, led by the Marquis of Rockingham, standing firm for justice to the colonials as well as constitutional freedom at home, in opposition to the imperious, despotic George III and his minister, Lord North. In this crisis the colonies rose to defend their liberties and the English constitution guaranteeing them. To their lasting glory, English Whigs such as Charles James Fox gave moral support. In the words of a recent editor of his work, the appearance of Trevelyan's *American Revolution* "constituted a bridge to renewed under-standing between the British and American peoples." The link will be apparent in the following selections. It is most openly expressed in the last extracts which contain the comments of Theodore Roosevelt on Trevelyan's interpretations.

ALEXANDER EVERETT

That the vast majority of nineteenth century American writers ignored the Loyalists is naturally a difficult point to prove by means of an extract from one man's writings. How does one include something which is hidden or absent?

Yet being forgotten was indeed the lot of the Loyalists, whether in general histories or special speeches. Daniel Webster flighted an oration at the laying of the cornerstone of the Bunker Hill monument and again at its completion. On neither occasion did he mention the Tories, even to abuse them! In another commemoration of the battle Alexander Everett (1790–1847), a less distinguished speaker, did the same thing. A brief extract from his words* conveys the atmosphere and shows very well why those who opposed the Revolution were lucky to be left in oblivion.

We are assembled, fellow-citizens and friends! to celebrate the return of a great and glorious day.† As Americans we hold it sacred; as children of the Pilgrim Fathers who subdued and settled our own beloved New England we regard it with a deeper and more peculiar interest. While we cherish with pride the memory of every gallant achievement performed in our country's defence,—of every generous sacrifice in her cause,—wherever the scene of action may have been laid, and whoever may have been the heroes of the day;— while we claim it as an honor to take our places side by side and shoulder to shoulder with our brothers of the south and west whenever duty calls us to the post of danger;—their noble spirits will understand and sympathise with us if we dwell with more than ordinary emotion upon those events in our history, of which our immediate neighborhood was the theatre and in which our own fathers were the actors and the sufferers. Filial tenderness joins her fond appeal to the graver voice of public duty which invites us to commemorate them. The fine chords of domestic love mingle their sweet and touching harmonies with the loud pæans of patriotic pride and martial enthusiasm with which we greet the return of this high national holiday. The heroes of the day we celebrate were our fathers: the noble matrons who sustained and encouraged them in their toils and sacrifices were our mothers: and we, their sons and daughters, are now met together on the spot which was the scene

---

* Alexander H. Everett, *An Address Delivered at Charlestown, Mass. on the 17th of June, 1836* (Boston, 1836) pp. 5–6.

† Sixty-first anniversary of the battle of Bunker, more accurately Breed's, Hill.

of their trial, their glory,—to many of them, alas! of their mortal agony,—to offer to their memories our united tribute of respect, admiration and grateful love.

Who could hesitate to join in so holy a work? We meet without distinction of party. No little shades of difference created by the passing events of the day, are permitted to disturb the harmony of feeling with which we now come together as brothers, as citizens of a common country, as joint heirs of a common inheritance in the glory of our ancestors and the blessings which they have bequeathed to their posterity.

GEORGE LIPPARD

The next selection is entirely different from Everett's speech. In a strange work, **Washington and His Generals** (1847), George Lippard (1822–1854) created and presented a series of dreamlike "legends of the Revolution." The moralistic quality of this extract* clearly owes much to the New Testament and also, perhaps less obviously, to the deistic position Washington already occupied in American mythology.† A Loyalist or Tory enters the story only to serve as a foil to the inspirational picture of the "Father of the Nation." The legends first appeared as articles in the **Saturday Courier** of Philadelphia; before they were over the paper had more than doubled its circulation, apparently in large part because of Lippard's writings. In itself this is an excellent proof that the view of the Revolution which he offered was what the people wanted to read.

THE TEMPTATION OF WASHINGTON

There are days in winter when the air is very soft and balmy as the early days of summer, when, in fact, that glad maiden May seems to blow her warm breath in the grim face of February, until the rough old warrior laughs again.

It was a day like this that the morning sunshine was streaming over a high rock, that frowns there, far above the Wissahikon.

A high rock—attainable only by a long, winding path—fenced in by the trunks of giant pines, whose boughs, on the coldest day of winter, form a canopy overhead.

---

* George Lippard, *Washington and his Generals: or, Legends of the Revolution* (Philadelphia, 1847) pp. 107–109.

† On this subject see the beautifully written analysis by Marcus Cunliffe, *George Washington, Man and Monument* (Boston, 1958).

This rock is covered with a carpet of evergreen moss.

And near this nook—this chamber in the forest, for it was nothing less—sate an old man, separated from it by the trunks of the pines, whose boughs concealed his form.

That old man had come here, alone, to think over his two sons, now freezing at Valley Forge——for, though the father was a Tory, yet his children were Continentals. He was a well-meaning man, but some half-crazy idea about the Divine Right of the British Pope, George the Third, to rule this Continent, and murder and burn as he pleased—lurked in his brain, and kept him back from the camp of Washington.

And now, in this bright morning in February, he had come here, alone, to think the matter over.

And while he was pondering this deep matter over, whether George the Pope or George the Rebel was in the right—he heard the tramp of a warsteed not far off, and, looking between the trunks of the pines, he saw a man, of noble presence, dismount from his grey horse, and then advance into the quiet nook of moss-carpeted rocks, encircled by giant pines.

—And now, leaving that aged Tory, to look upon this man for himself, let us also look on him, with our own eyes.

As he comes through those thick boughs, you behold a man, more than six feet high, with his kingly form enveloped in a coarse grey overcoat; a chapeau on his bold forehead—and beneath the skirts of that grey coat, you may see the military boots and the end of a scabbard.

And who is this man of kingly presence, who comes here alone, to pace this moss-covered rock, with drooped head and folded arms?

Come, my friends, and look upon him—let me show you—not this figure of mist and frost-work, which some historians have called WASHINGTON—but Washington, the living, throbbing, flesh and blood, Washington!—Yes, WASHINGTON THE MAN.

Look upon him, as he paces that moss-covered rock—see that eye burn, that muscular chest heave under the folded arms.

Ah, he is thinking of Valley Forge! Of the bloody foot-prints in the snow—of those three hideous figures that sit down in the huts of Valley Forge together—Disease, Starvation, and Nakedness!

Look, as those dark thoughts crowd on his soul, he falls on his knees, he prays the God of Heaven to take his life, as an offering for the freedom of his native land!

And as that prayer startles the still woods, that grey coats falls open, and discloses the blue and gold uniform—the epaulette and the sword-hilt.

Then the agony of that man, praying there in the silent woods—praying for his country, now bleeding in her chains—speaks out, in the flashing of the eye, in the beaded sweat, dripping from the brow!

—Ah, kings of the world, planning so cooly your schemes of murder, come here, and look at George Washington, as he offers his life, a sacrifice for his country!

Ah, George of England, British Pope, and good-natured Idiot, that you are, now counting, in your royal halls how many more men it will take to murder a few thousand peaceful farmers, and make a nation drink your tea, come here to this rock of the Wissahikon, and see, King and Pope as you are, George Washington in council with his God!——

My friends, I can never think of that man in the wilds of Wissahikon—praying there, alone: praying for his country, with the deep agony in his heart and on his brow, without also thinking of that dark night in Gethsemane, when the blood-drops startled from the brow of Jesus, the Blessed Redeemer, as he plead for the salvation of the world!

Now look! As Washington kneels there, on that moss-covered rock, from those green boughs steps forth another form—tall as his own—clad in a coarse grey coat, with the boots and scabbard seen below its skirts, with the chapeau upon his brow.

That stranger emerges from the boughs—stands there unperceived, gazing in silence upon the kneeling warrior.

A moment passes!

Look! Washington has risen to his feet—he confronts the stranger.

Now, as that stranger, with a slight bow, uncovers his forehead, tell me, did you ever see a stronger or stranger resemblance between two men than between these two, who now confront each other in silence, under the shade of those dark pines?

The same heighth, breadth of chest, sinewy limbs, nay, almost the same faces,—save that the face of the stranger, sharper in outline, lacks that calm consciousness of a great soul, which stamps the countenance of Washington.

That resemblance is most strange—their muscular forms are clad in the same coarse grey coat—their costume is alike—yet hold——

The stranger throws open his overcoat—you behold that hangman's dress, that British uniform, flashing with gold and stars! Washington starts back, and lays his hand upon his sword.

And as these two men, so strangely alike, meet there by accident, under that canopy of boughs,—one wandering from Valley Forge, one from Philadelphia—let me tell you at once, that the stranger is none other than the Master Butcher of the Idiot-king—Sir William Howe.

Yes, there they meet, the one the impersonation of Freedom—the other the tinselled lacquey of a Tyrant's Will!

LYMAN C. DRAPER

From his early life in Lockport, New York, until his death in Wisconsin as one of the country's most prodigious librarians, Lyman Draper (1815–1891) was imbued with a passion for the lore of the frontier. He did not have a particularly advanced education, but few men have matched his love of books. From his reading he came to realize, when he was still in his early twenties, that the literature dealing with the West was poor in quantity and quality.

He began to collect relevant materials and did not stop for half a century. In addition he practised what we would now term "oral history," seeking out the old pioneers, like Colonel William Martin of Tennessee, and writing up their stories. He balanced their accounts with material from other sources such as newspaper reports, court transcripts, financial accounts, and legal records. He also was adept at talking owners of old manuscripts into giving them up to him.

The long volume, **King's Mountain and Its Heroes** (1881),* stems directly from Draper's interest in the frontier of the colonial period. The material had been in his library for some forty years, and it included pension statements from militiamen (129 of them) and the testimony of 23 witnesses who had said their piece in 1823 during a quarrel between descendants of some of the Patriot participants in the battle. He also had the papers of Isaac Shelby and William Campbell, two of the Patriot leaders at King's Mountain. His material amounted to eighteen volumes, but his book did the research only partial justice.† Draper had taken the topic because it was such a fine example of pioneer valor triumphing over British tyranny. Although he deplored the tendency, then growing in the United States, to pursue historical "laws," i.e., to shape facts to fit a theory, he himself was guilty of shaping facts to fit his romantic view of the Revolution and his passionate commitment to the American cause. **King's Mountain** was lively, full of anecdotes—indeed the great historian Parkman warned Draper about trusting too much to personal remi-

---

* Lyman C. Draper, *King's Mountain and its Heroes: History of the Battle of King's Mountain, Oct. 7, 1780, and the events which led to it* (Cincinnati, 1881), pp. 134–135; 336; 337.

† An intriguing insight into the working habits of Draper, the historian, is provided in William B. Hesseltine, *Pioneer's Mission: The Story of Lyman Copeland Draper* (Madison, Wisconsin, 1954).

niscences—but overly detailed and somewhat overblown in its style. While there was much gold from Draper's diggings, he was so utterly in the grip of Patriotic fever, so eager to glorify the raw courage of American frontiersmen, that the Loyalists receive very short shrift. They are by no means forgotten, as they were by many historians of Draper's time, but he seems deliberately to malign them to heighten the virtues of the Patriots.

In what was originally a part of Tryon, now Lincoln County, North Carolina, were many Loyalists. Among them was Samuel Brown, who had been reared there, and proved himself not only an inveterate Tory, but a bold and unscrupulous plunderer. He had a sister, Charity Brown, who must have been a rough, reckless, bad woman. For quite a period, the two carried on very successful plundering operations— including horses, bed-clothes, wearing apparel, pewter-ware, money, and other valuable articles. Sometimes they had confederates, but oftener they went forth alone on their pillaging forays. About fifteen miles west of Statesville, North Carolina, three miles above the Island Ford, there is a high bluff on the western side of the Catawba river, rising three hundred feet high, at a place known as the Look-Out Shoals. About sixty feet from the base of this bluff, under an over-hanging cliff, was a cave of considerable dimensions, sufficient to accommodate several persons, but the opening to which is now partially closed by a mass of rock sliding down from above. This cave was the depository for the plunder taken by stealth or violence from the poverty-stricken people in the country for many miles around; for their depredations extended from the Shallow Ford of Yadkin to the region embracing the several counties of the north-western portion of South Carolina. . . .

So notorious had become the robber's achievements that he was known in all that region as *Plundering Sam Brown*. Among the Tories he was designated as Captain Sam Brown. As early as the Spring of 1778, he was associated with the Tory leader, David Fanning; and they were hiding in the woods together on Reaburn's creek, in now Laurens County, South Carolina, for the space of six weeks, living entirely upon what they killed in the wilderness, without bread or salt. . . .

The Southern country was then in a very critical condition, and there seemed to be a grave necessity for checking, by stern and exemplary punishment, the Tory lawlessness that largely over-spread the land, and impressing that class with a proper sense of the power and determination of the Whigs to protect their patriot friends, and punish their guilty enemies. . . . War, in its mildest form, is so full of horrors, that the mind recoils from vindicating any act that can, in the remotest degree, increase its miseries. To these no act contributes more than that of retaliation. Hence no act should be ventured upon with more solemn deliberation, and none so proper to be confined to a commander-in-chief, or the civil power. But the brave men who fought in the affair at King's Mountain, are not to be left loaded with unmerited censure.

The calmest and most dispassionate reflection upon their conduct, on this occasion, will lead to the conviction, that if they committed any offence, it was against their own country—not against the enemy. That instead of being instigated by a thirst of blood, they acted solely with a view to put an end to its effusion; and boldly, for this purpose, took upon themselves all the dangers that a system of retaliation could superinduce. . . .

GEORGE BANCROFT

Brief passages on the Loyalists do not fully convey the rabid chauvinism permeating George Bancroft's **History of the United States,** a paean to the Patriot leaders and a hard-hitting attack on the muddling, yet tyrannical British government. More than anyone else, Bancroft (1800–1891) was responsible for planting the seed of Germanic scholarship in American historiography, but his **History** was conceived in that hotbed of revolutionary tradition, New England, and developed as a lusty child of Liberty. Although it was the product of diligent research, especially in English depositories, the central element in Bancroft's interpretation of the Revolution was the division of men and forces for and against Freedom. Since the United States was a chosen nation, those who had opposed its formation were, at best, misguided. This inevitably was the view of an author who could say "the history of our colonization is the history of the crimes of Europe." One of Bancroft's most serious defects was his unhistorical viewpoint that independence supplied the key to the whole colonial period.

The following selection* shows the very different way in which Bancroft described the leadership of Sam Adams on the one side and Thomas Hutchinson on the other.

---

* George Bancroft, *History of the United States* (Author's last ed., 6 vols., New York, 1885), III, 306; 357–358; 376–377.

HOW BRITAIN ESTRANGED AMERICA

The approach of military rule convinced Samuel Adams of the necessity of American independence. He gave himself to his work as devotedly as though he had in his keeping the liberties of mankind. "He was," said Bernard, "one of the principal and most desperate of the chiefs of the faction;" "the all in all," wrote Hutchinson, who wished him "taken off," and who has left on record that his purity was always above all price. To promote the independence of his country, he was ready to serve, and never claim the reward of service. From a town of merchants and mechanics, Boston grew with him to be the hope of the world; and the sons of toil, as they perilled fortune and life for the liberties they inherited, rose to be, and to feel themselves to be, the champions of human freedom. . . .

His [Hutchinson's] advancement to administrative power was fatal to Britain and to himself; for the love of money, which was his ruling passion in youth, had grown with his years.

A nervous timidity, which was a part of his nature, had been increased by age as well as by the riots on account of the stamp act, and at times made him false to his employers. While he cringed to the minister, he trembled before the people. At Boston, he professed zeal for the interests and liberties of the province; had at one time courted its favor by denying the right of parliament to tax America either internally or externally; and had argued with conclusive ability against the expediency and the equity of such a measure. He now redoubled his attempts to deceive; wrote patriotic letters which he never sent, but read to those about him as evidence of his good-will; and professed even to have braved hostility in England for his attachment to colonial liberties while he secretly gave in his adhesion to the absoluteness of metropolitan authority, and suggested a system of coercive measures, which England gradually and reluctantly adopted.

Wherever the colony had a friend, he would set before him such hints as might incline him to harsh judgments. Even to Franklin he vouched for the tales of Bernard as "most just and candid." He paid court to the enemies of American liberty by stimulating them to the full indulgence of their malignity. . . .

Samuel Adams came out from the council chamber, and, baring his head, which was already becoming gray, moved through their ranks, inspiring confidence.

To the people, who crowded even the gallery and [a]isles of the spacious meeting-house, he made his report, and pronounced the answer insufficient. On ordinary occasions he seemed like ordinary men; but, in moments of crisis, he rose naturally and unaffectedly to the highest dignity, and spoke as if the hopes of humanity hung on his words. . . .

Hutchinson had done all he could to get Samuel Adams shipped to England as a traitor; at this most important moment in their lives, the patriot and the courtier stood face to face. "It is the unanimous opinion of the meeting," said Samuel Adams to him, "that the reply made to the vote of the inhabitants in the morning is unsatisfactory; nothing less will satisfy than a total and immediate removal of all the troops." "The troops are not subject to my authority," repeated Hutchinson; "I have no power to remove them." Stretching forth his arm, which slightly shook, as if "his frame trembled at the energy of his soul," in tones not loud, but clear and distinctly audible, Adams rejoined: "If you have power to remove one regiment, you have power to remove both. It is at your peril if you do not. The meeting is composed of three thousand people. They are become very impatient. A thousand men are already arrived from the neighborhood, and the country is in general motion. Night is approaching; an immediate answer is expected." As he spoke he gazed intently on his irresolute adversary. "Then," said Adams, who not long afterward described the scene, "at the appearance of the determined citizens, peremptorily demanding the redress of grievances, I observed his knees to tremble; I saw his face grow pale; and I enjoyed the sight." . . .

WILLIAM E. H. LECKY

William E. H. Lecky (1838–1903) was born in Ireland to a family of Scottish origin. At the age of thirty-one he published his sixth work, which he always considered his favorite, the **History of Morals from Augustus to Charlemagne** (2 vols., 1869). Almost immediately afterward he started research on his largest study, the **History of England in the Eighteenth Century** (8 vols., 1878–90). Lecky, an amateur in the sense that he held no academic position and had been given no special training as a historian, freely indulged his fancy as to what should be included. The results were somewhat strange. His long study may be divided into two sections: a series of essays on English history between 1714 and 1793 and a more connected account of Irish history between 1714 and 1801.

Most of Lecky's analysis of the American Revolution can be found in the third and fourth volumes of the original edition.* He was little interested in blood and glory, so he skipped quickly over military matters and concerned himself mainly with political affairs. These he presented in a clear style which related the story without excessive discussion. He was not shy of making judgments or expressing his interpretations forcibly, and according to William Gladstone, four times Prime Minister of Britain, he had "real insight into the motives of statesmen," even more so than Carlisle or Macaulay.†

Misgivings of this kind must have passed through many minds, and the older colonists were not of the stuff of which ardent soldiers are made. Among the poor, vagrant, adventurous immigrants who had lately poured in by thousands from Ireland and Scotland, there was indeed a keen military spirit, and it was these men who ultimately bore the chief part in the war of independence; but the older and more settled colonists were men of a very different type. Shrewd, prosperous, and well-educated farmers, industrious, money-loving, and eminently domestic, they were men who, if they were compelled to fight, would do so with courage and intelligence, but who cared little or nothing for military glory, and grudged every hour that separated them from their families and their farms. Such men were dragged very reluctantly into the struggle. The American Revolution, like most others, was the work of an energetic minority, who succeeded in committing an undecided and fluctuating majority to courses for which they had little love, and leading them step by step to a position from which it was impossible to recede. . . .

That strong dislike to military life which pervaded the colonial population was nowhere more conspicuous than in the class of society in which loyal sentiments chiefly prevailed, and the American loyalists risked much more than the American insurgents. In addition to the Acts punishing with death, banishment, forfeiture of goods, or imprisonment, those who assisted the English, every State passed Acts of Attainder, by which the properties of long lists of citizens who were

---

* William E. H. Lecky, *A History of England in the Eighteenth Century* (8 vols., New York, 1878–90), III, 481–482; IV, 10–12, 288.

† Quoted as coming from a chat Gladstone had with John Morley, later his biographer, by James F. Rhodes "Tribute to William E. H. Lecky," *Proceedings,* Mass. Hist. Soc., 2nd Series, XVIII (1903, 1904), 22.

mentioned by name were confiscated. Pennsylvania and Delaware, following the example of the Irish Jacobite Parliament of 1689, gave the attainted person the option of appearing to take his trial for treason by a specified date, but usually the confiscations were absolute and unconditional. In Connecticut the simple offence of seeking royal protection or absenting himself from his home and country made the loyalist liable to the confiscation of all his property. In New York, in addition to an Act confiscating all the goods of fifty-nine persons, three of whom were women, and making them liable to the penalty of death if they were found in the State, a heavy tax was imposed on every parent who had a loyalist son. One of the first acts of the revolutionary party when they occupied Boston was to confiscate and sell all property belonging to loyalists, and in a country of farmers and yeomen most property was immovable. The loyalist exposed himself to the undying animosity of a large proportion of his neighbours; he exposed his family to those savage mobs who by plunder and torture were everywhere supporting the Revolution, and he was certain to incur absolute ruin not only in case of the defeat of the English cause, but even in case of the temporary evacuation of the district in which his property was situated. If the rebellion collapsed, it would probably do so speedily through the want of men and money and through the burden of the sufferings it produced, and it was not necessary for him to intervene and to excite against himself the hatred of those who would continue to be his neighbours. If the rebellion was prolonged, an American resident could estimate more truly than Englishmen how difficult it was to subdue an enormous, half-opened country, how absolutely impossible it was that the English power could be, for purposes of protection, a living reality over more than a very small section of it. Nor were the moral inducements to enter into the struggle very strong. Thousands who detested the policy of the New Englanders, and who longed to see the colonies reconciled to England, reprobated the Stamp Act and many other parts of English policy, and felt in no way bound to draw the sword against their countrymen, or to add new fuel to a civil war which they had done their utmost to avert. . . .

The civil war between Whigs and Tories had, as we have seen, been much more savage than the war between the English and the Americans; and the revolutionary party attributed with some reason the long continuance of the struggle to the existence and to the representations of the great loyalist party in America. The power of Congress was still extremely uncertain; there was much difficulty in inducing the States to obey its mandates, and the restoration of the most active and enterprising leaders of the party disaffected to the new state of things might be very dangerous. The country was exhausted and impoverished and in no mood to pay anything, and strong personal and class interests were hostile to a restoration. The loyalists to a great extent sprang from and represented the old gentry of the country. The prospect of seizing their property had been one great motive which induced many to enter into the war. The owners of the confiscated property now grasped the helm. New men exercised the social influence of the old families, and they naturally dreaded the restoration of those whom they had displaced.

It remained for England to discharge her obligations to her exiled partisans.

GEORGE O. TREVELYAN

George Otto Trevelyan (1838–1928) possessed the proud distinction of having the great English historian Lord Macaulay as his uncle and George M. Trevelyan as his son. All three rank among the most distinguished names in the Whig historical school.

Trevelyan's father was a senior government officer, and George Otto also spent a good deal of time in public service. At Cambridge University he acquired a reputation which long outlasted his undergraduate years. He was an excellent scholar, but his mark was more obviously made through what his son called "intellectual high spirits." He reveled in literary writings of a topical and satirical kind and in many ways demonstrated that combination of lively wit and disciplined writing which is a mark of an acute intellect. Such an attitude, even in someone with Trevelyan's eminently respectable background, did not commend itself to the staid authorities at Cambridge. He was not awarded a fellowship (the first step toward becoming a university teacher), losing to others less able but also less troublesome.

From about 1862 until 1865 he worked for his father in India, then spent the next three years in Parliament. He became closely identified with the liberal reformer John Bright and was present as the House of Commons strenuously debated the very important Reform Bill of 1867. In 1868 he became a member of the first ministry of William Gladstone but resigned two years later over a domestic issue which he regarded as a matter of principle. During the 1870's either he was not given a Cabinet post or his party, as a minority, did not form the government. This decade became, not surprisingly, one of considerable literary achievement and in particular saw the publication of his **Life and Letters of Lord Macaulay** and the **Early History of Charles James Fox**. From 1881 to the end of the century he was very deeply involved in British politics, but managed to publish the first part of **The**

American Revolution in 1899. Between the beginning of this century and the beginning of World War I, four more volumes completed the story (the last two carrying the title **George III and Charles Fox**).

Because of the important impact on contemporary attitudes, the selections from Trevelyan's works* are followed by brief extracts from a few of the letters written to him by the most notable of his American admirers, Theodore Roosevelt. †

They [the Loyalist refugees] honestly believed that the fitness of things required the established method of distribution to last for ever. Their best feelings were hurt when a new man, with newfangled political opinions, put in his claim to a share. The inspiring motive, according to their story, of every Revolutionary leader was the need and greed for office; and their posterity across the Canadian frontier continued, in filial good faith, to repeat the same tale for the benefit of our own generation.

In their view Congressmen and Committee-men were "a set of rascals, who only sought to feather their own nests, and not to serve their country." An unlucky Loyalist who happened to use those expressions in ill-chosen company got himself inside a jail; and the words have a natural, and almost elemental, ring about them which irresistibly suggests that it was not the first time, by a hundred, that they had been uttered with emphasis in Tory circles. According to the theory accepted by those circles, Otis started the agitation, which started everything, because his father had missed a judgeship. Joseph Warren was a broken man, and sought to mend his fortunes by upsetting those of others. John Hancock, too rich to want a place, suffered from wounded vanity when walking behind his betters in the order of precedence. Richard Henry Lee had been baulked of an appointment as Distributor of Stamps under the Act which then, and only then, he came forward to denounce. John Adams turned rebel because he was

* George O. Trevelyan, *The American Revolution* (new ed., 3 vols., London, 1905–1907), I, 374–375; 377; II, 187–188. Reprinted by permission David McKay Company, Inc.

† Reprinted by permission of the publishers from *The Letters of Theodore Roosevelt*, edited by Elting E. Morison (8 vols., Cambridge, Mass.: Harvard University Press, 1951–54), III (1951), 667, 706–708; V (1952), 840; VI (1952), 881–882. Copyright by the President and Fellows of Harvard College.

refused a Commission of the Peace; and Washington himself never forgave the British War Office for having treated him with the neglect which was the natural portion of Provincial military officers. It was an argument with two edges; and there is now little doubt which of the two cut the sharpest. What claim to perpetuity, (it has been finely asked,) had those institutions under which John Adams could not be a magistrate, and any stripling who had purchased a pair of colours took rank of George Washington? Disappointed men perhaps they had been; but their day arrived; and, if they could not be justices or majors in a marching regiment, they both obtained a post for which they were not less competent, and became each in his turn the chief governor of a nation.

The Loyalists were a prosperous and enjoying set, free with their cash; hearty with their fellows; just, and something more, towards those who had a claim on them; and very indulgent to their negro slaves. They were not ascetics; and, if they had stayed in the country, it is possible that the march of Temperance legislation would have been seriously delayed in some of the New England districts. The breaking of his punch-bowl was the worse damage to his property which Doctor Peters of Hebron had to deplore, when his angry parishioners came to search his house for arms. . . .

The Loyalists were fully persuaded that they were more estimable than the majority of their fellow-subjects; and they attributed their superiority, whether real or fancied, to themselves and not to their circumstances. They spoke and wrote of their opponents in a tone of class arrogance which, when once the rift came, made reconciliation impossible. In the rhymed satires and political catechisms which issued from the Tory press the most respected members of the popular party were held up to scorn as the refuse of mankind. The delegates to the Congress were described as pettifogging attorneys, disbarred advocates, outlawed smugglers, bankrupt shopkeepers; and, at the best, as innkeepers and horsedealers who had not as yet gone through the Court. The world was told how a bricklayer or carpenter would lie down at night, and awake in the morning a Lycurgus or a Solon. As each demagogue in turn, by rope or otherwise, went to his appointed place, he would be hailed as a brother by Catiline, Jack Cade, and Cromwell; an ill-assorted trio, it must be allowed, who would have found some difficulty in establishing fraternity among themselves. History,—or what in the days before Niebuhr and Mommsen passed for history, was ransacked for humiliating parallels to the statesmen of the American Revolution. . . .

But, though there were more black sheep than could be wished among the American militia, the great majority of them were as decent, worthy people as ever marched out of step. They had the virtues of civilians; and many of them, when they joined the camps around New York, to all intents and purposes were civilians still. Some battalions arrived at the front without having learned the rudiments of training. In Virginia, the most military community of the whole continent, a spectator who had seen one of the independent companies put through what, at that distance from Berlin, was called the Prussian exercise, spoke of the performance as a mere burlesque. The General Orders, which Washington issued in rapid succession to his New York army, dealt for the most part with very elementary points of discipline. Captains were instructed, over and over again, to see that, in the presence of the enemy, every man had twenty-four cartridges in his pouch, and a good flint well fixed in the lock of his piece; colonels were informed that they must break sentries of the habit of sitting down, and laying by their muskets, before they could shoot them for sleeping at their posts; and subalterns were desired, when the line was turned out on ceremonial occasions, to salute by taking off their hats, until they had mastered the correct method of presenting their fusees.

A very diligent reader of American annals has remarked that it must always prove a source of wonder to the scientific soldier, and of mystery to the historical student, how the Revolutionary war could ever have been carried through. At the critical moment of each campaign the militia habitually evinced a desire to go back to their homes; and they belonged to a people who usually take the shortest way to get whatever they may want. It must be admitted that a military life presented itself to them under the least seductive aspects. The pride and pomp of war were often represented in their case by a strip of cloth, which once had been red or yellow, sewed on to the sleeve of their upper garment. Comforts they had none. The men of the contingent, which marched for Canada under General Sullivan, possessed one shirt apiece, and often not a waistcoat in a company; and that expedition was fitted out as lavishly as the slender resources at the command of Washington would admit. . . .

TO GEORGE OTTO TREVELYAN

Personal   *December 12, 1903*

My dear Sir George: I have finished the second part of the *American Revolution,* and I have enjoyed it so much that I must send you a line to say so. I feel that it is far and away the best account of the Revolution written by anyone. For interest, for delightful humor, for absolute fair mindedness, for exactness in narrative, for profound insight, (and for its English!)—why, my dear sir, no other book on the Revolution so much as approaches it. . . .

TO GEORGE OTTO TREVELYAN

January 25, 1904

. . . True impartiality, true justice, is as far as possible removed from the dreadful habit of painting all character drab-colored. Hamden and Washington are doubtless not pure white, and here and there it might be possible to find touches of gray in the character of Philip of Spain and Louis the XVth of France; but we do violence to the facts, and ethically we sin if in comparing the four men we fail to show that by every canon of the higher life—social, political, spiritual—two are white and shining souls and two stand in that black circle which numbers the meanest and most contemptible and yet sometimes the most dreadful enemies of mankind. The "impartiality" which would only study the flaws in the character of the two great and good men and set forth the occasional tricks of virtue in the two evildoers would be a shame and a mockery.

TO GEORGE OTTO TREVELYAN

November 11, 1907

My dear Sir George: I have now read thru your last volume. It is a little difficult to say just what I feel about your history without subjecting you to the discomfort always felt by a fastidious man when he suspects he is overpraised. Yet I cannot refrain from expressing my sincere opinion that you have not only written the final history of our revolution, but that you have done what is given to so very, very few men to do—that you have written one of the few histories which can deservedly be called great. I do not want to be misled by national feeling; and yet I cannot help believing that the American Revolution was one of the great historic events which will always stand forth in the story of mankind; and now we have been fortunate enough to see that rare combination of a great historic event treated by a great writer, a great student, a great historian. . . .

TO GEORGE OTTO TREVELYAN

January 1, 1908

. . . It seems to me that there has never been a more satisfactory summing up of Washington as a soldier than is contained in your pages 284 to 286. How well you have done Benedict Arnold! How will you deal with his fall; with the money-paid treason of the rider of the war storm? What a base web was shot thru the woof of his wild daring! He was at heart a Lucifer, that child of thunder and lover of the battle's hottest heat; and dreadful it is to think that when he fell his fall should have been, not that of the lightning-blasted Son of the Morning, but that of a mere Mammon or Belial. . . .

In Canada, for instance, Wolfe and Montcalm are equally national heroes, now, because the English conquered the French and yet live in the country on terms of absolute equality with them; so that of necessity, if they are to have a common national tie, they must have as common heroes for both peoples the heroes of each people. So in a very striking fashion it is with us and the memories of the Civil War. My father's people were all Union men. My mother's brothers fought in the Confederate navy, one being an admiral therein, and the other firing the last gun fired by the *Alabama* before she sank. When I recently visited Vicksburg in Mississippi, the state of Jefferson Davis, I was greeted with just as much enthusiasm as if it had been Massachusetts or Ohio. I went out to the national park which commemorates the battle and siege and was shown around it by Stephen Lee, the present head of the Confederate veterans' organization, and had as a guard of honor both ex-Confederate and ex-Union soldiers. After for many years talking about the fact that the deeds of valor shown by the men in gray and the men in blue are now the common heritage of all our people, those who talked and those who listened have now gradually grown, first to believe with their minds, and then to feel with their hearts, the truth of what they have spoken. But where such results flow from battles as flowed from Bannockburn and Yorktown, centuries must pass before the wound not only scars over but becomes completely forgotten, and the memory becomes a bond of union and not a cause of division. It is our business to shorten the time as much as possible; and no one has done better work toward this end than you yourself.*

---

* This passage excellently demonstrates Roosevelt's ability to turn a blind eye to the facts and his tendency to regard voluble optimism as manifest policy.

Part Three

The Twentieth Century

An Early Survey

By the beginning of this century a handful of American voices had been raised in defense of the Loyalists and some well written pleas for a more objective view of the Revolution had been produced. On the other hand, the comment of Edward Ellis that American schoolchildren were taught "in their histories and readers, as well as in speeches and orations, that the one being to be scorned above all others was he who being born in this country took sides with England in the war for liberty" seems quite accurate.

At the University of Pennsylvania a graduate student, challenged by what had already been written, perhaps most directly by the article of Moses C. Tyler already cited, chose the Loyalists as his dissertation topic. In 1902 Claude Van Tyne's work was published in book form. It is a sad commentary on twentieth century historiography that with all its imperfections it remains even today the standard general account. There are a number of reasons for this situation, which may be mentioned briefly.

The United States, as much as any country and more than many, wants its history told as a story of success; both American readers and writers have normally been chary of giving much attention to losers, whatever their field. Secondly, there has been a strong and consistent desire to proclaim the American Revolution as a people's uprising against tyranny. Although the work of the "imperial school" of historians, now extending through more than half a century, has gone far to dissipate the image of the British ministers as vicious and oppressive rulers, the same has not been done for those colonials who remained true to their allegiance to Britain even when they disagreed with their government. Thirdly, there is to some extent a paucity of historical sources, perhaps only to be expected in view of the dangers involved for a Loyalist in keeping his papers. Fourthly, the most voluminous body of manuscript material consists of the petitions (and supporting documents) presented before the British government, material that is therefore *post facto,* prejudiced and, in some cases, padded. Even more important perhaps is that these petitions came from only about three percent of the Loyalist exiles (or about eight percent of the exiled men) and, of course, they do not tell us about those who did not go into exile (very roughly equatable with those who were not very active). Therefore, they do not constitute quite the representative sample we would like, yet they remain the most valuable single collection of available data. Fifthly, to bring accounts of the Loyalists up to the highest standard of contemporary scholarship it would be necessary to dig deeply into local records. We need to know much more about American life in the late Colonial and Revolutionary periods before we can markedly advance the analysis of the Loyalists, by fully documenting and thereby proving, refuting, or modifying the customary generalizations about their social position, economic resources, and political motivations.

So that changing views of the subject may be presented in systematic fashion, we have included only excerpts from specific studies of the Loyalists. To see how the gradually developing interest in the Loyalist cause is reflected in more general works it would be instructive to peruse the standard textbooks of American history (for example, the one used by the student in his introductory course) and recent treatments of the Revolution as a whole. (See works by Alden, Palmer, Morgan, and Jensen, noted in the bibliography.)

CLAUDE VAN TYNE

In **The Loyalists in the American Revolution*** Van Tyne bit off more than he could chew. The rarity, range, and quality of the studies already in existence precluded a satisfactory general study and the author's lack of experience precluded his writing a broad, analytical account. By comparison with Alexander Flick's study of **Loyalism in New York**, also derived from a doctoral dissertation and published in 1901, Van Tyne, the more able man, produced a work which less adequately met the historiographical needs of the time even though, by default, his work today is the more likely to be read.

He shied away from the difficult task of minutely examining the formation of the Loyalist side or party, if that term can be used to mean only a faction or political position and not a united, organized political group. He declared that in the years before 1776 "loyalty was the normal condition . . . and it was the Whigs [Patriots] who must do the converting," which is simply not a good enough explanation of how men chose their sides. There were those who were conservatives in 1771 who became Loyalists and others who became Patriots. Van Tyne did not show how this came to be and, although his rather pedantic contention—that the Loyalist party was not created—is worth making, it hardly explains his major omissions.

The study is much better as a treatment of what happened after the war began. The events included extend through times of battle and into the first year of exile. In appendices Van Tyne included a Loyalist "declaration of independence" (copied from a New York newspaper, November 17, 1781) and tables listing and briefly analyzing the laws passed against the Loyalists during the war. Here in cold, documentary form he brought home to his countrymen the fact that much wrong had been done to the upholders of loyalty by the upholders of liberty, and thereby he performed a valuable service. Although his scholarly apparatus was creaky and he frequently failed to use important sources, for example the newly available transcripts of Loyalist claims which he especially noted in his preface, Van Tyne's study entered the stream of general historical literature in America. Thereby the place of the Loyalists in the Revolution received more attention than before, at least from respectable scholars and responsible readers.†

---

* Claude H. Van Tyne, *The Loyalists in the American Revolution* (New York, 1902) pp. 2–3; 25–26; 87; 89–90. Quoted by permission.

† The qualification at the end of the sentence is important. The sort of special pleading which some groups wished to substitute for history is mentioned in Bessie L. Pierce, *Public Opinion and The Teaching of History in the United States* (New York, 1926), especially pp. 236–41, 293, noting the banning in Battle Creek, Michigan, of Van Tyne's textbook for schools. A broader based study for the nineteenth century is Ruth M. Elson, *Guardians of Tradition* (Lincoln, Nebraska, 1964). More recent examples may perhaps occur to students. Biased studies have received scholarly analysis, for both the United States and the United Kingdom, in Ray A. Billington *et al.*, *The Historians' Contribution to Anglo-American Misunderstanding*.

. . . The great majority of men could be regarded as indifferent, ready to stampede and rush along with the successful party; yet, even among the masses, this traditional love of kingship had to be reckoned with and combated. Loyalty was the normal condition, the state that *had* existed, and *did* exist; and it was the Whigs,—the Patriots, as they called themselves,—who must do the converting, the changing of men's opinions to suit a new order of things which the revolutionists believed necessary for their own and their country's welfare.

It is only when we realize this truth that we can see the folly of John Adams' theory of the *creation* of the Loyalist Party. He failed to understand that it was his party that was created and not the Loyalist party. . . .

Before the coming of the British soldiers, the elements of the active Tory party may be fairly represented in a few well-defined classes. There were the office-holding Tories, whose incomes depended upon the existing régime. Closely linked with these were those gregarious persons whose friends were among the official class. Doubtless many of the Anglican clergy had motives similar to those of the crown officers. With these men drifted the conservative people of all classes, who glided easily in the old channels. Another type of man, who listened and yielded rather to metaphysical considerations than to concrete facts, was the dynastic Tory, the king-worshipper. Others, who were convinced that Parliament had a right to tax, may be defined as legality Tories. Both these types were reinforced by the religious Tory, whose dogma was "fear God and honor the King." Finally there were the factional Tories, whose action was determined by family feuds and old political animosities. The DeLancey party in New York, of which we shall hear more, was forced into opposition because the Livingston party, its ancient enemy, embraced the Whig principles. In Massachusetts, the antipathy of the Otis's to Governor Bernard doubtless aided the formation of revolutionary parties. With the actual outbreak of war came new accessions to the active supporters of the British, as we shall see when the issues arise on the subjects of the Continental Congress, the Declaration of Independence and the French Alliance. It must always be borne in mind, however, that content with the old order of things was the normal state, and that men had rather to be converted to the Whig or Revolutionary views than to the Tory or Loyalist position. The classification only shows what elements of society tended to remain steadfast in the old faith. . . .

THE DOWNFALL OF THE OLD FAITH

The policy of the Tories, if they may be said to have had any policy, seems always to have been a negative one. Instead of taking part in the colonial politics, they withdrew, in many cases, and looked frowningly on while rebellion advanced by leaps and bounds. The more influential disdained to enter into controversy with the "noisy, blustering and bellowing patriots." By such conduct they failed, except in one or two colonies, to make their influence felt against the assembling of delegates to the Continental Congress. The arch-Tory of them all, Galloway, who spoke the truth when he knew it, or when it was not obscured from him by passion, testified upon oath, that in the election of delegates very small proportions of the people turned out to vote. Only the more violent, he asserted, took part in the elections which determined the appointment of the delegates. . . .

In failing to prevent the Continental Congress, the Tories had lost their last political opportunity. When Democracy and Union had once created a regulating body like Congress, they were sure to be led far afield by their creation. The audacity of the second Continental Congress will ever be a matter of wonder. Without unity in instruction, with no power to form a government, without jurisdiction over an acre of territory, with no authority to administer government in an acre if they had it, with no money, no laws and no means to execute them, they entered upon the task of regulating a society in the state of revolution. . . .

Sectional Histories

For forty years after Van Tyne's book appeared there was a trickle of works about the Loyalists. All of these were in one way or another specialized studies and only a handful were the products of outstanding historians. The majority were concerned with local affairs, for example the study of Massachusetts Loyalists by James Stark (1910), of New Hampshire Loyalists by Otis Hammond (1919), of New Jersey Loyalists by Edward Jones (1926–27), and an economic study of Virginia Loyalists by Isaac Harrell (1926). There were also a few biographies ranging, chronologically, from an article on Galloway in the *Pennsylvania Magazine of History and Biography*, XXVI (1902) to John Alden's account of "John Mein: Scourge of Patriots" in the Colonial Society of Massachusetts *Publications*, XXXIV (1942). Most were brief, but an important exception is the scholarly study of Jared Ingersoll, a prominent Connecticut Loyalist, written by Lawrence H. Gipson (1920).

During this same period one part of Loyalist history was extensively tackled. Their tribulations, especially the confiscation of their estates, their departure, and exile were the subject of a stream of articles by Wilbur Siebert. Many are in fairly obscure publications, but two which are usually accessible are "Dispersion of American Tories" and "Loyalists in West Florida," in the *Mississippi Valley Historical Review*, I (1914) II (1916). In the 1930's two fairly good studies were published. Lewis Einstein's *Divided Loyalties* (1933) was composed of a number of attractive essays about the Loyalists in England. He told good tales of spies and secret agents as well as delineating the lives of three of the most important figures in the early history of American painting. Arthur G. Bradley's *Colonial Americans in Exile* (1932) was, to put it fairly, a bad book. He was often inaccurate in presenting his facts, and this was made even more unforgivable because his prejudices were so strong and his coverage so unbalanced. Far better, although again not very original, was George M. Wrong's *Canada and the American Revolution* (1935). The quality of source material available in printed form also improved. In 1905 the Archives of Ontario had published the notes of some of the commissioners on the claims of the Loyalists. A decade later the notes of D. P. Coke, another of the commissioners, were edited and published in London. Then in the 1920's and the 1930's, the pace of publication picked up and the journals of a number of Loyalists appeared. Especially useful were Jonathan Boucher's *Reminiscences* (1925), Alexander Chesney's *Journal* (1921), Ann Hulton's *Letters* (1927), and Samuel Seabury's *Letters* (1930).

Therefore, by the beginning of World War II new information had been made accessible, but clearly the Loyalists had not attracted much or the best attention. There was still a great deal of research to be done and around 1940 a few professional historians looked at the topic again. Unlike Van Tyne, some four decades before them, they were reluctant to undertake a general analysis and limited themselves to exploring the Loyalists within a particular state. Some examples follow.

Robert O. DeMond's **The Loyalists in North Carolina during the Revolution** (1940)* was the first modern attempt to deal with the subject. His study made abundantly clear the fact that local issues played a major, even dominant part in forming the decisions taken by groups and individuals. In particular, DeMond gave a significant role to the Regulator movement, a series of up-country uprisings (not confined to North Carolina) which protested the lack of representation in the assembly and the lax, often criminal conduct of public affairs by royal officials. It is now clear that he pushed too far the connection between Regulators before and Loyalists after the Revolution. We can name nearly nine hundred Regulators and of these better than 8:1 were Patriots.†

Despite this hole in the argument, DeMond's analysis is valuable for the note of complexity and diversity which it brings into its discussion of the Loyalists. More recent studies have sustained his other classifications, for example the general Loyalist partisanship of the Scots of North Carolina.

. . . There were two political parties or groups in North Carolina. The governor and council made up the Government party, while the Assembly represented the People's or Popular party. A large number of the people in the state had no part in the Government party and were equally unrepresented in the political machine which controlled the assembly and county offices. Whether this vast group would support the governor and remain loyal to the King or would join in the rebellion was an open question.

Generalizations are dangerous in treating any phase of history and doubly so in writing of the Loyalists. We cannot say that any one section or group was wholly loyal. The Tidewater region, in which lived most of the justices and small officials, in general tended to support the Revolutionary cause. These counties had more than a just share of the representatives, but worked in harmony with the justices, lawyers, and sheriffs of the back counties. Since the Tidewater region was in the majority in the Assembly, this section determined to raise most of the

---

* Robert O. DeMond, *The Loyalists in North Carolina During the Revolution* (Duke University Press, Durham, N.C., 1940), pp. 34–35; 48; 51–55; 58. Quoted by permission.

† Hugh T. Lefler and Albert R. Newsome, *North Carolina; the History of a Southern State* (Chapel Hill, N.C., 1954), p. 178. For South Carolina a similar relationship between the Regulator and Loyalist movements was widely accepted, but it has been finally destroyed in Richard M. Brown, *The South Carolina Regulators* (Cambridge, Mass., 1963), especially pp. 123–24.

money by poll taxes, which fell especially hard on the people of the back country, where money was scarce.

Dissensions between the two sections led to armed conflict. Governor Tryon, the officers, and the people of the Tidewater and the officers of the back country arranged themselves against the common people of the back country. The remembrance of the struggle between the two sections was fresh in the minds of the people when the Revolution broke out. To understand why so many people in this back country decided to remain loyal to the King, one must have a knowledge of the War of the Regulators. . . .

The causes are briefly summed up under three heads as follows: (1) unlawful exaction of fees by clerks and county registerers of deeds, (2) unlawful exaction of taxes under the color of legislative authority, and (3) directly the unequal distribution of benefits and burdens of the Provincial Government.

One recent writer emphasizes taxes, dishonest sheriffs, and extortionate fees as the cause of the uprising. A still more recent historian believes the background to have been the scarcity of money, taxation, and the land policy of the Granville district. To these might be added religious intolerance. . . .

The exact number of the Regulators who remained true to England and fought in the Revolution as Loyalists will never be known. When one reads the accounts of the engagements fought within the state the names of the Regulators appear constantly. Only two or three Regulators of prominence were Patriots. One of these, Thomas Persons, became famous as aiding the cause of the colony and later was a member of the provincial council. . . .

The question may now be raised, what caused the Scotch people for the most part to remain true to the Home Government when the contest with the colonies came? Those who came after 1745, the date of the defeat of the Scotch at Culloden in the war between England and Scotland, were bound by a solemn oath to become good and faithful subjects of King George II of England. Extremely religious people, they felt bound by this oath. They took the view that they owed their lives to the fact that a gracious king had permitted them to migrate to North Carolina, and they were loath to turn against him.

Being accustomed to a government by a king, they could conceive of no other. The revolutionary idea of a democracy was foreign to them, since they were accustomed to obey their superiors.

The leaders were for the most part determined to support their King. Some of them left landed estates in Scotland which they still owned, and to join the Revolution meant forfeiture of their estates. They blamed the poor markets in the colony on the disturbance which their factious neighbors were creating with the mother country. Residing also in North Carolina at this time were many Scottish officers who had fought in England after the defeat at Culloden, and these were now on half pay and subject to call to service. All those whom the common people regarded as their superiors supported the King, and this naturally influenced them to do likewise. Their leaders stressed the fact that all their past efforts against the King had ended in defeat, and this was sure to do likewise. They were told that this was their grand opportunity to show their loyalty to a king who might yet lack entire confidence in them.

The Scotch merchants, like many other merchants of North Carolina and the South, were mostly Loyalists. They carried on trade directly with England, exchanging tobacco, lumber, and other native products for those wares of the mother country. War would destroy this trade and bring them ruin. The merchants of New England, on the other hand, received much of their raw materials from the West Indies, which they manufactured and sent to England. They were gradually ruined by the Navigation Laws and had much more reason to support the side that would free them from this burden than did the merchants of North Carolina. . . .

Some of the larger merchants . . . bought goods on time from the British merchants and sold them on credit to the planters. On their books they had listed the names of hundreds of debtors at the outbreak of the war. If they joined the Revolution and did not settle their accounts, their credit with the British merchants would be destroyed. Some of them, like Andrew Miller, had conscientious scruples against not paying their honest debts. Other merchants without cash of their own depended entirely upon their credit with the British merchants for the financing of their trade.

Although the majority of the merchants of North Carolina supported the Loyalist cause, a large number in the Cape Fear region were leaders in the rebellion. . . . The merchants of Cross Creek were almost unanimous in their support of the King. Those of the Albemarle region were also generally loyal, probably on account of the fact that many of them were under the control of British merchants because of their debts. The middle-class Scotchman was accustomed to following the leadership of the wealthier class, and when this element declared for the King, he unhesitatingly followed.

The Germans were also an important racial element in North Carolina, but were of much less importance than the Scotch in the Revolution. Many of them entered the colony by way of the back country from Pennsylvania in search of lands. They settled chiefly in Forsyth, Guilford, Randolph, Davidson, Stokes, Rowan, Cabarrus, Stanley, Lincoln, Gaston, Catawba, and Burke counties, these bordering the frontier from Virginia to South Carolina. These were the counties which were prominent in the War of the Regulation. In this war a large number of the Germans supported the Regulators.

When the Revolution continued, many of them remained loyal to the King; as a result of their activities, they suffered the confiscation of their estates. Of the one hundred and eighty-two people summoned before the Rowan County Inferior Court in 1783 to show cause why they should not have their estates confiscated, one fifth were German.

The Moravians, a religious sect, which was made up largely of Germans and which somewhat resembled the Quakers, had settled in North Carolina just previous to the war. Since it was contrary to their religious principles to take either an oath or to serve in the army, they found themselves in a difficult position. They claimed exemption also because of the "conscientious objections," and it was granted them. In lieu of this service large fines were collected from them at the beginning of the war, and later they were taxed threefold. Their neutral stand, though it was a friendly neutrality as far as the Patriots were concerned, gave both the Whigs and Tories an excuse for preying on them. The Tories claimed the Moravians were in sympathy with the Continental forces, while the committees of safety accused them of secretly aiding the Royal party. Although the Moravians always supplied the demands of the Whig soldiers by giving them everything they demanded and accepted in payment worthless money or promises to pay, they frequently found themselves in difficulties. At one time a band of Whig militia robbed and pillaged the people so badly that they were left like a conquered enemy. In fact, they suffered much more from this class than they did from the Tories. . . .

One method of discovering how widespread was the support of the King in the Province is to make a study of the record of the sale of confiscated estates. Such a study reveals the fact that between June 5, 1784, and November 15, 1787, tracts of land belonging to Loyalists were sold in twenty-nine counties of North Carolina: Anson,

Beaufort, Bertie, Bladen, Brunswick, Camden, Carteret, Chatham, Chowan, Craven, Currituck, Dobbs, Duplin, Edgecombe, Halifax, Hertford, Hyde, Montgomery, Moore, Nash, New Hanover, Orange, Randolph, Rowan, Sampson, Tyrell, Wake, and Wayne. These counties extended from Currituck in the east to Rowan in the west, and from Guilford in the north to Brunswick in the south. The number of estates sold in each of these counties varied all the way from one each in Wayne, Currituck, and Camden counties to fifty-four in Rowan, fifty-eight in Bladen, and ninety in Orange. This fact would indicate that loyal men of property, of the planter class, were to be found in practically every section of the state.

CONNECTICUT

When Connecticut celebrated its three hundredth anniversary in 1934, officially sponsored historical publications formed part of the state's observances. A slim volume on the Loyalists written by Epaphroditus Peck, a local lawyer and competent amateur historian, was included. Peck stated that in his state the boundary between the Patriots and the Loyalists "was more clearly marked than anywhere else, and coincided generally with the line of denominational cleavage." By this he meant that the vast majority of Anglicans were on the side of the Crown and the great bulk of Congregationalists were in favor of the Revolution. In the following selection this connection between religious persuasion and political allegiance is more fully developed. While the theory holds up quite well for Connecticut it is not applicable to all the colonies. Virginia is a clear exception. In our more secular age the importance of religious issues may be heavily downgraded, but in the decade before the Revolution few matters stirred up as much oratory and passion as the colonial fear that an Anglican episcopate was to be forcibly imposed upon America.

Perhaps Peck was reflecting the celebratory occasion a little too generously in his conviction that during the war "the conduct of both [Loyalists and Patriots] was usually governed by noble motives and seldom descended to brutal measures," but his brief piece, based largely on secondary sources, gives an unbiased picture of the Loyalists in Connecticut.*

This identification of loyalty to the king with devotion to the Church of England gave a degree of respectability, and also a quality of emotional fervor, to the loyalist cause in Connecticut that it may have

---

* Epaphroditus Peck, "The Loyalists of Connecticut," Tercentenary Commission of the State of Connecticut, Committee on Historical Publications (Yale Univ. Press, 1934), pp. 4–8; 15–18. Quoted by permission.

lacked elsewhere. Sabine, in his *American Loyalists*, says: "I feel assured that, in Connecticut, the number of adherents of the crown was greater, in proportion to the population, than in Maine, Massachusetts, or New Hampshire.". . .

The reason why the Anglican clergy of Connecticut and their people were so strenuous in opposition to the Revolution, while in Virginia most of the Revolutionary leaders, including George Washington, were loyal adherents of the Church of England, is to be found in the preceding century and a half of New England history. Massachusetts and Connecticut were originally settled by men and women some of whom had been actually driven out of England by the authorities of the Anglican Church, and others had been in conflict with those authorities, and had come to a bleak and unknown wilderness to escape ecclesiastical tyranny. Naturally, with this background, the first generation of settlers in Massachusetts and Connecticut had little affection for the Church of England, but had a constant fear that its prelates would seek to extend their power to the colonies, and close the independent churches here.

In the half century which followed the establishment of the first settlements a good many people had come to New England for other reasons than for "freedom to worship God." Most of these had less religious zeal than had the early Pilgrims and Puritans, and some had no religious zeal at all. To one who had been accustomed from childhood to the ritual services of the English Church, especially if he had lived in a large town where the services of the church were carried on with dignity and some degree of splendor, the barren and austere services of the New England meeting houses must have seemed a poor substitute; and doubtless many, who would have made no fervid expression of religious feeling, had an innate reverence for the sacraments, especially if administered by a priest in holy orders conferred by a successor of the apostles, which the long sermons and long prayers of the Puritan ministers did not inspire. Some of the ministers, too, in their reading of theology found the writings of the great English divines convincing and persuasive.

When Charles II, after his restoration to the throne, sent commissioners to ascertain the state of things in New England, the commission reported that the Connecticut colony "will not hinder any from enjoying the Sacraments and using the Common Prayer Book provided they hinder not the maintenance of the public minister." In 1689, the first year of the reign of William and Mary, an Act of Toleration was passed, which permitted Protestant dissenters to carry on without molestation their own forms of worship. This naturally gave the Anglicans a claim to similar relief in Connecticut, and at the May session of the general court in 1708, a statute was passed, which by its terms was based upon the English Act of Toleration and permitted "such as soberly dissent from the way of worship and ministrie established by the antient laws of this government" to appear before the county court and "qualifie themselves" in the same manner as provided in the English act, and thereupon to "enjoy the same libertie and priviledge in any place within this Colonie without any let, hindrance and molestation whatsoever," but with the proviso that they should not be exempt "from paying any such minister or town dues, as are now, or shall hereafter be due from them." Thus the situation in Connecticut was quite defined. The Congregational churches were "owned and acknowledged established by law," but toleration was granted to sober dissenters to worship God in their own way, provided they paid the taxes levied for the support of the Congregational ministers. . . .

Two facts in particular tended to create hostility between the Congregational majority and the Anglican minority. There was no American bishop, and men (many of them originally Congregational ministers) who desired Anglican orders had to go to England for ordination. A journey to England was then by no means the easy and safe procedure which it now is. Dr. Johnson wrote to the Archbishop of Canterbury that of the fifty-two men who had gone to England for ordination in little more than forty years, ten had lost their lives on the journey.

On the other hand, the rulers of Connecticut were determined in their opposition to the establishment of an American episcopate. It was from the tyranny of episcopacy that their fathers had fled to America. They were well aware that the Congregational churches of New England were looked upon by the English authorities as illegal, schismatic, and altogether pestiferous, and they felt that the arrival of a bishop in America would be the first step toward restoration of the despotism against which the very existence of New England was a protest.

While the question of establishing an American episcopate showed the existence of a fundamental antagonism between the contending parties, the question of taxation created more personal bitterness. Practically every Connecticut community was first organized as an ecclesiastical society, which had the right and duty to call a minister, build a meeting house, and conduct religious services. The cost was defrayed by taxation. In the great majority of cases the revenue that could be obtained by taxation was meager, and any attempt to evade payment of the minister's rate or the meeting house rate on conscientious grounds was looked upon with great suspicion, and often resulted in legal proceedings to enforce payment of the tax.

On the other hand, those who were sincere adherents of the Church of England, and were carrying a heavy load of expense to build a church and support a minister of that order, naturally thought it a great hardship to be compelled to pay taxes for the support of the Congregational establishment. Sometimes even the Anglican clergyman himself was called upon to pay taxes for the support of his Congregational rival. It can readily be seen that the enforcement of such demands would create a bitter feeling of oppression in the minds of the Anglican clergy and people.

It is evident that, when the contest between the king and parliament of Great Britain and the people of New England broke out into open warfare, the two groups of Connecticut citizens were certain to take opposite positions in the struggle. The dominant majority held firmly to a form of religious worship and organization established here by law, but barely tolerated in England; the minority professed no less devotion to a church established by law in England, but only tolerated in Connecticut. The basic civic virtue to the mind of the majority was zeal for liberty; to that of the minority it was loyalty. . . .

The Anglican clergy of the state, who were not likely to be personally guilty of acts of treasonable violence, found themselves in a very painful position. The Church of England was intensely nationalistic in its attitude. When the colonies had openly resisted the Stamp Act, the Society for the Propagation of the Gospel had refused to create any new missions in New England. To the appeals of the American Churchmen that a bishop should be consecrated for the colonies, the church authorities at home gave repeated refusal. Now, if the Declaration of Independence were maintained, New England had ceased to be a part of the territory over which the Church of England claimed or was even willing to exercise jurisdiction. The Connecticut clergy had braved the wrath of their neighbors to show their devotion to a church which was barely tolerated by the authorities of the state, and was bitterly hated by a great majority of the people, only to find themselves abandoned and repudiated by the rulers of that church.

An especial point of difficulty was the *Book of common prayer,* by which the form of their worship was rigidly prescribed. The Anglican prayer-book of that day was full of extreme expressions of loyalty to the king, who was looked upon as the anointed and inspired representative of God. On every 30th of January prayers declaring the national penitence and humiliation for the "Martyrdom of the blessed King Charles the First" were to be read. On every 29th of May there was "to be read publickly in all Churches at Morning Prayer" a thanksgiving for the restoration to the throne of King Charles II. This prayer went on to beseech God to "Strengthen the hands of our gracious Sovereign King GEORGE . . . with judgment and justice, to cut off all such workers of iniquity, as turn Religion into Rebellion, and Faith into Faction." The daily orders for morning and evening prayer included "A Prayer for the King's Majesty," desiring "that he may vanquish and overcome all his enemies." It may be imagined that if those prayers were read with emphasis by a zealous clergyman in full sympathy with their sentiments, any Sons of Liberty who were in the congregation might feel it their duty to prevent or punish such treasonable utterances. . . .

Some of the clergy removed to more friendly colonies or confined their activities to the private administration of the sacraments or performance of pastoral duties. Others could not refrain from non-clerical activities, and did not escape the hand of the law. At the same term of the superior court at which Moses Dunbar was condemned to death, the Reverend James Nichols, missionary at Waterbury, who also had parishes in Northbury (now Plymouth) and New Cambridge (now Bristol), was tried for treason but acquitted; and the Reverend Roger Viets of Simsbury was convicted of having assisted loyalist prisoners to escape and received a sentence of imprisonment for one year. Four months later the general assembly ordered him to be released from prison and to be confined within the town of Simsbury for the remainder of his term upon his giving a bond of one thousand pounds not to ". . . do or say anything against the United States of America or detrimental to their interest."

Whether the loyalists suffered more from the irregular and illegal violence which they often endured at the hands of overzealous patriots, or from the imprisonments and other penalties imposed upon them by authorized process of law, it may be difficult now to tell. . . .

New Points of View

During the last quarter of a century there has been some sporadic interest in the Loyalists on the part of American historians. While limited local studies have continued to appear, more significant has been a small number of sophisticated analyses from various standpoints. Although nothing like a historical school has developed and the Loyalists continue to be neglected in general accounts of the Revolutionary period, they have benefited greatly from the attention of superior historians.

The Loyalists have been seen not as total reactionaries blindly opposing the enlightened thought of their era, but rather as personifying, in a time of crisis, conservative tendencies which were firmly rooted in Colonial America (see the following selection by Labaree). In 1941 Philip Davidson placed their writing in the context of the propaganda battles of the Revolution. More recently, there has been a re-assessment of their role in support of the British armies (see Smith selection). In Canada increasing attention has been given to what happened to those Loyalists who went into exile there.

A more difficult problem, what happened to the Loyalists who stayed here or who crept back in the first years of the Republic, is dealt with in Zeichner's selection. In the last decade there have been two general studies dealing with the Loyalist mind (see Nelson excerpt) and Loyalist claims for material losses.*

---

* Wallace Brown, *The King's Friends: The Composition and Motives of the American Loyalist Claimants* (Providence, R.I., 1965).

LEONARD W. LABAREE

One of the most sophisticated and coherent statements of the philosophical, psychological, and historical roots of Loyalism was presented in 1944 by Leonard Labaree. It may seem obvious, but one of the key virtues of this piece is that it looks back to 1763 for the origins of Loyalism, just as historians have usually done when tracing the rise of the opposition to Britain and the formation of Patriot attitudes, views, and ideology. In Labaree's **Conservatism in Early American History** (1948) this theme was broadened, deepened, and extended in time to take in the century before independence. Tackling the ambiguous and elastic term "conservatism" he decided to use it as meaning "an attitude of resistance to change shown in varying degrees by a variety of people with reference to any issue of the day." This was still a very broad gauged net through which a great variety of political fish could swim. To recognize that conservatism "may be present in different individuals in different degrees" is well and good, so far as it goes. Two questions arise immediately: is such a definition narrow and distinct enough to be useful in analyzing a historical situation, and is anything more precise possible?

Labaree himself seemed to answer "no" and "yes" respectively. In his book he tended to use a tangible denominator. After stating that conservatism may be seen in all strata of society he found it "most pronounced among the economically and socially privileged." The question also arises: Is a definition of conservatism as resistance to change entirely satisfactory? Weren't the wealthy, who may have been obtuse in the face of political developments, the trend setters in fashion, manners, and ways of life? Or is that explained sufficiently by saying they copied London? Labaree believed colonial education was inclined to be conservative, a claim supported by the absence of curricular changes. Yet the American colleges did not become bulwarks of Loyalism, even though Loyalist leaders were well educated and the Loyalists as a group were the best examples of the colonial conservative.*

In the article from which this selection is taken† Labaree first indicates how Loyalism developed between 1765 and 1775. He then identifies five groups in which Loyalism was most strongly, but not exclusively, apparent: office holders, Anglican clergymen, Quakers and other pacifists, large landholders, and merchants. These groups are then given detailed treatment in a graceful and insightful analysis. He concludes by indicating the characteristics of the Loyalist mentality.

---

* The strength of the Patriotic cause in the colleges is briefly summarized in Richard Hofstadter and Walter P. Metzger, *The Development of American Freedom in the United States* (New York, 1955), pp. 205–206.

† Leonard W. Labaree, in *Proceedings* of the American Antiquarian Society, N. S. Vol. 54, 1944 (Worcester, Mass., 1945), pp. 15–17; 52–53; 55–57. Used by permission.

THE NATURE OF AMERICAN LOYALISM

During the century or so before 1765 conservative tendencies had been apparent in many aspects of colonial life. America was a new and growing country and it was natural that new and liberal—if not radical —ideas and attitudes should appear. But at all times and in every sphere of interest a conservative force had also been present and men of a conservative attitude had prevented the frontier environment from effecting too marked a change upon colonial thinking and upon the face of colonial life. The Old World idea that political leadership was the province of men of rank and substance still prevailed in nearly every colony. Established churches still held their place in several colonies and even such a widespread movement as the Great Awakening could only make inroads upon, but not destroy, the orthodox worship and organization of the various denominations. Social levelling gained some headway in a land where every white man might aspire to economic independence, but class distinctions were far from being obliterated and the term "gentleman" was not one to be used carelessly or indiscriminately. The political thinking of nearly all men was still founded on the premise of a "balance" between the royal, aristocratic, and democratic elements of a "mixed monarchy," and few radicals there were who dared challenge the right of the first two of these three to a place in any decent government. In these and in other respects conservative attitudes had persisted and, in fact, had greater strength in 1765 than might have been expected in view of the new environment in which colonial life had developed. As the Revolutionary Era began, conservatism held a strong and respected place in the American scene. This fact must be recognized if we are to understand why many Americans became Loyalists at the time of the Revolution.

The years from 1765 to 1783 brought many changes. What had been basic assumptions of many men's lives were rudely challenged. Not only was there questioning of the authority of Parliament over colonial taxation, but there was also denial of the very basis of the British connection, and a repudiation of the principle of monarchy itself. Further, these years brought new elements of society into political prominence and power—the previously unenfranchised town laborer and the under-represented frontier farmer. These men and their leaders were vigorously to challenge the leadership of their "betters" and to attempt to weaken the aristocratic, as well as destroy the royal, element in government. Along with all this was a revolutionary tendency to substitute public clamor and even mob violence for the "decent" procedures of civil government. A trend toward social levelling and an attack upon the position of privileged religious groups were important by-products of a movement which seemed to many Americans to go much too far beyond the issues which had brought it into being. All in all, the period was one in which society seemed to be shaken to its very foundations.

Naturally, in such times, many men of a conservative temperament refused to follow the lead of radical agitators. They might—as most of them did—believe that Britain was pursuing a mistaken policy in beginning to tax the colonies by act of Parliament. Here was an innovation, on principle quite as distressing to colonial conservative as to a radical. But when the reaction to the parliamentary and ministerial measures went beyond the stage of respectful protest and led to violence and civil disobedience, some of the colonials drew back. When civil disobedience was followed by armed resistance, and then by a declaration of independence, and these were accompanied by an internal revolution in the institutions of colonial society itself, many Americans found themselves siding with the mother country. Not only was Britain the rightful claimant to their allegiance, but she was also the only agency which could be relied on to restore society to its proper foundations. . . .

Part of the uncertainty over the future of an independent America came directly out of the experience of the years which just preceded the outbreak of warfare. Those years did little to bring assurance that Americans would of their own volition reestablish a government of decency and order. Attention has already been given to the attitude of the men of great wealth to the radical's disregard of property rights. Many others shared this feeling without apparent regard to the extent of their personal fortunes. And if to the actual destruction of merchant's ships and goods be added the lootings of houses like Thomas Hutchinson's, the tarrings and featherings, the intimidation of officials, the general rioting and mob rule, the setting up of extra-legal committees and associations, the "demagogery" of the radical leaders, and the enfrancisement of the propertyless common people, then the prospect that a government of law and wisdom could be established in America seemed remote indeed.

From the very start of the troubles there were men to denounce the resort to violence. The Stamp Act disturbances aroused protests from as far apart as South Carolina and New Hampshire. One of the most emphatic newspaper attacks upon the act itself and upon its British authors came from "Philo-Patriae" in the far South, but a good share of his criticism was diverted to the violent disorders in the northern colonies. Whether these disturbances had come from the "misguided zeal" of true patriots, he wrote, or from "the villanous cunning of those who took the opportunity of the public discontent to promote and increase the tumult" for criminal purposes, in either case "the true lovers of liberty and their country" heard the rioting "with concern and sorrow." Such behavior did injury to a just cause and might well alienate "men who have been accustomed to venerate and obey lawful authority and who delight in peace and order."* . . .

The writings of the men called Loyalists reveal that, in spite of individual and group differences, there were several features of their thinking which were general enough among these men to be safely called aspects of the common Tory mind. Apart from the special factors that influenced the loyalty of officeholders and members of certain religious bodies, and the economic and political considerations that affected the position of merchants, great landowners, and men of wealth generally, certain common attitudes of the Loyalists are clear. For many, if not for most, a position of out-and-out loyalism was something arrived at only slowly. They reached it after a long and unhappy course of events had led them from general agreement that the British policy of taxation was unwise to a belief that their duty bound them to support the mother country against her disobedient colonial children. More than any other one thing it was the radical's resort to violence and extra-legal action that brought conservatives to this position. Many of these Loyalists were essentially moderates who preferred to take a neutral stand in the controversy and abandoned that only when compelled to do so by men or circumstances. Individually and as a group, the Loyalist were deeply attached to England and the crown. They were sincere admirers of the British constitution and of its system of government balanced between the monarchical, the aristocratic, and the popular elements. They were staunch believers in the value to America of the British connection. While many recognized that sometime the colonies would outgrow their dependent status, they were unwilling to believe that the inevitable day had come. Most of the Loyalists were men who could not look forward with any

---

* *The South-Carolina Gazette, and Country Journal,* Feb. 11, 1766 (no. 9).

equanimity to a future of independence. The changes, both external and internal, which would come if the Revolutionists had their way, seemed, even at best, too uncertain to command the trust and confidence of conservatives. On the contrary, if the future could be gauged by the present and the immediate past, it offered a prospect of anarchy and disorder rather than of stability, since mobs and violence would probably hold sway and demagogues would lead into political power an uncultured and emotional rabble. Aside from all considerations of the constitutional rights of parliament and of America, such were the views that influenced the minds of most men who ultimately declared themselves as Loyalists.

Participation in revolution—except for those whose motives are most narrowly selfish—requires a special kind of imaginative courage, one compounded of a general bravery in the face of an uncertain future, faith in that future, a power to imagine vividly how it may be molded to a desired end, and an optimistic disregard of the possibilities of loss or of failure to attain the hoped-for goal. All great revolutionaries have had that sort of courage, whether or not the movements they led have, in the long perspective of history, been successful, or have sought ends to the real interest of humanity. The conservatives who have opposed such revolutions—again apart from those whose motives have been primarily ones of self-interest—have seldom been endowed with this sort of courage. Again and again they have displayed a different group of virtues: a strong sense of the values in the contemporary order of society which are in danger of being lost, an imagination keen enough to see the possible harm as well as the good in the changes proposed, and a personal bravery in the face of suffering and persecution.

Thus it was with the sincere Loyalists of the American Revolution. They saw more clearly than did some of their opponents the values inherent in their colonial past, in the tradition of government by law which was theirs under the British constitution, and in the strength and external security afforded by the British connection. They recognized the dangers threatening a future state founded in violence and disorder by a group of leaders many of whom were quite inexperienced in the art of government. . . .

PAUL H. SMITH

Could the Loyalists, aided by the British, have won the war? Their military potential was initially taken for granted by British ministers and generals and then abused during the actual conflict. Naturally, their role was a function or derivative of total British military policy, and it is in this context that they are examined by Paul H. Smith in **Loyalists and Redcoats** (1964).* In an excellent study, making heavy use of the voluminous manuscript collections of British materials at the University of Michigan, the author deals with each year of the war and the actions or inaction of the Loyalists. His task was difficult because British policy was ambivalent, shifting as the war turned in and out of their favor; at times the Loyalists were disregarded almost completely, at other times they were wooed almost despairingly.

Smith explains that the British government's treatment of the loyal colonials was in keeping with its generally uninspired conduct of the war. The Loyalists "never occupied a fixed, well-understood place in British strategy. Plans to use them were in the main **ad hoc** responses to constantly changing conditions." Nor were they always organized for military purposes. On some occasions there was "practically no other reason than to afford them protection and to provide for their useful employment." At other times it was merely to keep them occupied, to lower costs, or to preserve support in Parliament for what many members came to believe was a futile war. Indeed, Smith suggests that the very use of Loyalists, who could have been a source of British strength, was so mismanaged that it contributed to the British defeat.

. . . Most Loyalists patiently awaited Britain's guidance and leadership. It was precisely this situation that Britain failed to grasp; unaware of the possibilities of loyalist support, government only halfheartedly asserted that leadership in the early months of the contest. Of the many mistakes Britain made with her American colonies, none was more costly or had more far-reaching consequences than her assumption that numerous Loyalists would without encouragement continue after 1775 to accept responsibilities as they had during the preceding decade. The error was easily made and difficult to correct; it followed readily from several basic British beliefs. Most Englishmen believed the majority of Americans to be essentially loyal, the bulk of the rebels too cowardly and poorly trained to face the British army, and Loyalists resolutely determined to prevent the overthrow of imperial authority. Before 1778, the Loyalists' assistance was simply presumed to be unneeded. Thus without seeking to determine the precise contribution

---

* Paul H. Smith, *Loyalists and Redcoats* (Chapel Hill, N.C.: University of North Carolina Press, 1964), pp. 168–174. Used by permission of The Institute of Early American History and Culture and the publisher.

they might make, government from the outset failed to make adequate preparations to organize them effectively.

Surprisingly, this initial failure in no way weakened government's confidence in the ultimate usefulness and dependability of the Loyalists. Indeed, during the first two years of the war, when little official effort was directed to mobilizing Loyalists, their eagerness to form provincial corps and participation in a few hastily conceived loyalist projects strengthened that confidence. What officials failed to perceive, however, was that this response was not merely the result of loyalist zeal or British plans but largely of conditions which were unlikely to persist. Loyalists at this time acted not because of, but in absence of, positive encouragement. The initiative in every case came from America, not London. Their motives were conditioned by fear of rebel reprisals, proximity of the British army, and a presumption that the war would be of brief duration. Britain's policy was as yet inchoate, consisting of little more than a few regulations to govern the first Loyalists who early forced their unwonted attentions upon the administration. It was impossible from their initial response to assume that mere policy changes and more liberal inducements would readily elicit decisive loyalist participation.

The ambivalence of Britain's early loyalist policy—which coupled reluctance to organize them with surpassing confidence in their usefulness—made the administration's subsequent plans appear contradictory. Furthermore, in light of her meager efforts to mobilize Loyalists before 1778, Britain's paralyzing dependence upon them in later stages of the war appears incomprehensible. Careful examination easily resolves the confusion. British overconfidence, the tendency to underestimate the enemy, and the North ministry's reluctance to expand the Provincial Service, which marked British policy during Howe's command, no longer crippled British planning after 1778. Saratoga and the French entry combined to destroy government's propensity to employ half-measures against the revolutionists. Thus, Britain subsequently turned to every resource at her command and eagerly sought aid from every feasible quarter, which included above all cooperation of the American Loyalists. . . .

Not until Clinton embarked an expedition for South Carolina during the winter of 1779–80 did another British offensive get under way.

By the time a full-scale expedition was dispatched to South Carolina, British strategy had become securely tethered to the southern

Loyalists—a consequence of basic political factors in London as well as military developments in the colonies. For while government painstakingly reformulated American policy during the months following Saratoga, the emergence of effective political opposition forced the ministry increasingly to develop basic strategy with an eye to its Parliamentary majority. The fundamental weakness of the ministry contributed importantly to opposition efforts to discredit the war in America. The 1778 naval crisis, the Lord Chancellor's resignation, failure of the Carlisle Peace Commission, Admiral Keppel's court martial, Suffolk's death early in 1779, and the continued paralysis of British operations in America enhanced every opposition attack. When ministerial mismanagement opened the way for an inquiry into Sir William Howe's conduct in America, the North ministry very nearly fell. Only by insisting that the war in America could be continued with token reinforcements and greater support from the Loyalists was it able to maintain a majority in support of continuing the war. Subsequently, the political situation in Parliament loomed as large in formulation of British strategy as purely military factors.

Just as the prospect of loyalist support decisively shaped over-all policy, so too did that anticipated support mold actual southern operations. Indeed, after 1779, continuation of the war against the colonies depended upon the cooperation of Loyalists in re-establishing royal government in the South. Although decisive victory at Charleston appeared to destroy opposition in South Carolina, Cornwallis nevertheless soon found that Britain's loyalist plans were in peril. . . . By September [1780] the Loyalists were in control of very little territory outside the immediate vicinity of Charleston, and the backcountry was aflame with revolt. Thus in October Cornwallis started northward to rally the North Carolina Loyalists and to cut off all outside support for the South Carolina revolutionists, but the incredible rebel victory at King's Mountain disrupted his march.

Before Cornwallis resumed the campaign, the situation in the South had changed completely. The destruction of Loyalists under Major Ferguson at King's Mountain and arrival of another American army in the South under General Greene practically destroyed all prospects of organizing the Carolina Loyalists. . . .

Blindly striking out after Morgan and Greene—a maneuver which lost him both his baggage train and the crucial race to the Dan—Cornwallis in February suddenly found himself several hundred miles from his nearest support and totally unequipped to complete his original plans with the North Carolina Loyalists. Although he paid lip service to this project during the following weeks, he gradually abandoned the loyalist experiment—and with it the primary purpose of the southern campaign. A bloody engagement with Greene at Guilford Courthouse failed to improve his position. Seemingly unaware that his army's condition and the presence of Greene's troops rendered it unlikely that Loyalists would now foolhardily expose themselves, he nevertheless once again called them to the royal standard. Upon encountering a very meager response he precipitately abandoned the Carolinas to Greene, convinced that any campaign dependent upon cooperation from the Loyalists was completely unsound. . . .

Both Cornwallis's conduct in North Carolina and the loss of his army at Yorktown have obscured British strategy in 1781. From initial formulation in Germain's orders to Clinton on March 8, 1778, until the war's end, Britain's basic strategy after Saratoga (although frequently blurred and at times temporarily endangered by short-range tactical decisions) rested squarely upon participation of Loyalists in the reestablishment of royal authority in America. The French entry, which produced the plans formulated in Clinton's revised orders of March 21, 1778, and various incidental delays thereafter, only temporarily interrupted efforts to execute that strategy. Not until Cornwallis marched to Virginia did a high official repudiate this plan, and then Sir Henry steadfastly adhered to it in the face of Cornwallis's objections. Nor did the administration waver in support of that policy. Confused instructions emanating from Whitehall in 1781 appeared to support Cornwallis against Sir Henry, but actually they merely demonstrated that at the time Germain completely misunderstood their plans for continuing the war.

Government proposed no fundamental strategic changes after 1780. Unable to acquire new support in Parliament, the ministry refused to hazard its precarious position by altering basic designs in America. Laboring under severe censure, at war with powerful European enemies, and beset by financial woes, government doggedly clung to the hope that Loyalists might yet rally vigorously and thereby convince the revolutionists of the futility of remaining in rebellion. In light of the ministry's plight, no other course was open. . . .

In dealing with the Loyalists, Britain made two palpable errors: she turned to them for assistance much too late, and then relied upon them much too completely. Basic ignorance of colonial conditions and sheer incompetence, to be sure, lay at the core of these errors. Equally, however, they were committed because government was not at any time entirely at liberty to conduct the war on purely military grounds. Thus foreign intervention, political pressures, and poor intelligence led to adoption of a policy which had major limitations at best and grave defects at worst. Never free to wage total war in America, Britain inaccurately gauged the possibilities and limitations of the restricted warfare which alone she was free to pursue. Only vaguely aware of these subtle limitations, she relied upon a series of inconsistent plans, of which her loyalist policy was the least well managed. That confused policy stands as a monument to the hazards which inhere in the conduct of limited war.

OSCAR ZEICHNER

At the close of the Revolution many Loyalists quietly stayed on in America. Others had little choice but to leave, and still others felt that nothing must come between them and their loyalty to the King. As the war came to an end there were many glib ideas about where these "displaced persons" could be relocated within the British empire. Australia, South Africa, Great Britain, the West Indies, and Canada were all mentioned. Actually, the vast majority of the approximately 100,000 who went into exile stayed in the western hemisphere.* Because of the Loyalist migration the population of Nova Scotia was almost doubled, and New Brunswick and Upper Canada (created when the old province of Quebec was divided in two in 1791 and roughly equivalent to present-day Ontario) were established as new provinces with a preponderance of American exiles for their inhabitants.

More than people were transported. Many Loyalists reoccupied positions of political power similar to those they had held in the American colonies and exercised a strong influence on the course of the Dominion's history. In the United States they were despised by contemporaries and neglected by historians and popular writers, but in Canada they became heroic figures.† Perhaps too much so! Modern Canadian historians have spent a fair amount of time separating the Loyalist myth from the facts, and reassessing their influence on nineteenth-century Canada.

---

* On the subject of the total number of Loyalists, the reader is referred to the Appendix.

† In 1789, Lord Dorchester (formerly Sir Guy Carleton, commander-in-chief of British forces at the end of the War of Independence and good friend of the Loyalists) suggested that those "families who had adhered to the unity of the Empire" should as a mark of honor have the right to add U.E. after their name.

The subject of the next extract, by Oscar Zeichner,* is the position of the Loyalists in New York after 1783. The main group consisted of those who had not been sufficiently anti-Patriot to make departure imperative. A much smaller number, having found the new settlements in Canada not to their liking, silently crept back into New York and other states. How many we shall never know. The reception they received depended upon a host of personal factors, just as their original decision to become Loyalists had done. In general the states made it plain that in the peace treaty of 1783 Congress had only agreed to suggest restitution and they (the states), having noted this advice, were paying no heed to it. A Loyalist who, by vigorous attitude or open action, had created a lasting current of animosity did well to stay away or at the very least pick a different state in which to settle down. In New York, where they had been most heavily concentrated during the war, the prospects of the Loyalists being peaceably reaccepted into society were not great.†

During the war the state adopted a consistent anti-loyalist policy. Legislation systematically deprived the Tories of their property, jobs, and political rights. In March, 1778, they were disfranchised; in October, 1779, Tory lawyers were excluded from the practice of their profession; and in the same year fifty-nine loyalists were attainted and their property confiscated. Thomas Jones wrote that Governor Clinton "had rather roast in hell to all eternity than consent to a dependence upon Great Britain or shew mercy to a damned Tory." Hamilton admitted that the severe policy of repression had reduced the proportion of Tories in the state population from one-half in 1775 to a third in 1783.

This legislation induced many of the loyalists to leave their homes for the British lines or to quit the country. A large number went to New York City where the British army offered them a temporary refuge. Here they hoped and worked for the failure of the Revolution. On the other hand those Whigs who had suffered at the hands of

---

* Oscar Zeichner, "The Loyalist Problem in New York after the Revolution," *New York History*, XXI (New York State Historical Association, Cooperstown, N.Y., 1940), 286–289; 292–293; 295–296; 301–302. Used by permission.

† A brief summary of the return of the Loyalists, especially the rejection of the loyalty oaths as a meaningful test, can be found in Harold M. Hyman, *To Try Men's Souls: Loyalty Tests in American History* (Berkeley, California, 1959), pp. 108–119. Another approach is Allan Nevins, *The American States during and after the Revolution* (New York, 1924), pp. 645–651. Merrill Jensen, *The New Nation* (New York, 1950) underestimates the difficulties encountered by Loyalists, particularly between 1783 and 1785.

armed Tory bands or had also been forced to move by the coming of the British army became even more hostile to the "renegades." . . .

There were certain Whigs, however, who because of personal, economic, and social ties were opposed to the extreme measures urged by the radicals against the loyalists. These Whigs were, in general, the moderates of 1774 who had failed to check the revolutionary movement, but who were now determined to put an end to radical supremacy. They were "men of education and wider knowledge of the world," and during the "Critical Period" their objectives were "union, public credit, and the dominion of law." To them "the people were still, as in the colonial days, turbulent, self-willed, and lawless," and one of the first fields in which the reign of the law must be reëstablished concerned the treatment of the Tories.

The conservative Whigs realized that the great majority of the Whig population were hostile to the loyalists. They discreetly refrained, therefore, from voicing their moderate views in the first few months after the establishment of peace. Soon after, however, they wrote and spoke in favor of allowing the loyalists to become adjusted to the new conditions with as little friction as possible. . . .

Alexander Hamilton . . . became the chief advocate of conciliation and moderation in the treatment of the Tories. Basing his arguments on the principles of abstract justice and, more particularly, on the clauses of the peace treaty and international law, he maintained that differences between the loyalists and the Whigs, now that the war was over, should be removed. Popular sentiment, however, agreed with Isaac Ledyard that Hamilton's opinions were "opposed to common understanding." More violent was the "Mechanic" who castigated Hamilton for his defense of "the most abandoned and flagitious scoundrels in the Universe" and accused him of being "under the golden influence." . . .

The conflict between radical and conservative Whigs over the loyalists centered in the struggle to control the state legislature, and the Tory question usually became especially prominent when election dates approached. Early in 1783 "Publius" warned the citizens of New York that, now the war was at an end, the loyalists would endeavor to secure control of the government. He therefore advised the voters to retain Governor Clinton in office. On the other hand, in the 1784 elections the conservative Whigs attempted to line up the Tories behind them by hinting at the possibility of removing loyalist disabilities and restoring Tory property. In 1786 "Brutus," incensed at the proposed repeal of restrictions on the franchise to loyalists, warned the "Independent Electors . . . to guard [the] country from the intrigues of a number of knavish men who will most assuredly endeavor to put in a set of tory gentry." As late as 1787, despite the fact that in general anti-loyalist sentiment had subsided, feeling against the Tories was still utilized at election time.

The efforts to drive the loyalists from the state and prevent their return were by no means completely successful. Immediately after the war was over, the Tories tried to participate in political life. In 1783 they voted for governor and other officers, but the new legislature was dominated by the radicals, who soon deprived Tories of the franchise. This action was in accord with direct demands of the people. In August, 1783, for example, the electors of Ulster County advised their assemblymen to take the anti-loyalist resolutions "of the country for the rule of your conduct on this subject." They also demanded speedy enforcement of the existing confiscation laws and the enactment of severer penalties on Tory property. . . .

The events of 1784 marked the high point of anti-loyalist legislation and sentiment in New York. Although the radicals continued to control the legislature during most of the "Critical Period," Gouverneur Morris' prediction that "the rage against the loyalists will . . . give place to more favorable sentiments" began to be fulfilled. The bitter struggle between the two wings of the Whig party was shifted to other issues. Even in 1784 there were signs that the tide in the anti-loyalist feeling had begun to turn. In 1785 the assembly still refused to repeal legislation hostile to the Tories, but in the following year the act which required lawyers suspected of loyalism to take an oath of abjuration was repealed, and John Jay observed that the anti-loyalist measures were being less seriously enforced. In 1787 the legislature refused to pass a bill, introduced by an extreme Whig, which would have disabled any person who had been on the side of the British, or had voluntarily given them provisions, or aided or encouraged others to do so, from holding any office in the state. Jay wrote John Adams on February 21, 1787, that "all discriminations inconsistent with the peace treaty will gradually be abolished," and in the following year all laws contrary to the treaty of peace were repealed, thus completely emancipating the former loyalists from the restrictive legislation which had curbed their freedom since the outbreak of hostilities. . . .

New York tried hard to punish its Tories for their anti-revolutionary position. Hostile legislation enacted during the war forced thousands to flee the state, while extra-legal action and the fear of further punitive measures added many more to the number of refugees who left New York with the British. When the war ended the Tory question became an important issue between conservative and radical Whig. In the years after 1783 the radicals secured control of the legislature and, following in the footsteps of many local communities, adopted severe anti-loyalist measures. Petitions of Tories who asked to return to the state were refused. Although the conservatives protested, they were as yet impotent to do anything else. Compared with the policy of Connecticut, New York's attitude was rather harsh. This judgement, however, must be tempered by the realization that some of the most bitter phases of the long and severe civil war had occurred in New York. In comparison with the treatment of the losing side in recent European civil struggles, New York's policy toward its defeated foes was relatively humane.

Shortly after the anti-Tory feeling reached a climax it began to subside. The discriminatory laws were repealed, new hostile legislation was voted down, and the prayers of the "renegades" were listened to more favorably. In the meantime most of New York's Tories continued to reside in the state, while some of those who had fled quietly attempted to come back. Not all of the radicals were willing to forget the bitter conflict, and they pointed out the injustice and danger of permitting their former enemies in the state. Although Tory baiting continued to be an effective political weapon into the early nineteenth century, it lost its original purpose. Like a scar it indicated how severely the Revolution had cut through the population. But the state recovered, and the great majority of the loyalists in New York remained to contribute their energies to its post-war development.

WILLIAM H. NELSON

While Smith analyzed what Loyalists did and did not do during the Revolution, William Nelson's **The American Tory** (1961)* delved into their thoughts. The book consists of a series of essays with more limited aims than their headings indicate. For example, under the title "The Moderate Men" there is an examination of Loyalist preparations for the First Continental Congress,

---

* William H. Nelson, *The American Tory* (Oxford, England, 1961; paperback, Boston, 1964), pp. 85–91. Used by permission of the Clarendon Press, Oxford.

and "The Crisis of Allegiance" deals essentially with attacks made by four leading Loyalists on the authority of Congress. The book therefore cannot be regarded as the badly needed successor to Van Tyne's general survey, but on the basis of the printed materials which almost exclusively form his "sources" Nelson has offered some interesting observations.

The reader should, however, beware of accepting uncritically some of the statements which are made very casually. For example, what does the author mean when he blandly says that in contemporary England there was a "decay of a genuine aristocratic tradition." Is his contention accurate? What is the proof of the decay? How rapid was it? If it existed, why did England have to suffer riots and wait for half a century after the American Revolution was over before there was any substantial change in the suffrage?

Nelson persists in differentiating between Britons and Americans. Possibly this is reading back into history what wasn't there. After examining the selections in Part One do you think that the Crown and Britain can be equated? Were the Loyalists loyal to both, to the first, or to the second? Isn't it true that the sense of allegiance to the sovereign was so strong that both Jefferson and Paine made systematic attacks on the Crown in order to strengthen the Patriot cause? What does it mean to speak of "Americans" in 1775? Was there a sense of nationalism? Can one differentiate between Americans and Britons, as Nelson does, even though Charles Inglis, one of the better political philosophers among the Loyalists, decidedly did not? These are the sort of troubling questions which arise when reading **The American Tory**. Nevertheless the book remains probably the best general analysis of recent times. For this reason it has seemed useful to ask such direct questions to indicate what needs to be done if the history of the Loyalists is to be incorporated into our general history of the Revolution and if it is to add measurably to a clarification of that period in both American and Western history.

Of all the approaches that might be used in an attempt to separate intelligibly the Loyalists from their Patriot kinsmen, that of occupation or social class seems the least fruitful. There was indeed a Tory oligarchy, but there was also a Whig oligarchy, and if in New England the Tory proportion of ruling families was greater than the Tory proportion of the total population, in the Southern Colonies the reverse was true. Even in New England the Loyalists were hardly the gentry pictured in legend. When an Act of Banishment was passed against some three hundred Loyalists in Massachusetts in 1778, they were listed by trade or profession. About a third were merchants, professional men, and gentlemen; another third were farmers, and the rest were artisans or labourers with a sprinkling of small shopkeepers. . . .

Clearly, none of the simpler economic determinants was at work separating Whigs from Tories. Economic influences, however, may account in part for the pattern of geographical distribution that appears when the Loyalist strongholds are considered. The main centres of Tory strength fall into two distinct regions: The first was along the thinly settled western frontier, from Georgia and District Ninety-Six in South Carolina, through the Regulatory country of North Carolina and the mountain settlements of Virginia, Pennsylvania, and New York, to the newly-occupied Vermont lands. The other was the maritime region of the Middle Colonies, including western Long Island and the counties of the lower Hudson Valley, southern New Jersey, the three old counties of Pennsylvania around Philadelphia, and the peninsula between Delaware and Chesapeake Bays. There were also locally important concentrations of Tories elsewhere along the Atlantic seaboard: at Charleston, around Wilmington and Norfolk, and around Newport and Portsmouth in New England.

In the West and in the tidal region of the Middle Colonies Loyalists and neutrals may have formed a majority of the population. In the areas of dense agricultural settlement, however, including the plantation country of the Southern Colonies, the thickly settled parts of the Piedmont, and most of New England, Loyalists were comparatively scarce. All that the Tory regions, the mountain and maritime frontiers, had in common was that both suffered or were threatened with economic and political subjugation by richer adjoining areas. The geographical concentration of the Tories was in peripheral areas, regions already in decline, or not yet risen to importance.

It is not difficult to explain the Loyalism of the West. The Appalachian frontiersmen—hunters, trappers, and fur traders—feared the advance of close settlement which would destroy their economy. Like the Indians of the region, many of the frontiersmen were loyal to Britain because the British government was the only force they could rely on to check the rapid advance of agricultural settlement. The tidal region of the Middle Colonies, on the other hand, still had political power, but was in danger of losing it to the more populous districts inland. Moreover, this region formed part of an Atlantic community. It looked eastward; its ties with Britain were closer than its ties with the new West. Even in New England the truly maritime regions seem to have been less than enthusiastic in their support of the Revolution. Newport lacked zeal; Nantucket and Martha's Vineyard were opportunist or neutral, and the Maine coast grew steadily less faithful to the Revolution, until Nova Scotia's Loyalism of necessity was reached.

Whether the St. Lawrence Valley should be considered a separate province, or whether it merely combined the characteristics of a thinly settled and a maritime region, it too was indifferent or hostile to the Revolution. Undoubtedly some of Vermont's capriciousness during the period may be ascribed to the pull of the St. Lawrence. In any case, wherever regions newly or thinly settled touched the sea, there the Revolution was weakest: in Quebec, in Nova Scotia, in Georgia, and in New York where the Hudson carried the Atlantic world into the mountains. Wherever sailors and fishermen, trappers and traders outnumbered farmers and planters, there Tories outnumbered Whigs.

Of course a major insufficiency of such a geographical analysis is that it takes no account of important cultural influences, differences in nationality and religion mainly, that played a great role in the Revolution. The Canadians of the St. Lawrence Valley were suspicious of the Revolution, not only because they lived far outside its physical homeland, but also because they were French and Catholic, and the Revolution seemed to them English and Protestant. No geographic or economic considerations can explain the Tory villages on Long Island, intermingled with Whig villages. The Tory villages were Dutch, while the others had been settled by New Englanders. Here again, legend has done a disservice to students of the Revolution. The Loyalists were seldom more English than the patriots. There were, of course, many British-born Tories whose allegiance to England was habitual and natural. But, apart from these, the Tories more commonly drew their recruits from the non-English than from the English parts of the community. The two most purely English provinces, Virginia and Massachusetts, were the strongholds of the Revolution. It was in the patchwork societies of Pennsylvania and New York that the Tories were strongest.

Among almost all cultural minorities, the proportion of Tories seems to have been clearly higher than among the population at large. The Dutch and Germans seem to have inclined towards supporting the Revolution where they were already anglicized, but not where they had kept their language and separate outlook. In New York, for example, the English-speaking Dutch Reformed congregation was Whiggish, but the Dutch-speaking congregation was Tory, and on such cordial terms with the Anglicans that they were allowed to use St. George's chapel during the British occupation. The Tories praised the loyalty of the French Calvinists at New Rochelle, the only place in the colonies where they had preserved their language, while elsewhere the descendants of the Huguenots were conspicuously active revolutionists.

There seems to have been reason for John Witherspoon's lament that his fellow Scots made bad revolutionists, whether Highlanders in the back country of New York and North Carolina, or Lowlanders along the Virginia and Carolina coast. Even the Ulstermen were tainted with Toryism in the Regulator districts of North Carolina and in the frontier districts of South Carolina. The Loyalism of the Indians is well known, and contemporary opinion held that the Negroes were dangerously Toryfied. Of course people like the Brooklyn Dutch or the South Carolina Germans and Scots may have remained loyal to Britain partly out of political quietism. It is difficult not to believe, however, that they were Loyalists also because they thought Britain would protect them from the cultural aggression of an Anglo-American majority.

In religion, the lines that divided Tories from Whigs were quite clearly drawn. Adherents of religious groups that were in a local minority were everywhere inclined towards Loyalism, while adherents of the dominant local denomination were most often Patriots. In New England not many Congregationalists, in the Middle Colonies not many Presbyterians, in the South not many Episcopalians, were Tories. Conversely, most of the Anglicans in the North were Tories; so were many Presbyterians in the Episcopalian South. Of the smaller religious groups, most of the Quakers and German Pietists were passive Loyalists, and in New England even the Baptists were accused of 'not being hearty' in the American cause. The reputation the Methodists had for being poor rebels was perhaps not entirely due to the influence of Wesley and other English ministers.

The Catholics and Jews apparently form an exception to the rule that religious minorities leaned towards Toryism. Both seem generally to have supported the Revolution, although among the Jews there were notable exceptions like the Hart family in Newport and the Franks family in Philadelphia. Jonathan Boucher observed that although the Maryland Catholics supported the Revolution in its later stages, they had taken little part at first. It is possible that the Jews and Catholics were in such suspect and habitual minority, that they felt obliged to follow what seemed majority opinion for their own safety.

Taking all the groups and factions, sects, classes, and inhabitants of regions that seem to have been Tory, they have but one thing in common: they represented conscious minorities, people who felt weak and threatened. The sense of weakness, which is so marked a characteristic of the Tory leaders, is equally evident among the rank and file. Almost all the Loyalists were, in one way or another, more afraid of America than they were of Britain. Almost all of them had interests that they felt needed protection from an American majority. Being fairly certain that they would be in a permanent minority (as Quakers or oligarchs or frontiersmen or Dutchmen) they could not find much comfort in a theory of government that assured them of sovereign equality with other Americans *as individuals*. Not many Loyalists were as explicit in their distrust of individualism as, say, Jonathan Boucher, but most of them shared his suspicion of a political order based on the 'common good' if the common good was to be defined by a numerical majority.

A theory that the Loyalists were compounded of an assortment of minority groups does not, of course, preclude their having in total constituted a majority of Americans. Without the social and religious homogeneity, without the common purpose, and without the organic and efficient leadership of the revolutionists, the Loyalists might still have outnumbered them. In this case the Revolution would have been, as it has sometimes been claimed to have been, the achievement of an organized and wilful minority. . . .

Part Four

The Nature of Loyalty

Diverse Remarks

"PARADOXICALLY, LOYALTY IN A FREE SOCIETY DEPENDS UPON THE TOLERATION OF DISLOYALTY. THE LOYALTY OF FREE MEN MUST BE FREELY GIVEN."*

There is a strong tendency to take for granted two basic emotions, love of a partner in a long established marriage and loyalty to one's country. In both cases this attitude may prove dangerous! For example, if we become dubious about the existence or effectiveness of the emotion, we then try by simple means to measure and gauge its absolute strength. Shakespeare's remark, "that love is merchandized whose rich esteeming the owner's tongue doth publish everywhere," may be applied to loyalty as well as love. But each year in America while a million or more people break their marital ties without too much trouble, examination of the bonds of loyalty calls forth hypersensitive responses. Possibly this is because loyalty is a central feature of the republic's covenant and therefore not fully open to scrutiny. We have adopted instead a method of testing loyalty that is less than commendable. We believe that by requiring citizens to affirm their allegiance under oath, their loyalty may be proved or disproved. The futility of such a procedure as an antisubversive device may seem logically obvious, but it has not consistently appeared so in the history of the United States.† This simple, rigorous, but highly ineffective method becomes a substitute for an atmosphere, hoped for by thinking men and women, that would indeed permit examination of loyalty, but one which would lead from increased knowledge through deeper understanding to clearer appreciation. We leave aside any discussion of the trust, dignity, and naturalness which should hallmark the most essential relationship between a citizen and his state in a free, democratic society.

---

* Alan Barth, *The Loyalty of Free Men* (New York, 1951), p. 231.

† A very full discussion of the loyalty oath in American history is Harold M. Hyman, *To Try Men's Souls* (Berkeley, 1959).

157

In this section some challenging observations on the nature of loyalty are taken from recent commentaries. Not every viewpoint can be represented, nor can we deal with such closely related topics as Nationalism, Patriotism, Sovereignty, and World Order. All that is possible is to point out, by grouping together a few remarks, that loyalty, however much it is unthinkingly assumed by both citizen and state, is in reality a very complicated matter. What men do in unpredicted situations, the choices they make based on considerations of personal ethics, inculcated traditions, fear of authority, self-interest, and patterns of group response, remain questions to which we have only incomplete answers. Loyalty, in keeping with some of the other intangibles which are key elements in social relationships, is sometimes more appreciated when absent, but its origin and character dictate that when present it may proceed in many, sometimes conflicting, directions.

LOYALTY'S COMPLEXITIES

The brief, clear observations Francis Biddle makes on what loyalty means to an American are deceptively simple. The following extract is from his book, **The Fear of Freedom,** * which was concerned with the scare climate in the United States in the late 1940s. Many, many Americans believed that the safety of their nation was in jeopardy, and a few pushed the country into an unfortunate mood of despair and insecurity. The result was a witchhunt through the halls of academe and the corridors of politics. To his semihysterical country Biddle brought a few words of sanity and wisdom.

He could not be written off as an idealist, a liberal, a "perfessor," or a pinko, then terms of opprobrium in many circles of American life. His lineage was long and distinguished and his career of public service had been capped by holding the position of Attorney General of the United States. During his period in this office (1941–1945) the country could have undergone another attack of jitters similar to the one she passed through during World War I and the years immediately following. Under Biddle's control of the Department of Justice there were, with the notable exception of the Japanese Americans on the West Coast, no sustained outbursts of guilt by association or innuendo tactics. His book is mainly a tract for his own times, but the comments on loyalty distinctly transcend any such limitations.

. . . The simple loyalty of the medieval world, as I have just suggested, was a personal relationship involving duties on each side, defined by the long practice of the little-changing centuries. It was far more like the relation of a citizen of the great Russian empire today to his Government than what we mean by loyalty. The Soviet citizen yields allegiance by surrendering, or, put perhaps more accurately, by never claiming any political rights or any individual freedom; and for this he receives from his master, the State, whose commands must not be questioned, the promise of economic security. In such a relation, as in the medieval, loyalty to the country and loyalty to the Government mean in substance the same thing. Under such a conception there does not —there cannot—exist the loyalty which Americans have in mind when they use the word.

What do Americans mean by "loyalty"? I do not think the word can be defined, any more than "patriotism," or than many of the words which, in spite of the way they have been rubbed down like worn coins, still hold for us the cherished reality of an inner meaning which

---

* From *The Fear of Freedom,* by Francis Biddle. Copyright 1951 by Francis Biddle. Reprinted by permission of Doubleday & Company, Inc., pp. 189–193.

we find hard to express and perhaps cannot define at all. A "loyal American" does mean something very definite to each of us. Yet to each of us the meaning will be different.

And it could not be otherwise in our rich and teeming country, drawing its blood and bone and mind from so many races of men; our impulses flowing from such varied streams of life; our memories searching back into pasts so divergent in their beauty or their sorrow or their strength; the half-forgotten dreams which our fathers brought with them to build here into fabulous castles of reality which, having never lived in, they could create with such unfettered imagination; or failing to build, or seeing them fall to the ground, knew their children or their children's children might someday fashion. We were all immigrants once.

The very essence of loyalty to country in a democracy, and particularly in this democracy, with its varied backgrounds and its severance from feudal traditions, dependent on no single class authority, without even the unifying symbol of a crown as in England, is that it may find expression in a dozen forms, in countless aspirations or activities. Loyalty must know such unhampered outlets if it is to be the free and dynamic force which holds together our democratic life. It is a life which we have freely chosen, which has not been forced on us, or inherited by us. We must therefore be allowed to select or to reject our own forms of loyalty. If our conception is based on the exciting free play of thought and idea, not only as the best means of creating self-government, but as a good in itself, worth all other goods, we shall permit endless varieties of loyalty. They will conflict with and contradict each other in the give and take of our lives, which are constantly changing and growing as the community grows and changes. Individual lives will feed and strengthen and make whole the common life, draw strength and serenity from the common purpose.

Yet loyalty is more than the recurring recollection of an emotion. We cannot write out in words the undefined and undefinable memories and aspirations which make up our loyalty to America. But they are essentially ours, cultivated in a firm ground of decision and purpose. For loyalty grows daily as we live. It may flow from that simple human need to love the earth where we live together, the earth which, as Bossuet says, is a mother and a common nurse, the earth remembered as something strong and elemental, which has carried and nourished us living and will receive us in her bosom when we die.

That long-remembered love of earth is a part of our loyalty, even here in America, holding our life together in a queer world of gadgets, in the blare of radio and the meaningless intensity of movies, beneath the strident machines, the automatic voices that chatter and are never silent, the assembly lines, our hands unused, forgotten the gracious spacing of time and the rhythm of the seasons. . . .

But loyalty is more than these. It is intrinsically a moral concept, and for that reason involves moral choice and the exercise of personal will, since for social human beings—and but for the abnormal we are all social entities—the individual self-assertion cannot be enough, and loyalty involves self-control, and the devotion to some common group: family, club, labor union, Church, and finally to country, when loyalty becomes patriotism, which, as Lord Acton has suggested, is in political life what faith is in religion, the development of selfishness into sacrifice. Loyalty translates, as does religion, the mechanical and the minute into the spiritual and the eternal. To modern man this need can best be fulfilled through the sense of sharing his ideal with others— "the pursuit of a remote and ideal object," as Acton says, "which captivates the imagination by its splendour and the reason by its simplicity." Thus imagined, the object of loyalty transcends the life of the individual, although the cause to which devotion is to be given must be *his* —*his* club, *his* country. There is a final fusion between the instinct to rebel and the longing to submit. When the cause becomes ours we experience a sense of completion. . . .

If our democracy is bound to the certainty that a government of free men must rest on free thought, and thence on unrestrained public opinion, the greater the variety of opinion, the greater the ultimate resource of the State. Our State is not identical with our society, but is subservient to it, and not a little at arm's length. The very distribution of power among the constantly changing social agencies in our American community tends not only to give it a dynamic energy of free play in ideas and purposes, but to keep the State off a pedestal and on the level where it belongs—the level of the people. The sources of power are diversified and multiplied, and countless institutions become the cohesive bonds between individual and State.

Here we begin to recognize the enormous importance of loyalty in a democratic country, not only to the State, but to the people. Americans of our time are profoundly in need of finding spiritual values, are ripe for idealism, as Royce said, often knowing that they have not found their way in the blind clash of great industrial and mechanical forces, between which they are uncertainly aware of the malaise which must have plagued primitive man into propitiating the reckless and unpredictable forces of nature—the sun and the fury of the sea, rain and death and the untamed beasts which prowled about him. . . .

A SATIRICAL LOOK AT LOYALTY

Few countries have been more ready to use a sworn statement as a test of allegiance than the United States in recent years. We are speaking of course of times when a nation is not at war and when no special situation arises, such as induction into the armed services or high political office. During the 1950's the extent of this practice, the pervasive nature of its effect, and the harrassment undertaken in the name of loyalty, led many Americans to examine and frequently criticize federal and state loyalty oaths. Usually their writings said little about loyalty **per se** but simply addressed themselves to the matter of the moment. Many were vitiated by an excess of romantic idealism or righteous indignation, and it was fairly easy to brush aside these high decibel commentaries. Satire is a trickier weapon, but often it is more successful in challenging prejudices and stirring up reform. Here is an excellent example applied to the federal loyalty program.*

The loyalty probers are missing a good bet. To date they have confined themselves to searching for disloyalty among present and prospective employees of the federal government. But they have done nothing whatever about the disloyalty which may have been rampant among those employees who have resigned or passed into eternal rest. The problems to them are grave, to say the least. It ill befits a patriotic citizenry to pay homage to a former public servant as to whose loyalty there may be reasonable doubt. And the security of our populace is poorly served by permitting the memoranda, letters and other work products of the disloyal dead to permeate government files, infecting anyone who chances to use them today.

It is accordingly suggested that the President issue a new executive order extending the loyalty program to all who have served the

---

* Eugene Gressman, "How Disloyal was Thomas Jefferson?" *New Republic,* Vol. 127 (July-Dec. 1952), 13–14. Reprinted by permission of The New Republic, © 1952, Harrison-Blaine of New Jersey, Inc.

government in any capacity since its inception in 1789. This would not involve sailing too far on uncharted seas. Existing departmental loyalty boards could be utilized to a large extent, though some special boards might be created to deal with certain historical periods like the Civil War. Much the same investigatory techniques now in use could be employed. Thus a door-keeper who served briefly in the Treasury Department in the Polk Administration would receive a preliminary screening. His name would be checked against a vast collection of dubious personalities carefully culled from historical tracts, yellowed newspapers and periodicals, ancient gossip and fertile imaginations. Only if some serious question arose from this screening would he be subjected to a full-scale investigation by historical agents of the FBI.

All of the substantive evils which form the matrix of the present program would lend themselves with ease to this projected inquiry. Such ingrained principles as guilt by association and disloyalty due to non-conformity could readily be applied to many prominent ex-employees who at one time were un-American enough to identify themselves with a dissident group or with libertarian or unpopular ideas. Moreover, all the procedural inequities which have so convincingly demonstrated their brutal efficiency under the present program could be carried over intact. In fact, most of the troublesome nuisances which have been sentimentally maintained up to now could be eliminated under this new project. Little if any purpose, for example, would be served by continuing the pretense of a fair hearing. The subjects of this inquiry would be in no position to object, especially since most of them are deceased and since none of them had any constitutional right to feed at the public trough in the first place. Appeals from adverse decisions would be cut to a minimum. And the percentage of such decisions could be raised so high that Senator McCarthy's eyebrows would not even quiver.

Still there may be a squeamish few, desirous of maintaining some of the maudlin procedures which for generations have masqueraded under the guise of due process. Some may wish, for instance, to have formal charges preferred against the individual and/or his present-day descendants, followed by an appropriate counterpart of the hearing farce now employed. Should such mawkishness prevail, it is suggested that the following type of charges be utilized, though with considerably less informative detail.

REVOLUTIONARY LOYALTY BOARD

MR. THOMAS JEFFERSON, HIS HEIRS AND ASSIGNS,
MONTICELLO, VIRGINIA.

July 4, 1952

"As a result of a recent investigation made of you as a former employee of this government under the provisions of Executive Order 9835, which establish a Federal Employees Loyalty Program, and Executive Order 10241, which established a new standard for determining suitability for federal employment on the basis of loyalty, and Executive Order 12345, which extended the foregoing orders to all past employees of the government, information has been received which indicates that a reasonable doubt may exist as to your loyalty to the Government of the United Staates and that you were therefore unsuitable for federal employment. More specifically, it is alleged:

"1. That over a period of many years you wrote revolutionary tracts, such as 'A Summary View of the Rights of British America' and the 'Declaration of Independence,' in which you advocated and encouraged citizens to alter or abolish established forms of government, by force if necessary.

"2. That on November 13, 1787, you wrote to one W. S. Smith a letter in which you advocated the violent overthrow of government every 20 years. In that letter you allegedly said: 'God forbid that we should ever be 20 years without such a rebellion . . . what country can preserve its liberties if their rulers are not warned from time to time that their people preserve the spirit of resistance? Let them take arms. . . . What signify a few lives lost in a century or two? The tree of liberty must be refreshed from time to time with the blood of patriots and tyrants. It is its natural manure.'

"3. That over a period of many years you maintained a sympathetic association with many persons alleged to be ardent revolutionists. Said persons resided in the United States, France and England. Included among them was one Thomas Paine, a notorious atheist and advocate of world revolution. In May, 1791, you publicly praised a pamphlet written by Paine, entitled 'The Rights of Man', in which he defended world republican revolution.

"4. That over a period of many years you advocated that no constitution or law should be permanent, that it 'naturally expires at the end of 19 years' and that 'if it be enforced longer, it is in an act of force not of right'.

"5. That over a period of many years you proclaimed and adhered to the revolutionary motto—'Rebellion to tyrants is obedience to God' —and advocated the divine right of revolutions.

"6. That on January 30, 1787, you wrote to one James Madison a letter in which you said: 'A little rebellion, now and then, is a good thing, and as necessary in the political world as storms in the physical. . . . It is a medicine necessary for the sound health of government'.

"7. That, according to Confidential Informant A. H., you were 'actuated by views . . . subversive of the principles of good government and dangerous to the Union, peace and happiness of the country', and that, furthermore, you consistently opposed the Constitution and expressed a desire of not paying the public debt.

"You or your descendants have a right to answer these charges in writing within 10 days from the receipt of this letter. Your reply, setting forth in detail all matters you consider pertinent, must be sworn to or affirmed before a notary. You may support your answers by affidavits if you wish. In addition, you have a right to an administrative hearing before the Loyalty Board. At such appearance you have a right to be accompanied by an historian of your own choosing and to present evidence, in your own behalf, through witnesses or by affidavit."

It should be added that, since secrecy is of no moment to an ex-employee like Jefferson, such a charge—though not the answer—could be given full publicity in the press and other means of mass communication. And certainly a finding of reasonable doubt as to Jefferson's loyalty should be given every possible publicity. Only in that way can we avoid the embarrassment of honoring disloyal Americans and perpetuating their soiled reputations and labors. Only in that way can the loyalty program, as it gradually exhausts its current and prospective live victims, stir up enough interest to keep itself alive with a steady flow of appropriations.

PATRIOTISM

One of the approaches to the question of loyalty is by reference to patriotism. This is probably an even more difficult word to define, and most people are content to say that it is a feeling of love for one's country.

The genre of patriotic literature is immense, heavily weighted in favor of emotional statements rather than cool analysis. Instead of quoting the flatulent oratory of typical commemorative speakers, the following extract* contains the answers of four fairly average Americans to the question "What is Patriotism" when it was put to them during the not particularly jingoistic days of September, 1929.

WHAT IS PATRIOTISM?

Forum definitions. [Three different conceptions of patriotism were evident.] The first was the attitude of "jingoism," or blind patriotism— "My country right or wrong!" The second was the point of view which advocates observance of the law only so long as the individual is convinced that the law works in the best interests of his country. The third, and least frequent, view was that which holds in contempt all patriotism as an expression of egotism and selfish insularity.

In selecting the winning definitions this month we have tried to include each of these categories. . . .

1. Patriotism is that spiritual force in a man which causes him to act, and to advocate that his government act, in such a way that his country will be admired, loved, and respected by the thoughtful citizens of all countries, including his own.

2. Patriotism is a love for one's country which prompts one to give the fullest allegiance and yet enables one to realize when the policy of the government is incompatible with her truest welfare, and at such a time to work against the generally accepted policy, even at the risk of persecution, striving always for her highest good and progress. . . .

3. Patriotism—inherent love of country, expressed by devotion to its welfare, strict adherence to its laws and traditions, and constant support of its authority and interests. . . .

4. Patriotism is a conviction, fostered by generations of propaganda, that the people who comprise one's nation are superior to all others, one's government the finest, one's army and navy the greatest; that other inhabitants of the earth are "foreigners" and inferior, to murder whom in warfare is a virtue, and to be killed by whom insures national immortality.

---

* *Forum*, Vol. 82 (1929), Supplement LIII–LIV.

LOYALTY AND THE PRESIDENCY

If we are forced to name a point in time when Loyalists and Patriots had to take sides, it must be the drawing up of the Declaration of Independence. It was then that the issue of allegiance to the King had to be squarely faced. Many of those who chose to remain loyal had been positive, if not vehement or violent, in their opposition to British policies during the 1760's and 1770's, but "to take up arms against a sea of troubles and by opposing end them" seemed neither good sense nor good citizenship. For the Loyalist, therefore, his loyalty centered upon the Crown and the person who at that moment occupied the throne.

The United States defiantly proclaimed itself a republic and although there were some widespread misgivings, no one among the Patriots, not even Alexander Hamilton or John Adams, ever seriously thought of reintroducing monarchy. As a result, in this country the question of loyalty has usually been less personally focused. Whereas Britain still speaks of Her Majesty's Navy and citizens receive passports asking foreign countries to grant the bearer free passage in the name of Her Britannic Majesty, the president's position as commander-in-chief is temporary and even his term in office is now specifically limited by constitutional amendment.

Although the two countries share the cherished tradition of free speech, one has a sovereign who must remain above politics and the other a president who must combine the functions of party political leader and president of all the people. It becomes no easy matter to determine in practice when an attack upon the policies of the president is not also damaging to the interests and possibly the security of the country. The line of demarcation cannot be rigidly and permanently drawn. The issue has a long history, and it would be foolish to assume that it has yet been solved, or that it ever will be, in any absolute sense. But however troublesome, this flexibility is not a bad thing. Surely the intention of the Founding Fathers was that each generation would reexamine the fundamental assumptions of the American republic and constitution in the light of its own needs and circumstances.

So that contemporary issues do not intrude and weaken our understanding, let the point of opposition to the president and opposition to the nation be made by noting one of Theodore Roosevelt's last speeches and an equally partisan reaction.*

WHAT IS LOYALTY?

"Every public official from the President down is entitled to have the truth told about him and entitled to nothing else. The only proper slogan is 'Stand by the Country' and to stand by the President or against the President exactly to the degree to which he does well or

---

* *The Bellman,* XXIV, No. 612 (April 6, 1918), pp. 369–370.

does ill as a servant of the country. The man who tries to substitute the cry of 'Stand by the President' for the doctrine of 'Stand by the Country' is preaching a basely un-American principle and occupies a position both shameful and contemptible."—*From Colonel Roosevelt's speech before the Maine Republicans on March 28.*

The man who in this manner substitutes the President for the country may be preaching a "basely un-American principle," and he may also occupy "a position both shameful and contemptible," to use Colonel Roosevelt's own redundantly intemperate language, but the man who holds that, in such a time as this, to stand by the President is to stand by the country, that the two are inseparable, and that it is impossible to do one without also performing the other, occupies much firmer ground in respect of his loyalty than that most unfortunately taken by one who aspires to be, and, if he lives, probably will be, the next Republican candidate for President.

At this time, one cannot assail the President without also assailing the country. Colonel Roosevelt would be the first to charge high-handed and punishable treason against those who attacked the President, if it happened that he and not Mr. Wilson was the occupant of the office.

This inconsistency is impressed upon those of restrained and moderate partisanship who read what Colonel Roosevelt permits himself to say in these times; they cannot fail to believe that the billingsgate* of Colonel Roosevelt, who for months has been railing at the President like an infuriated fishwife, is actuated less by loyalty to his country than by a very petty and unworthy jealousy of the man who holds an office that he hopes himself to fill, and by a strong desire to undermine the good repute of that man among the people to the one end—that he may succeed him.

The difference would have been, had Colonel Roosevelt and not Mr. Wilson been President during this critical period in the nation's history, that being necessarily, inevitably and infallibly right in all things, to assail him would obviously have been treasonous, whereas, the incumbent not claiming infallibility, it follows that opposition becomes a patriotic duty, which Colonel Roosevelt is only too delighted to perform to the full measure of his lungs and the limits of his pen.

---

* Meaning bad or intemperate language. Billingsgate is the central fish market in London, England. Comparison of Roosevelt to a fishwife is therefore very apposite.

As to what is right and what is wrong, what constitutes "standing by the Country" and what becomes miserable, cowardly, unfair criticism of an overworked President who, by reason of his office, is unable to retaliate in his own defense, there can, of course, be but one competent and unbiased judge, and Colonel Roosevelt is the supreme and not-to-be-disputed It. . . .

Had any one written or spoken of him when he was President as he has both written and spoken of President Wilson, there is no doubt whatever that long since he would have found a way to have locked him up. Indeed, Colonel Roosevelt has deliberately taken advantage of his position as an ex-President to say things concerning the government and its Chief Executive that would undoubtedly have caused the arrest, prosecution and punishment of a less prominent and distinguished person, and the country would have indorsed and applauded the act as being both wise and just. Many an obscure I.W.W.* has said less and been sentenced to imprisonment for it.

Here in the West, the people joyously tar and feather and ride on rails gentlemen who claim they are "standing by the country" and its best interests, and are far more sincere in their contention than he, when they take occasion to emphasize their particular views of the President's errors. If Colonel Roosevelt has the inalienable right, if it be his patriotic duty, to assail the President's course, why has not the be-feathered soap-box orator an equal right to air his opinions? Or perhaps this is not a republic, and what would be treason if uttered by the ordinary, irresponsible windjammer becomes laudable zeal for the country's welfare when spoken by the elect of the opposition. . . .

The truth is, Colonel Roosevelt is a very poor judge of loyalty. With all his collection of great qualities, and it is a large one, loyalty is not among them. It is obvious that he does not know what loyalty means, and he has never shown it except to himself. He was not loyal to his best and closest friend, nor was he loyal to the party that gave him his preferment and made him President. With him, loyalty to his country means decrying its Chief Executive during a war, belittling his efforts, attempting to discredit him, seeking his discomfiture, trying to annoy and harass him.

---

* Member of the Industrial Workers of the World, a radical labor reform union created in 1905 under the leadership of Eugene Debs and others. Members were nicknamed the "Wobblies."

This is his conception of "standing by the Country," but fortunately it is not shared by the American people, who have a higher, clearer, better ideal, and one less tinged with political selfishness and partisan ambition.

Insights from the Social Sciences

What do disciplines other than history have to say about loyalty? The next three selections are taken from a sociologist (Bloch), a social psychologist (Guetzkow), and a political scientist (Grodzins). Each has been chosen to reflect a particular way of approaching the problem although, inevitably, there will be some overlapping of coverage. Together they present us with a large number of interesting, even provocative, suggestions. They are not easy reading since each writer uses the constructs of his discipline as the framework for a tightly organized analysis. On the other hand, a few unfamiliar words should not frighten us away from the possibility of discovering new ideas. Because they are more theoretically construed and more qualitatively regarded, these concepts of loyalty are possibly more precise.

HERBERT A. BLOCH*

We are not always conscious of our loyalties: to an extent, we are content to take them at their face values. But a loyalty must always be crystallized and defined to some point of view by our attitudes. It can never in itself be inchoate and aimless. It is the necessary locus in our social definition as individuals. Though an individual may express himself as being in doubt as to what course to follow, his very doubt is being fomented by his loyalties. As soon as he resolves these, he integrates himself by a newly-formed loyalty to the social fibre. The implication follows that a loyalty may be not outwardly articulate but latent. So thoroughly habituated do we become to the conventional and usual in our ordinary social intercourse that the bonds of unity which compose much of the warp and woof of society are taken for granted. The consciousness of the attachment arises only when the need for prerogative action and choice presents itself.

The loyalty, however, can always be perceived by observing the fundamental subscription of the individual to some code or group. These social agents are the chief means by which man seeks realization of his ends. They are the conveyances which he utilizes to bring him social satisfaction. There can be no social being devoid of adherence to some code or group. The criminal, as is well known, is very much a conformatory being, though the codes and mores to which he subscribes are indicative of a criminal group and not the group at large. Splendid virtues can be practiced in the sequestered outlines of some socially disapproved unit: thus bravery, self-sacrifice, even compassion may perhaps be more consistently practiced under the criminal code than under our own. It is interesting to note how these highly-esteemed and universally approved attributes can exist in any community and under any code. If these generally approved characters can exist in almost any social setting, it evidently means that we approve these things only in the benevolent aura of our own loyalties and convictions. The enemy is not a man who lacks these splendid qualities but is one who practices them only in connection with that group with which he feels himself a vital part. The connections in which these traits are exercised may be highly revelatory of the loyalties sustained. . . .

---

* Herbert A. Bloch, *The Concept of our Changing Loyalties* (New York: Columbia Univ. Press, 1934), pp. 38–39; 61–63. Used by permission.

Our beliefs are always the expressions of our agreements with certain modes of conduct. Taking our cue from this, we may now attempt to establish certain criteria whereby the fundamental texture of our loyalties may be ascertained. It is maintained that first, there must be an essential and consistent unity in practice with some institutional factor. It is the presence of some such factor or group of factors which establishes our loyalty to some group or code even when the particular group or code appears to further ends inimical to our own. We find, frequently, groups which *appear* to incorporate many of the practices and ways which we happen to favor. A loyalty may be, therefore, more apparent than real. A predatory political organization, whose sole purpose is to reap political spoils, may assume for me a symbolic character of highly commendable political purpose and resultantly may become an object of my allegiance. This cannot, certainly, be conceived as a true loyalty except in a limited sense, for my place in the group is falsely conditioned. Furthermore, this inharmonic situation can persist only just so long as the group, symbolic of my predilections and chosen preferences, is enabled to remain falsely representative or as my own peculiar behavior habits remain what they are. My attachment to individuals may take the same course.

The whole insidious art of propaganda is conceived upon this basis. In order to evoke our adherences, our public figures are transformed into many-faceted, and ofttimes irreconcilable personalities before our eyes. Our political candidates do the two-faced Janus to shame in their efforts to make a universal appeal to a heterogeneous population. They become humble sons of the soil, firm believers in trade unionism, literateurs, devotees of baseball, proponents of corporate activity in business—beside expounding as a reiterated fundamental theme those homely virtues which an entire society regards as especially its own even when these have often come to be incompatible with contemporary factors. Where a dominating issue has arisen and where it is unknown wherein lies the balance of power, we have learned to resort to poorly-drawn distinctions, to the ambiguous and to the vague, hoping that by innuendo and by giving a doctrine some approved stamp such as the nebulous concept of Americanism, our loyalties will, somehow or other, settle upon the doctrine being manoeuvered into power. . . .

However, the loyalty can be sought for only in the meaning with which the individual endows his own conduct. It is true that he may dream he is king and actually be a slave but the fact remains, nevertheless, that the whole relation depends upon the way he dreams. The context of his relationships depends upon his imagined status and this, in turn, is always both an approval and a condemnation, either tacit or expressed, of certain ways of group activity.

HAROLD GUETZKOW*

THE ADAPTIVENESS OF LOYALTY DEPENDS UPON
THE NATURE OF THE SOURCE

The very process of generating loyalties may have an influence on the way in which the attitudes are expressed. When the sources involve rewarding processes, the loyalties are expressed as constructive, adaptable, positive acts of support. When the sources involve punishing processes, the loyalty attitudes predispose the individual to conformity and obedience with rigidity. My seven different sources of loyalty all involve punishment and/or reward as the basic underlying devices by which the mechanisms are made operative.

Contemporary psychologists find increasing evidence to support this notion that reward and punishment create quite different kinds of responses. These differences have been summarized as follows:

Reward Process	*Punishment Process*
1. Consequent behaviors are flexible and plastic, free to adapt to changes in the external situation.	Consequent behaviors are more rigid and stereotyped, unable to change with shifts in the environment.
2. Approach is sustained, even when goal is remote.	Avoidance is more immediate, effective when punishment situation is encountered.
3. Behavior is cast with a problem-solving, outward-going orientation.	Behavior is defensive, with a strong endeavour to preserve things as they are.

---

* Harold Guetzkow, *Multiple Loyalties: Theoretical Approach to a Problem in International Organization* (Publ. No. 4, Center for World Political Institutions in the Woodrow Wilson School of Public and International Affairs, Princeton, 1953), pp. 32–33; 61–62. Used by permission.

The identification, self-avoidance, and autonomy roots seem to generate loyalty mainly through rewards, while the sanctions root involves punishment. Perhaps the attachment-to-means, inculcation, and legitimation mechanisms involve a mixture of both reward and punishment. To what extent will empirical research confirm my prediction that the reward-generated loyalties are acted out in supportive behaviors which are flexible, sustained, and problem-oriented? And contrariwise, to what extent does loyalty which has its roots in punishment tend to be stereotyped, short-sighted, and defensive?

I would hypothesize along the following lines. When loyalty is generated through rewards, the result is a patriotism which tolerates. Such loyalty allows for diversity of expression. When loyalty is reared through fear and punishment, its expression is more stereotyped, more of the flag-waving type. When loyalty is positively rooted, it has time perspective and encourages patience in accomplishment of the nation's goal. When it is fear-induced, it is short-visioned and demands that the object of loyalty be supported here and now in the thick of the present crisis. Such fear-ridden loyalty is not sustained. When the crisis is over, the patriotism is forgotten. Loyalty developed through the reward mechanism has higher aspirations than loyalty developed through punishment. Disciplined loyalty tends to be less bold, because it is generated as a defensive device. These characteristics markedly color the supportive behaviors which are expressed toward the object of national loyalty. . . .

There are a few important implications for the policy-maker in this concept of multiple loyalties. But before these implications can be taken seriously, it is imperative that the theories presented be tested more directly than has ever been done. Findings from the study of loyalty of the private citizen must not be lightly generalized so as to encompass the loyalty of elites or of professional secretariats, and vice-versa. For the multiple loyalties of the private citizen are undoubtedly colored by apathy and remoteness; the patriotism of the elite is embedded in the struggle for influence; the allegiance of the international civil servant is filtered by his professional identifications and his career needs.

These are some implications of this theory for the policy-maker in international affairs.

1. Loyalty is not a single entity—once used up, then exhausted. It is, rather, an expandable quantity which can be generated in increasing amounts

toward a variety of objects. Thus there is no need to think that increases in loyalty to a supranational group necessarily mean decreases in loyalty to the nation-state.

2. It should be just as feasible to go from loyalty to nation-state toward loyalty to universal organization as to go from loyalty to nation-state toward loyalty to regional organization. Except for introducing a time delay, loyalty to a regional organization (*if* it contains no exclusiveness norm) should not hinder or accelerate development of loyalty to a universal organization.

3. The exclusiveness norm seems to be the great barrier to expanding loyalties where a barrier exists. But to build a new loyalty one need not necessarily destroy other loyalties.

4. Doing a common job together in a face-to-face group composed of members of different nationalities may not be the most effective way to generate broader loyalties. The members may see more clearly their conflict of interest under such conditions, as compared with a face-to-face situation in which no particular job has to be accomplished.

5. There is probably no single way by which loyalty to a supranational level can be built. But to do so, a policy-maker would be well-advised to draw upon certain sources of loyalty before other sources, because loyalties seem often to occur as means before they have become attached to objects as end-values. Once loyalties have been established with certain spreads and strength, they seem to be self-enhancing and no longer need nurturing by the policy-maker.

MORTON GRODZINS*

It is a contradiction in terms to speak of a man without loyalties. He does not exist. The human qualities that differentiate man from other mammals are the products of his social life. . . . And society—social structures of every sort—rests upon loyalties: upon systems of mutual rights and duties, common beliefs, and reciprocal obligations. To accuse one of being devoid of loyalty can have only one meaning. His loyalties are antagonistic to your own. . . .

---

* "The Basis of National Loyalty" by Morton Grodzins is reproduced with permission from the January 1951 issue of the *Bulletin of the Atomic Scientists.* Copyright 1951 by the Educational Foundation for Nuclear Science. (Vol. VII, 356–357; 359; 362)

FUNCTION OF LOYALTIES

Loyalties are a part of every individual's life because they serve his basic needs and functions. They are a part of his indispensable habit patterns. Loyalties provide him with a portion of that framework through which he organizes his existence. In the absence of such a framework, he could establish no easy, habitual responses. He would be faced with the endless and hopelessly complicated task of making fresh decisions at each moment of life. He would soon degenerate into wild and random inconsistencies or into a brooding state of confusion and indecisiveness, conditions that soon merge into the psychotic. . . .

Loyalties are thus the source of great personal gratification. They contribute to making life satisfying. They protect the individual, reducing the area of his uncertainty and anxiety. They allow him to move in established patterns of interpersonal relations with confidence in the action expected of him and of responses that his action will evoke. By serving the group to which he is loyal, he serves himself; what threatens the group, threatens the self. There is no self outside group activity. "In so far as one identifies himself with a whole, loyalty to that whole is loyalty to himself; it is self-realization, something which one cannot fail without losing self respect."

Complete identification between individual and group does not often exist. Totalitarian governments attempt to accomplish this end by destroying all intermediary loyalties, or by fusing the activities of all other groups with those of the state.

In the Western democracies the case is different. Except in periods of extreme crisis, freedom to form and maintain group ties is cherished and encouraged, and individuals preserve strong loyalties to numerous non-national groups. These loyalties are given to family, friends, neighborhood, church, ethnic society, job, class, and to a host of other institutions, groups, and idea systems. They exist most frequently in situations that bring the individual face-to-face with others who share his views and situation; they may also exist where this immediate human contact does not exist. The relative strength and weakness of these numerous loyalties change with age, with shifts in life situation, with new experience, and especially under stress of crisis. They change as old relationships no longer serve biological needs or as they no longer supply satisfaction and security to the individual in the total network of his social existence. . . .

Democratic nations cannot exist unless the "interests"—the life goals—of its citizens are at least approximately achieved. And these achievements are in areas where there is little or no direct nation-person relationship. National loyalty here becomes a by-product of satisfactions achieved in non-public spheres of activity.

Indeed, from this view a generalized national loyalty is a misnomer. It does not exist. Loyalties are to specific groups, specific goals, specific programs of action. Populations are loyal to nation only because the nation is believed to symbolize and sustain these values.

Leon Trotsky once remarked that revolutions were not caused by the poor. If they were, he said, there would be revolutions going on all the time. This is one way of expressing the important fact that "life expectations" or "life goals" are not fixed or static concepts. Individuals define these terms in various and divergent fashions; their definitions are influenced in many ways, not least of all by parents, profession, sex, and social class.

To say that loyalty is dependent upon the achievement of life satisfactions is therefore not to say that the poor are the disloyal, the rich, loyal. The individual's own definition of satisfaction is of crucial importance. The fat men who do not make easy converts are those fat in satisfactions, not necessarily in body or other material possessions. A subtle tool to measure these satisfactions would be an index of the discrepancy, if any, between life expectancy and life achievements, as defined by the individual. Where the spread is a big one, deprivations are experienced and loyalty to the nation (not considering direct nation-person ties) is presumably less strong than where expectations are actually or approximately achieved.

This variety in definition of life satisfactions is crucial to understanding the interplay between those satisfactions and national loyalty. . . .

The principal loyalties of men in democratic states are directed toward these non-national groups and interests. Their very existence provides possibilities for sharp clashes between national and other loyalties. But these other loyalties are also the most important foundation of national loyalty.

Why this is so has already been suggested. The nation is the most important group with which all persons in a given geographic area are associated. It gives all citizens a common point of reference. It sustains their groups. A threat to a nation is interpreted as a threat to all groups within the nation and to the gratifications derived from those groups. The satisfactions springing from smaller groups are thus related to the nation and to national loyalty.

But in times of crisis, the national demands may easily conflict with the demands of non-national groups. Family welfare, professional status, career and job stability may be threatened or thwarted by governmental policy. In such circumstances, clean choices need not always be made. When they do, national loyalty may mean family or professional disloyalty. Where loyalty to family or to career or to profession is held foremost, then the result is national disloyalty.

The total configuration is a fine paradox: non-national loyalties are the bricks from which national loyalty is constructed; they are also the brickbats by which national loyalty is destroyed. . . .

The view presented here rejects the contention that national allegiance is a simple conditioned response to political symbols. It equally rejects the idea that loyalty is a cool and rational choice of one way of life over another. It emphasizes that loyalty can be explained, like other social phenomena, in terms of life situation (discussed here) and personality attributes (neglected here).

This view also recognizes how ambiguous the concept of national loyalty is in Western democracies. Does "nation" mean administrative programs or national ideology or a specific leader or a system of government? The variety in answers to this question makes it possible for traitors to act in the name of patriotism and patriots to perform the role of traitors. Traitors, for example, can wreck great programs of government in the service of lofty slogans and honored principles; and the patriot can subvert principle while honoring program.

This ambiguity becomes crucial when linked to the tendency, already mentioned, of all groups to validate their conduct in terms of national values. This is a near-universal phenomenon. Ku Klux Klansmen and racial equalitarians, high tariff and low tariff proponents, management and labor, all link their efforts to national welfare. Even traitors do the same.

Disloyalty to the nation therefore does not emerge as a simple act of rejection. With rare exception it also requires a positive act of identification, sometimes identification with the nation itself, though in one of the meanings not recognized as valid by others. Despite the many social impediments discussed above, people thus slip into disloyal action. A new loyalty becomes primary: to family, to labor union, to profession, to Marxist study club. What sense of evil or betrayal they may feel as the result of subordinating national to other demands becomes overshadowed by the positive values of serving a cause.

This is so even for the most blatant traitor. He regards his acts as an expression of loyalty to, not disloyalty against. He is almost always supported by some group with which he is in intimate, daily, face-to-face contact. There are few Iagos who glory in villainy. "No man at bottom means injustice," Carlyle said. "It is always for some distorted image of a right that he contends." . . .

The loyalty thus engendered is different from the religious-like quality of direct nation-person relationships, those dominant in totalitarian states. In the latter case, loyalty emerges from the poverty or absence of participation in voluntary groups. It is mobilized by state leaders, and it is marked by a high emotional content. In democracies national loyalties are largely by-products of participation in voluntary groups. They do not emerge as a consequence of manipulation from above. They are not submissive. They are more studied, less emotional, more qualified, less completely mobilized at any given moment.

This explains the greater intensity of totalitarian loyalties, in comparison with democratic ones. It also suggests the greater duration and stability of democratic loyalties. They are based upon human satisfactions derived from numerous overlapping but independent group contacts. Barring complete social catastrophe, no single cause can bring widespread dissatisfaction, widespread disloyalty.

To sustain such loyalties, democracies in practice must supply some achievement of the expectations promised in the democratic creed. The danger, among scientists as well as others, is not that of individual persons becoming disenchanted and turning to disloyal acts. Nor is the danger that democracy will fail because it is inherently unable to supply the immediate life satisfactions that, indirectly but solidly, lead to strong national allegiance. The danger is that democracy may fail, not on its merits, but because it fails to be democratic. . . .

A Historian's Summary

Henry S. Commager has been a productive and distinguished historian of America for some thirty-five years. He quotes approvingly Santayana's remark: "To be an American is of itself almost a moral condition, an education, and a career." His own life has personified all three points.

There is inevitably a certain "conservatism" in a historian's wisdom. Heritage is treasured with a decent respect for the opinions of mankind past. Commager, as a self-confessed "Jeffersonian liberal," is also quick to remind his countrymen of the moral character of America and to ask that the ideals on which this nation was founded should prevail, in different contexts, today. The historian in him leads him to say that most of our contemporary problems are new forms of the ones previously encountered. "Circumstances change profoundly, but the character of the American people has not changed greatly or the nature of the principles of conduct, public and private, to which they subscribe."

In analyzing the question of loyalty in the United States as it arose in the 1950's, Commager brings to bear his sweeping historical knowledge, not merely details of individual events but also the broad currents which have flowed together in the turbulent river of American life. It is therefore fitting that we end, as we began in the Preface, with an assertion of the consistency in man's experience and with the implication that the problem of loyalty remains, long after the Loyalists have gone.

HENRY STEELE COMMAGER*

And this is what is significant—the emergence of new patterns of Americanism and of loyalty, patterns radically different from those which have long been traditional. It is not only the Congress that is busy designing the new patterns. They are outlined in President Truman's Loyalty Order of March 1947; in similar orders formulated by the New York City Council and by state and local authorities throughout the country; . . .

In the making is a revival of the Red hysteria of the early 1920's, one of the shabbiest chapters in the history of American democracy; and more than a revival, for the new crusade is designed not merely to frustrate communism but to formulate a positive definition of Americanism, and a positive concept of loyalty.

What is the new loyalty? It is, above all, conformity. It is the uncritical and unquestioning acceptance of America as it is—the political institutions, the social relationships, the economic practices. It rejects inquiry into the race question or socialized medicine, or public housing, or into the wisdom or validity of our foreign policy. It regards as particularly heinous any challenge to what is called 'the system of private enterprise,' identifying that system with Americanism. It abandons evolution, repudiates the once popular concept of progress, and regards America as a finished product, perfect and complete.

It is, it must be added, easily satisfied. For it wants not intellectual conviction or spiritual conquest but mere outward conformity. In matters of loyalty it takes the word for the deed, the gesture for the principle. It is content with the flag salute, and does not pause to consider the warning of our Supreme Court that 'a person gets from a symbol the meaning he puts into it, and what is one man's comfort and inspiration is another's jest and scorn.' It is satisfied with membership in respectable organizations and, as it assumes that every member of a liberal organization is a Communist, concludes that every member of a conservative one is a true American. It has not yet learned that not everyone who saith Lord, Lord, shall enter into the kingdom of Heaven. It is designed neither to discover real disloyalty nor to foster true loyalty.

---

* From *Freedom, Loyalty, Dissent* by Henry Steele Commager. Copyright 1954 by Oxford University Press, Inc., pp. 146–149; 154–155. Reprinted by permission.

What is wrong with this new concept of loyalty? . . . The concept of loyalty as conformity is a false one. It is narrow and restrictive, denies freedom of thought and of conscience, and is irremediably stained by private and selfish considerations. 'Enlightened loyalty,' wrote Josiah Royce, who made loyalty the very core of his philosophy,

'means harm to no man's loyalty. It is at war only with disloyalty, and its warfare, unless necessity constrains, is only a spiritual warfare. It does not foster class hatreds; it knows of nothing reasonable about race prejudices; and it regards all races of men as one in their need of loyalty. It ignores mutual misunderstandings. It loves its own wherever upon earth its own, namely loyalty itself, is to be found.'

Justice, charity, wisdom, spirituality, he added, were all definable in terms of loyalty, and we may properly ask which of these qualities our contemporary champions of loyalty display. . . .

The effort to equate loyalty with conformity is misguided because it assumes that there is a fixed content to loyalty and that this can be determined and defined. But loyalty is a principle, and eludes definition except in its own terms. It is devotion to the best interests of the commonwealth, and may require hostility to the particular policies which the government pursues, the particular practices which the economy undertakes, the particular institutions which society maintains. 'If there is any fixed star in our Constitutional constellation,' said the Supreme Court in the Barnette flag-salute case, 'it is that no official, high or petty, can prescribe what shall be orthodox in politics, nationalism, religion, or other matters of opinion, or force citizens to confess by word or act their faith therein. If there are any circumstances which permit an exception they do not now occur to us.'

True loyalty may require, in fact, what appears to the naïve to be disloyalty. It may require hostility to certain provisions of the Constitution itself, and historians have not concluded that those abolitionists who back in the 1840's and 1850's subscribed to the 'Higher Law' were lacking in loyalty. We should not forget that our tradition is one of protest and revolt, and it is stultifying to celebrate the rebels of the past—Jefferson and Paine, Emerson and Thoreau—while we silence the rebels of the present. 'We are a rebellious nation,' said Theodore Parker, known in his day as the Great American Preacher, and went on:

'Our whole history is treason; our blood was attainted before we were born; our creeds are infidelity to the mother church; our constitution, treason to our fatherland. What of that? Though all the governors in the world bid us commit treason against man, and set the example, let us never submit.'

Those who would impose upon us a new concept of loyalty not only assume that this is possible but have the presumption to believe that they are competent to write the definition. . . .

What do men know of loyalty who make a mockery of the Declaration of Independence and the Bill of Rights, whose energies are dedicated to stirring up race and class hatreds, who would straitjacket the American spirit? What indeed do they know of America—the America of Sam Adams and Tom Paine, of Jackson's defiance of the Court and Lincoln's celebration of labor, of Thoreau's essay on Civil Disobedience and Emerson's championship of John Brown, of the America of the Fourierists and the Come-Outers, of cranks and fanatics, of socialists and anarchists? Who among American heroes could meet their tests, who would be cleared by their committees? Not Washington, who was a rebel. Not Jefferson, who wrote that all men are created equal and whose motto was 'rebellion to tyrants is obedience to God.' Not Garrison, who publicly burned the Constitution; or Wendell Phillips, who spoke for the underprivileged everywhere and counted himself a philosophical anarchist; not Seward of the Higher Law or Sumner of racial equality. Not Lincoln, who admonished us to have malice toward none, charity for all; or Wilson, who warned that our flag was 'a flag of liberty of opinion as well as of political liberty'; or Justice Holmes, who said that our Constitution is an experiment and that while that experiment is being made 'we should be eternally vigilant against attempts to check the expression of opinions that we loathe and believe to be fraught with death.'

There are further and more practical objections against the imposition of fixed concepts of loyalty or tests of disloyalty. The effort is itself a confession of fear, a declaration of insolvency. Those who are sure of themselves do not need reassurance, and those who have confidence in the strength and the virtue of America do not need to fear either criticism or competition. The effort is bound to miscarry. It will not apprehend those who are really disloyal, it will not even frighten them; it will affect only those who can be labeled 'radical.' It is sobering to recall that though the Japanese relocation program, carried through at such incalculable cost in misery and tragedy, was justified to us on the ground that the Japanese were potentially disloyal, the record does not disclose a single case of Japanese disloyalty or sabotage during the whole war. The warning sounded by the Supreme Court in the Barnette flag-salute case is a timely one:

'Ultimate futility of such attempts to compel obedience is the lesson of every such effort from the Roman drive to stamp out Christianity as a disturber of pagan unity, the Inquisition as a means of religious and dynastic unity, the Siberian exiles as a means to Russian unity, down to the fast-failing efforts of our present totalitarian enemies. Those who begin coercive elimination of dissent soon find themselves exterminating dissenters. Compulsory unification of opinion achieves only the unanimity of the graveyard.'

Who are those who are really disloyal? Those who inflame racial hatreds, who sow religious and class dissensions. Those who subvert the Constitution by violating the freedom of the ballot box. Those who make a mockery of majority rule by the use of the filibuster. Those who impair democracy by denying equal educational facilities. Those who frustrate justice by lynch law or by making a farce of jury trials. Those who deny freedom of speech and of the press and of assembly. Those who demand special favors against the interest of the commonwealth. Those who regard public office merely as a source of private gain. Those who would exalt the military over the civil. Those who for selfish and private purposes stir up national antagonisms and expose the world to the ruin of war. . . .

But if our democracy is to flourish it must have criticism, if our government is to function it must have dissent. Only totalitarian governments insist upon conformity and they—as we know—do so at their peril. Without criticism abuses will go unrebuked; without dissent our dynamic system will become static. The American people have a stake in the maintenance of the most thorough-going inquisition into American institutions. They have a stake in nonconformity, for they know that the American genius is nonconformist. They have a stake in experimentation of the most radical character, for they know that only those who prove all things can hold fast that which is good.

It is easier to say what loyalty is not than what it is. It is not conformity. It is not passive acquiescence in the status quo. It is not preference for everything American over everything foreign. It is not an ostrich-like ignorance of other countries and other institutions. It is not the indulgence in ceremony—a flag salute, an oath of allegiance, a fervid verbal declaration. It is not a particular creed, a particular version of history, a particular body of economic practices, a particular philosophy.

It is a tradition, an ideal, and a principle. It is a willingness to subordinate every private advantage for the larger good. It is an appreciation of the rich and diverse contributions that can come from the most varied sources. It is allegiance to the traditions that have guided our greatest statesmen and inspired our most eloquent poets —the traditions of freedom, equality, democracy, tolerance, the tradition of the Higher Law, of experimentation, co-operation, and pluralism. It is a realization that America was born of revolt, flourished on dissent, became great through experimentation.

Independence was an act of revolution; republicanism was something new under the sun; the federal system was a vast experimental laboratory. Physically Americans were pioneers; in the realm of social and economic institutions, too, their tradition has been one of pioneering. From the beginning, intellectual and spiritual diversity have been as characteristic of America as racial and linguistic diversity. The most distinctively American philosophies have been transcendentalism— which is the philosophy of the Higher Law—and pragmatism—which is the philosophy of experimentation and pluralism. These two principles are the very core of Americanism: the principle of the Higher Law, or of obedience to the dictates of conscience rather than of statutes, and the principle of pragmatism, or the rejection of a single good and of the notion of a finished universe. From the beginning Americans have known that there were new worlds to conquer, new truths to be discovered. Every effort to confine Americanism to a single pattern, to constrain it to a single formula, is disloyalty to everything that is valid in Americanism. . . .

Appendix

A Note on Numbers

It would clearly be advantageous if one could say precisely how many people were Loyalists. Unfortunately there can be no definite answer to this vital question because the tabulation depends on the definition of Loyalism. If we count only those who actually bore arms we arrive at one approximate figure; if we count only those who went into exile during or after the war we obtain another. With the first computation we have to leave out the quieter people, loyal in mind and heart but not in deed; some were perhaps not given much chance of serving the King. With the second we are leaving out the many who passively wanted the status quo ante Revolution and cried a plague on both armies, those Loyalists who stayed on in the new United States (in all probability a majority), and those who left the country but came back later.*

The best known estimate is the one made by John Adams, who appears to have divided the American people into three parts, the Patriots, the Loyalists, and the neutral group. This is very neat, too neat obviously, and even in conflict with an earlier assessment by Adams himself.†

---

* A famous example is Samuel Curwen. Less well-known, but more important in American history, is Philip Barton Key who served with the British, was declared an outlaw by the Maryland legislature, sought and received a pardon, and was elected to Congress. Ironically, Francis Scott Key, who wrote "The Star Spangled Banner" was his nephew. I owe this reference to my former colleague, H. Dan Piper.

† Adams' three-way division of the population is quoted back to him in a letter from Thomas McKean to Adams, January 1814. This is the citation most usually made by historians. A more explicit statement will be found in a letter from Adams to McKean, August 31, 1813 where the former president concluded that it was an "ample" allowance to say that "two thirds of the people" were "with us in the revolution." Yet while the war was actually taking place, he wrote that "the tories throughout the whole continent do not amount to the twentieth part of the people." References are, respectively, to John Adams, *Works*, edited by Charles F. Adams 10 vols., Boston, 1850–56), X, 87; X, 62–63; VII, 270.

Quite a few contemporaries offered their observations on the number of Loyalists, but because of the cloudiness about what constitutes Loyalism their results are not easy to evaluate. Some certainly ring truer than others. That tireless news-gatherer, Ezra Stiles, president of Yale from 1778 to 1795, always kept himself informed. Yet in the following extract it is clear that he is making astute guesses to the nearest whole number. It should be noted that he is speaking of the period before the mass emigration of Loyalist refugees.

A calculation of Loyalist exiles made by Phineas Bond, a Pennsylvania Loyalist and later (1786) a British consul in America, has been roughly confirmed by modern scholarship. Bond believed that approximately 100,000 Loyalists migrated (out of a total population of two and a half million).* Wallace Brown, on the basis of Loyalist claims before the British commissioners and calculations based upon figures given in a number of secondary works, offers 80,000 as the round number of exiles. In a second suggestion which he labels tentative, and which inevitably will never be quite precise or uniformly accepted, Brown indicates that "active" Loyalists totaled between 160,000 and 384,000, that is "between 6.4 and 15.3 per cent of the total population of 2,500,000 on the eve of the Revolution, or between 7.6 and 18.0 per cent of the *white* population of 2,100,000."†

Lastly, in a book with the considerable merit of treating the American Revolution in an Atlantic context, Robert Palmer offers concrete figures on the scope of the conflict. His analysis raises the question of how much change the revolutionaries hoped to produce.‡

---

* "Letters of Phineas Bond" Amer. Hist. Assoc., *Annual Report for 1896* (2 Vols., Washington, 1897), I, 648.

† Wallace Brown, *The King's Friends: The Composition and Motives of the American Loyalist Claimants* (Providence, R.I., 1965), p. 250.

‡ The conservative nature of the revolution has been incisively argued by Daniel Boorstin in *The Genius of American Politics* (Chicago, 1953), pp. 66–98.

EZRA STILES*

March. [1783]

1. Read[ing] a Packet of London Prints sent to me from Boston. In one of 6 Aug. last thus—"One principal obstacle to the Completion of my propositions f[rom] G[uy] Carlton† to Congress, are the Terms to be given the American *Refugees* of wh[ich] there is not less than 4 or *five thous[an]d either in pay as embodied men in America, or pensioned in England.* G[uy] Carlt[on] contends that these unhappy p[eo]ple should be again admitted into their Country, & get their *confiscated* property; but Congress say—inadmissible." Rema[rks] 1. Here probably the Truth as to Numbers—which the Tories in America are or have been constantly magnifying the Numbers gone over to the En[em]y as if they were twenty or 30 Thous[an]d Men. 2. Should we suppose 5000 Men perhaps 1000 or 1500 with Families, the rest single men: so may be estimated 8 or 9000 souls. But it is most probable with me, 3. That the 4 or 5 Th[ousand] includes all the Souls. Lloyds Neck on L[ong] Isld. has been the place of Refugee Head Qu[arte]rs & here the largest Collection in America: and yet I never could learn there were above 150 or two hundred Hutts there and seldom above 3 or 400 Refugee Troops. Their numbers never were eno[ugh] considerable in any other part of America to have a *Board of Refugees,* as at New York. 4. I am confirmed in this by inspecting the Advertis[emen]ts in the respective States enumerat[ing] the Names of those whose Estates are confiscated. I think in Mass. there were about two hundred names. At the capture of Cornwallis, none were found—the Bonnetta sloop of War might carry off 4 hundred. The Evacuation of Phil[adelphi]a & Charlest[on] might carry off 50 or 60 families each. The flight fr[om] different parts of the interior Country, may have been for N. England perhaps 5 or 6 hundred during the War—from Jersy & the parts adjacent to N[ew] Y[ork] & Philad[elphi]a as many more—as for those who joynd L[or]d Cornwallis in his Itinerary Marches thro' the Carolinas & Virginia, the most of them left him as he left them in passing, altho' near half the Carolinas were *not* Whigs, yet neither were they risquing Tories. The whole State of So[uth] Caro[lina] is but thirty

---

* *The Literary Diary of Ezra Stiles,* ed. by Franklin B. Dexter (3 vols., New York, 1901), III, 60–61.

† Sir Guy Carleton, British commander-in-chief after 23 February, 1782.

thous[an]d souls Whites. About 30 sail evacuated Charlesto[n] of Kings Troops & Tories. Rem[arks]. 5. Returns of Refugees are duely sent to Engl[an]d, & it becomes part[icularl]y necess[ar]y for the King to know the true No of Amer[ican] Loyalists now at settling at Peace. There went last summer about two hundred Fam[il]ys to Florida, & as many to Nova Scotia and there may be two hundred more at N[ew] Y[ork] & L[ong] Isld, the only place within the XIII States now possessed by the British Troops. There may be one hundred fam. in Engl[an]d to be provided for. Death has reigned among the Refugees as well as others. Altho' there might be last summer 4000 souls liv[in]g, yet more have gone to the En[em]y. However I do not estimate the Total of the Refugees in all the States during this whole eight years War to exceed 15 or *twenty Thous[an]d Souls* out of *three millions.* In Truth I believe they are not twelve thous[an]d, & one third of these have shulked back again.

ROBERT R. PALMER*

My own view is that there was a real revolution in America, and that it was a painful conflict, in which many were injured. I would suggest two quantitative and objective measures: how many refugees were there from the American Revolution, and how much property did they lose, in comparison to the French Revolution? It is possible to obtain rough but enlightening answers to these questions. The number of émigré loyalists who went to Canada or England during the American Revolution is set as high as 100,000; let us say only 60,000. The number of émigrés from the French Revolution is quite accurately known; it was 129,000, of whom 25,000 were clergy, deportees rather than fugitives, but let us take the whole figure, 129,000. There were about 2,500,000 people in America in 1776, of whom a fifth were slaves; let us count the whole 2,500,000. There were about 25,000,000 people in France at the time of the French Revolution. There were, therefore, 24 émigrés per thousand of population in the American Revolution, and only 5 émigrés per thousand of population in the French Revolution. . . .

Revolutionary France, ten times as large as revolutionary America, confiscated only twelve times as much property from its émigrés, as

---

* Robert R. Palmer, *The Age of the Democratic Revolution* (2 vols., Princeton: Princeton University Press, 1959, 1964), I, 188–189. Used by permission.

measured by subsequent compensations, which in each case fell short of actual losses. The difference, even allowing for margins of error, is less great than is commonly supposed. The French, to be sure, confiscated properties of the church and other public bodies in addition; but the present comparison suggests the losses of private persons.

It is my belief also, John Quincy Adams notwithstanding, that the American and the French revolutions "proceeded from the same principles." The difference is that these principles were much more deeply rooted in America, and that contrary or competing principles, monarchist or aristocratic or feudal or ecclesiastical, though not absent from America, were, in comparison to Europe, very weak. Assertion of the same principles therefore provoked less conflict in America, than in France. It was, in truth, less revolutionary. The American Revolution was, indeed, a movement to conserve what already existed. It was hardly, however, a "conservative" movement, and it can give limited comfort to the theorists of conservatism, for it was the weakness of conservative forces in eighteenth-century America, not their strength, that made the American Revolution as moderate as it was. . . .

It must always be remembered, also, that an important nucleus of conservatism was permanently lost to the United States. The French émigrés returned to France. The émigrés from the American Revolution did not return; they peopled the Canadian wilderness; only individuals, without political influence, drifted back to the United States. Anyone who knows the significance for France of the return of the émigrés will ponder the importance, for the United States, of this fact which is so easily overlooked, because negative and invisible except in a comparative view. . . .

Guide to Further Study

Extracts from, or reference to, most of the important works by and concerning Loyalists have been made in this book. Some other titles will be found in Oscar Handlin *et al.* (ed.), *Harvard Guide to American History* (1954; paperback, 1967), pp. 301–2. Chapter 10 (pp. 294–315) deals with the Revolutionary period in general. The *Guide* clearly needs to be brought up to date and the process is under way, but given the slow rate at which new writings on the Loyalists appear, this problem is not critical. More recent references will be found in the bibliography to Wallace Brown, *The King's Friends* (1966). The still more recent book by North Callahan, *Flight from the Republic: The Tories of the American Revolution* (1967) is a work of sloppy, unreliable scholarship.

DICTIONARIES AND ENCYCLOPEDIAS

Mark M. Boatner, *Encyclopaedia of the American Revolution* (1967). Generally accurate, but references and bibliographical notations are sometimes out-of-date.

Thomas H. Johnson (ed.), *The Oxford Companion to American History* (1966).

Richard B. Morris (ed.), *Encyclopaedia of American History* (rev. ed., 1965).

BIBLIOGRAPHICAL AND HISTORIOGRAPHICAL ESSAYS

Wesley F. Craven, "The Revolutionary Era" in John Higham (ed.), *The Reconstruction of American History* (1962), pp. 46–63.

Jack P. Greene, "The Flight from Determinism: A Review of Recent Literature on the Coming of the American Revolution," *South Atlantic Quarterly*, LXI (Spring, 1962), 235–59.

Donald Higginbotham, "American Historians and the Military History of the American Revolution," *American Historical Review*, LXX (October, 1964), 18–34.

Edmund S. Morgan, *The American Revolution: A Review of Changing Interpretations* (American Hist. Assoc. Pamphlet, 1958) and "The American Revolution: Revisions in Need of Revising," *William and Mary Quarterly*, 3rd Series, XIV (January, 1957), 3–15.

GENERAL ACCOUNTS

Lawrence H. Gipson, *The Coming of the Revolution* (1954); the most readily available short statement of the "imperial" interpretation by the dean of that school of historians.

Edmund S. Morgan, *The Birth of the Republic* (1956); a brief, interestingly written survey from the modern nationalist or "conservative" point of view.

Richard Pares, *King George III and the Politicians* (1953) and Eric Robson, *The American Revolution in its Political and Military Aspects* (1955) reflect the pioneering research done by Lewis B. Namier. They may be said to belong to a "Namierist" school whose most important conclusions, for students of the American Revolution, are that George III was not a tyrant but a constitutional monarch, that Parliament was not composed of parties tied together by ideological bonds but rather of factions and family groups whose interests centered on privilege and office, and that, as a result, local rather than broad national or imperial concerns tended to dominate parliamentary activities. For a strong critique of this view see Herbert Butterfield, *George III and the Historians* (1957) and "George III and the Constitution," *History*, XLIII (February, 1958), 14–33.

H. Trevor Colbourn, *The Lamp of Experience* (1966) and Bernard Bailyn, *Ideological Origins of the American Revolution* (1967) are two outstanding recent analyses of the intellectual side of the Revolution. Howard H. Peckham, *The War for Independence* (1958) and Piers Mackesy, *The War for America* (1964) are lucid accounts of the military events by an American and a British scholar, respectively. A number of valuable essays are conveniently grouped together in Richard B. Morris, *The American Revolution Reconsidered* (1967).

MORE SPECIALIZED STUDIES

Social and economic forces as causes of the Revolution, either with regard to relations between the colonies and Britain and/or in terms of class conflict in the colonies themselves, are stressed in the following: Arthur M.

Schlesinger, "The American Revolution Reconsidered," *Political Science Quarterly*, XXXIV (March, 1919) and *The Colonial Merchants and the American Revolution* (1918); Charles and Mary Beard in Chapters V and VI of *The Rise of American Civilization* (1927) and Charles A. Beard, *An Economic Interpretation of the Constitution* (1913); J. Franklin Jameson, *The American Revolution Considered as a Social Movement* (1926) and the challenge to this by Frederick B. Tolles in *American Historical Review*, LX (October, 1954), 1–12. See also Oscar and Mary Handlin, "Radicals and Conservatives in Massachusetts after Independence," *New England Quarterly*, XVII (September, 1944), 343–55; Merrill Jensen, *The Articles of Confederation* (1948), *The New Nation* (1950); Elisha P. Douglass, *Rebels and Democrats* (1955).

Oliver M. Dickerson, *The Navigation Acts and the American Revolution* (1951) and Lawrence A. Harper, *The English Navigation Laws* (1939) come to opposite conclusions regarding the effect of British trade policies.

Benjamin W. Labaree, *The Boston Tea Party* (1964) is a good modern account throwing new light on an event which is heavily overlaid by myth.

The colonial fear of episcopacy is a main theme in Carl Bridenbaugh, *Mitre and Sceptre* (1962).

Leonard W. Labaree, *Royal Government in America* (1930) should be combined with Jack P. Greene, *The Quest for Power* (1963). Kenneth Coleman, *The American Revolution in Georgia* (1958) and David S. Lovejoy, *Rhode Island and the American Revolution* (1958) are two examples of solid regional studies by authors who do not feel that class conflict played a major part in bringing about the Revolution.

Robert E. Brown, *Middle-Class Democracy and the Revolution in Massachusetts* (1955) is a sharply argued study which raises some new questions about the causes of war.

On the West after 1763, Clarence W. Alvord, *The Mississippi Valley in British Politics* (1916) is a pioneer work still possessing many valuable insights. More recent are Thomas P. Abernethy, *Western Lands and the American Revolution* (1937) and Jack M. Sosin, *Whitehall and the Wilderness* (1961).

RECENT IMPORTANT ARTICLES

Bernard Bailyn, "Political Experience and Enlightenment Ideas in Eighteenth-Century America," *American Historical Review*, LXVII (January, 1962), 339–51.

R. Buel, Jr., "Democracy and the American revolution: a frame of reference," *William and Mary Quarterly*, 3rd Series, XXI (April, 1964), 165–90.

R. M. Calhoon, "William Smith Jr.'s alternative to the American revolution," *William and Mary Quarterly,* 3rd Series, XXII (January, 1965), 105–18.

Eugene R. Fingerhut, "Uses and Abuses of the American Loyalists' Claims" and Paul H. Smith, "The American Loyalists" in *William and Mary Quarterly,* 3rd Series, XXV (April, 1968), 245–258, 259–277, are two important articles dealing with the difficult problem of the number of Loyalists and estimates by historians.

Merrill Jensen, "Democracy and the American Revolution," *Huntington Library Quarterly,* XX (August, 1957), 321–41.

Cecelia Kenyon, "Republicanism and Radicalism in the American Revolution," *William and Mary Quarterly,* 3rd Series, XIX (April, 1962), 153–82.

Edmund S. Morgan, "The American Revolution Considered as an Intellectual Movement," in Arthur M. Schlesinger, Jr. and Morton White (eds.), *Paths of American Thought* (Boston, 1963), pp. 11–33.

William H. Nelson, "The revolutionary character of the American revolution," *American Historical Review,* LXX (July, 1965), 998–1014.

Thad W. Tate, "The Coming of the Revolution in Virginia: Britain's Challenge to Virginia's Ruling Class, 1736–1776," *William and Mary Quarterly,* 3rd Series, XIX (July, 1962), 323–43.

————, "Social Contract in America, 1774–1787; revolutionary theory as a conservative instrument," *William and Mary Quarterly,* 3rd Series, XXII (July, 1965), 375–91.

Clarence L. Ver Steeg, "The American Revolution Considered as an Economic Movement," *Huntington Library Quarterly,* XX (August, 1957), 361–72.